Sense and Nonsense in Homer

A consideration of the inconsistencies and incoherencies in the texts of the Iliad and the Odyssey

John Wilson

BAR International Series 839
2000

Published in 2016 by
BAR Publishing, Oxford

BAR International Series 839

Sense and Nonsense in Homer

ISBN 978 1 84171 044 0

© J Wilson and the Publisher 2000

The author's moral rights under the 1988 UK Copyright,
Designs and Patents Act are hereby expressly asserted.

All rights reserved. No part of this work may be copied, reproduced, stored,
sold, distributed, scanned, saved in any form of digital format or transmitted
in any form digitally, without the written permission of the Publisher.

BAR Publishing is the trading name of British Archaeological Reports (Oxford) Ltd.
British Archaeological Reports was first incorporated in 1974 to publish the BAR
Series, International and British. In 1992 Hadrian Books Ltd became part of the BAR
group. This volume was originally published by Archaeopress in conjunction with
British Archaeological Reports (Oxford) Ltd / Hadrian Books Ltd, the Series principal
publisher, in 2000. This present volume is published by BAR Publishing, 2016.

Printed in England

PUBLISHING

BAR titles are available from:

              BAR Publishing
              122 Banbury Rd, Oxford, OX2 7BP, UK
EMAIL   info@barpublishing.com
PHONE +44 (0)1865 310431
  FAX   +44 (0)1865 316916
              www.barpublishing.com

CONTENTS

Preface		v
Introduction		1
Part 1:	Comments on the Iliad	5
Part 2:	Comments on the Odyssey	21
Part 3:	Conclusions	61
References		75

PREFACE

I am concerned in this book with those passages in the Iliad and the Odyssey which present semantic or logical difficulties, and more particularly with those which might be thought incoherent or inconsistent: both individually in their own right, and as collectively shedding some light on Homeric composition. 'Incoherent' is a vague term, but I hope to make my criteria clearer in the Introduction which follows. Here I need only say, rather boldly, that there seem to be many such difficulties which have not been adequately discussed - often not even noticed - in the existing commentaries and other literature. I wanted to get a clear picture of the nature and distribution of these difficulties in both texts; and, again, more particularly, of those cases which might fairly be thought incoherent or nonsensical, where Homer was nodding (hence my rather dramatic title, 'Sense and Nonsense'). I do this in Parts 1 and 2. In Part 3 I offer a tentative picture of the origin and persistence of these incoherencies.

A strictly semantic approach to the Homeric texts is nowadays comparatively unfashionable, at least in many quarters. In the last few decades it has been overshadowed by other approaches and interests, concerned perhaps with formulaic composition, verse-structure, thematic composition, sociological study, aesthetic effect, any of the other aspects of Homer which the texts so fruitfully offer us. It may even be felt that we have had enough of the semantic approach, or that all the work necessary has already been done. This last at least I hope to prove false.

My references are throughout to the Oxford Classical Text. I have had to face the question of how much to refer to other commentators and semantically-orientated literature generally, and have thought it best to reduce this to a minimum, if only because not every reader will have all commentators to hand. In general I have confined my references to the two commentaries, by now perhaps standard works, most likely to be available to the reader: that is, the Cambridge University Press commentary on the Iliad (1985 and later) under the general editorship of G. S. Kirk and with notes by Kirk, Hainsworth, Janko, Edwards and Richardson, and the Oxford University Press commentary on the Odyssey (1988 and later) with notes by Heubeck, West, Hainsworth, Hoekstra, Russo and Fernandez-Galiano, from which the reader will be able to take up further references; and to a few other editions and commentaries where I have thought this helpful. (I shall refer to all these just by naming the commentator in the text: the reader may take up the references *ad loc.*) These and other works referred to are listed fully at the end of this book.

Finally I should like to say something about the origins and development of this book. The general need for this kind of work first struck me when I undertook a literal translation of the text in the light of modern scholarship; the translator (unlike the editor or commentator) is compelled ultimately to come down in favour of one interpretation as against any other - he cannot sit on the fence - and it became apparent that many passages either remained obscure or, as I said earlier, had simply not been noticed. Existing translations were in general unhelpful, since (understandably enough) translators were more concerned to produce a readable story than with literal accuracy. When one focusses on these passages, it also becomes clear that many of them resist all attempts to make any coherent sense; and that led me to my particular concern with sense and nonsense in the text.

That, I think, must be a legitimate concern for any Homeric scholar; but of course opinions will vary both about what particular passages are incoherent and about the cause of such incoherencies. The latter will depend greatly on one's views about Homeric composition in general. My own views (given in Part 3), though formed chiefly on the basis of the incoherencies themselves, have been developed (and I hope improved) in the light of the work of many other scholars, and I should like here to express my gratitude to those who have been most helpful and in some cases kind enough to give their personal time and trouble to an amateur scholar. They include G.S. Kirk, Jasper Griffin, Alfred Heubeck, Stephanie West, J.B. Hainsworth, Richard Janko, Nicholas Richardson, Mark W. Edwards and Joseph Russo, together with many others whose names are mentioned in the text. They are not of course to be taken as agreeing with any of my comments or conclusions; nevertheless I stand (if sometimes rather heavily) on their shoulders, and I hope their work has saved me from too much naivety.

JBW

Oxford 1998

INTRODUCTION

The reader is owed some fairly clear idea in advance of what I am trying to do in this book, and why I think it worth doing. I attempt this briefly below: but it has also to be said that, in this particular case, the proof of the pudding is in the eating. All I can do here is to explain what sort of pudding it is supposed to be.

I am concerned, then, solely with the meaning of certain parts of the text in a fairly strict sense of 'meaning': with how certain passages should be construed, what their exact sense is, and particularly with whether they do in fact make sense. 'Sense' and 'nonsense' themselves have different senses, but my criterion of selection has chiefly to do with logical or semantic incoherence: the paradigm case would be one in which what is said in a particular passage contradicts itself. My criterion obviates (1) cases where the meaning of some term is just obscure or unknown; (2) cases of vagueness (about Trojan or other topography, for instance); (3) cases of lack of realism (as in some of the 'fairy-tale' elements in the Odyssey); (4) cases where the grammar or syntax is peculiar or deficient, just so long as the meaning is clear and intelligible; (5) cases where the carelessness or economy of the text, or some other reason, makes a demand on our understanding in order to produce sense, but equally there is no question of incoherency or nonsense, and (6) cases where we may be uncertain about whether to take the meaning of a passage in one or another way, but where at least one way (perhaps either way) is coherent enough.

There is one type of case where the criterion is not so clear. Sometimes we can detect what might be called a long-term incoherence in the plot, or in some picture which the poet presents: something not just vague but positively inconsistent. The best known example is the reappearance of a warrior on the battlefield when his death has been reported earlier: and there are other examples (of Ithacan and other topography, for instance) where, if we carefully put together pieces of evidence from various widely-separated parts of the text, we may convict the text as a whole of incoherence. The selection of these passages is here more arbitrary. But as I shall use my criterion, it calls on us to judge whether the reader/hearer might reasonably be thought to react with surprise or bafflement at some point: and that seems to turn on just how short-term or long-term the inconsistency is. A very short-term inconsistency would on my criterion count as incoherent, because we would expect that amount of (short-term) memory on the part of both poet and reader/hearer: indeed all cases of incoherence entail some dependence on memory - A and not-A appear in different places in the poem (perhaps within a few lines) and cannot be judged as incoherent in my sense unless we conceive of them as being held together in someone's mind. Just how short-term or long-term a memory can reasonably be assumed is a matter of subjective judgement: in general I have not counted anything as an incoherency unless A and not-A appear within less than about 50 lines.

Even given these explications, 'incoherent' is still a rather imprecise term. But to discuss various kinds of incoherence, or different senses of the term, in more detail would take us into deeper philosophical waters than I want to swim in here. More importantly, there are difficulties in the application of this criterion to various passages. Most will perhaps be clear enough. But there are not a few in which 'incoherent' may (or may not) be too strong a word to use: in which such terms as 'careless', 'muddled', 'confused', or 'obscure' seem more natural. I have tried to make clear in the notes what description seems to me appropriate; and, in general, I have tried to include all passages which any reasonable person might see as incoherent.

There are quite a few borderline cases. It may perhaps help to view the criterion in terms of what a reasonably attentive hearer or reader would (as it were) say to himself when he heard/read these passages. He might say, for instance, "Well, that's a bit odd, but I see what he means", or "That's rather obscure, just how does the poet actually picture such-and-such?", or "He doesn't really make it clear whether he means such-and-such or so-and-so". These are (at worst) borderline cases. But he might alternatively say "But that doesn't really work", or "That's inconsistent", or "But there's a contradiction there" or "That makes no sense": and here we can speak of incoherence.

I should add that seeing the criterion in this sort of light does not involve making any specific empirical or historical assumptions about the attentiveness or acumen of the poet's audience (whoever these were: something of which we are largely ignorant), if only because we have also to consider the composer's (or reciter's) own attentiveness and acumen. I suppose it might be possible to think, at least *prima facie*, that neither the audience nor the composer/reciter minded at all about the obscurities or even the incoherencies, or even noticed them. But that is both implausible in itself, and also (as I shall show later) would make it very hard to account for various facts: particularly the fact that the vast majority of the text (especially in the Iliad) is free from incoherence, whereas incoherencies crop up quite thickly in other parts of it. Different standards of coherence seem to operate in different parts of the text. We have surely to believe that the poet took care to avoid incoherence in most of the text, rather than that he was indifferent to it. (When I say 'the poet', I do not commit myself to any view about multiple or single authorship: for that question see my Conclusions in Part 3.)

To enlarge a little on this: it might (just) be believed that the audiences who heard the initial recitations, or even who read the earliest written texts, adopted some attitude towards the words which either blinded them to incoherency or else allowed them to consider it as irrelevant: an attitude of mindless reverence, for instance, or of such bewitchment by the verses (and, when recited or chanted, rather than declaimed, their musical accompaniment) that the incoherency passed them by. There might be a parallel here with the way in which sacred texts were intoned or ritually spoken by or to a congregation that simply had no interest in their semantic consistency. Problems about coherence might well then be raised only by later generations of scholars; and that, *mutatis mutandis,* might be the case with the Homeric epics as with (for instance) the Christian scriptures. But it is much less easy to believe that those who composed or produced the texts were equally unconcerned with semantic incoherence, though they may of course have been careless or obscure. Of course the existence of serious incoherencies has to be shown; but I do not think it can be assumed in advance that such cases, if they exist, can simply be brushed aside on the *a priori* grounds that they are irrelevant. Whether anything like a mountain can be made out of these molehills must depend on how many, and how large, the molehills are.

In my selection of passages I have been chiefly concerned with (1) passages which on close inspection turn out to be incoherent, but have not been noted properly (or the nature of the incoherence not properly understood): most of my passages fall into this category. There are also (2) some passages which all or almost all commentators have thought to be incoherent, but are in fact not; I have included these because I want to get some kind of picture of just how much coherence and incoherence the text as a whole is liable to. Finally, there is (3) a category of cases where there is some kind of incoherence which has in fact been not only noted but adequately dealt with by previous commentators. I have to take these into account, for the reason just given: that is, in order to get some overall picture of coherence and incoherence in the text as it stands. There are in fact very few cases of (3): most of the cases fall under (1), with a small minority under (2). In the cases of (3), I need only note briefly what previous commentators have said, for the sake of completeness. That of course adds nothing to Homeric scholarship, but will help (a little) to present a rounded picture.

If one is concerned with the general question of the coherence or consistency or integration of each of the two epics as we have them in our text, as shedding some light on their composition, there are of course many different kinds of these in which one may be interested: consistency of language, for instance, or integration of the plot, or consistency of character, or of the way in which the gods behave, or topographical coherence, or consistency of moral values, or many other things. But I think there may be a special importance to be attached to logical coherence within certain passages, or between passages which are sufficiently close in the text to each other for us to feel safe in taking them together. For here we are asking under what conditions a passage could have been composed (orally or in writing), or transcribed, or put in order, or anyway used and produced eventually as part of our text, when it is logically incoherent or self-contradictory. At least this question relates to the conditions of composition (transcription, etc.) in a different, and perhaps a sharper or more challenging, sort of way. How could these (fairly frequent) cases of nonsense have been generated? With other cases, it is plausible to say things like "Homer writes as a poet, not as a geographer"; but if we say in these cases "Homer writes as a poet, not a logician" we come near to regarding Homer (or whoever we take to be responsible for the passages as we have them) as mentally incompetent. We have surely to assume, at least *prima facie*, that Homer was not, as it were, just irresponsible: that he meant what he said. Yet how can he have meant nonsense? I have myself been driven to a certain theory about the generation of these passages, which I offer (tentatively) at the end of this book. But whether or not this theory is at all on the right lines is comparatively unimportant. What is important is that we should first identify the cases of logical incoherence, and then face squarely the question of how they could have been generated.

It would be possible to formulate *a priori* views about how much (and what kinds of) sense and nonsense, coherence and carelessness, consistency and inconsistency could reasonably be expected from the text: provisional hypotheses about which of these the text would be likely to contain, to be subsequently checked against a more detailed study. But I doubt whether any such views or hypotheses would be worth very much, unless conceived in the most broad-minded way. The trouble is that there are too many unknown factors. We may perhaps know, for instance, that much or most of the text was originally composed orally, and by accretion from the contributions of many bards over a long period of time: and that in itself may offer some guidance. But we do not know, with any certainty, (a) at what stage the text was written down, (b) how much any bard had to remember on any particular occasion, (c) whether the bard could take advantage of a written text (i) to learn it or (ii) to make his own additions to it, (d) the exact position of any monumental 'Homer' in relation to the text as a whole, or (e) the kind of audiences who heard the recitations. Nor do we have any clear idea about the general possibility of interpolations, additions, alterations and so forth. Moreover, what we do

INTRODUCTION

know (or think probable) is itself mostly a result of detailed study of the text, rather than resting on external evidence; so that we cannot without circularity argue from particular passages to *a priori* opinions (they would not then be *a priori*). Nor is the comparative study of oral poetry of much use. That can indeed tell us (has in fact told us) quite a lot about formulaic composition, and a little about what a competent bard could remember without the benefit of a written text; but the trouble here is, obviously enough, that there is in fact no oral poetry of comparable length, background and complexity, or which draws on so many and varied layers of traditional recited song. The uniqueness of the Homeric text is here a fatal difficulty.

All we can say, I think, is that the methods of Homeric composition (insofar, indeed, as we have any clear idea of these) may in principle admit of different kinds of incoherence and inconsistency than those we should expect from a text composed under other conditions. That may be largely the result of differences between the spoken and the written word and the use of formulae in the *Kunstsprache*. It is undeniable that Homeric composition (whatever else we may think about it) was carried out by means of an artificial or stylised form of language-use, a *Kunstsprache* or 'artificial speech', chiefly or at least partly designed to make it easier for the bard to memorise and recite, and consisting in large part of formulae or standard phraseology which simplified the tasks of memorisation and recital. A good deal of work has been done on the general nature and details of this *Kunstsprache* (the best brief account is in Kirk (1985 onwards): see also Kirk (1965), with references): much may still be unclear, but on any reasonable view it will make a big difference to the way in which we see the text as a whole. We have at least to remember that, if I tell a story (especially a long story) orally, particularly if I use formulae or other methods of standardisation to assist me in the telling, I shall say things that are not always coherent, things which I should cut or alter if I were producing a written version. Moreover, my hearers will overlook or let me get away with things when I talk or recite which they would not overlook in a written text. Nevertheless we cannot use this point as a blank cheque or *carte blanche* to excuse ourselves from confronting the sense (or nonsense) of various passages. So what we have to do, and what I shall try to do in this book, is simply to press the various passages for sense and coherence and see what happens. Sometimes sense and coherence emerge; sometimes they are absent - and that, rather than anything else, may tell us something about the way they were composed and conceived.

The existence of the *Kunstsprache* may also suggest that the incoherencies which we shall meet are largely or wholly the result of this highly stylised - one might say, standardised - use of language. That is certainly occasionally the case: the (quite severe) demands of the metre, or the pressure to use formulae when they are not really applicable, sometimes results in incoherency or nonsense. I have noted these in the text. But in fact such cases seem to me to be few; most of the incoherencies cannot reasonably be ascribed to the *Kunstsprache* itself, or even to 'poetic licence' (unless that phrase is used to cover any kind of nonsense). The chief argument here is simply that the vast majority of the text, though always composed with the *Kunstsprache*, is in fact entirely free from incoherence or nonsense (particularly in the Iliad): there seems to be nothing in the *Kunstsprache* itself which generates incoherency or even carelessness. Most of the incoherencies are in fact structural, and cannot fairly be described as 'casual slips' or 'carelessness' at all.

Thus in Iliad 13.363 the formulaic ἔνδον ἐόντα makes no sense: as Janko says, it is a 'misused formula', no doubt carelessly added by the poet to fill out the metre of the line. But the vast majority of other cases are not like this at all. It is more than 'careless' to say (Odyssey 9.21-26) that there are many other islands around (ἀμφί) Ithaca, but that these islands lie apart or away from it (ἄνευθε). The whole passage (see my comments in the main text) is deeply confused. So too with Odyssey 1. 386-98, where βασιλεύς (either 'king', or 'prince', 'noble') seems to be used in different and contradictory senses, and there can be no coherent idea of a 'play upon words' on the part of the speaker. I hope to persuade the reader, in my detailed comments on particular passages, that almost all cases are more like the latter than the former.

One further point must be mentioned. When faced with a passage which seems not to make sense, we can of course always consider the possibility that part of the passage is 'an interpolation' or 'a later addition'. If we take this line, we thereby conceive of some 'original' text which made sense, but has subsequently been messed up. That of course then raises the problem of how, in principle, one can distinguish between what is 'original' and what is to count as 'an addition': a problem which, in the case of Homer, may well seem insoluble. We are already familiar, in Homeric scholarship, with the procedure of (as it were) stripping the text down so as to produce a clear-cut 'original' version which then presents no difficulties in relation to the plot or the topography or anything else: but we get rid of such difficulties only at the cost of getting rid of substantial amounts of the text. The process can easily be overdone, if we insist on our own ideals of coherence as against the text as we have it.

Nevertheless of course there are interpolations and additions (and other forms of messing up the text, for instance having the lines in the wrong order). Where the possibility of these bears on the passages to be analysed, I shall mention it. But fortunately this turns out to be a rare occurrence, for reasons which may not be obvious in advance. Most (nearly all) of the passages are, so to speak, too tightly woven in their logic and construction for their problems of meaning and logic to be solved by the possibility of simple interpolation or other such possibilities. That would not be the case where, for instance, the removal of a single line would produce coherence, or a simple change in the manuscript reading make sense of the passage. But these cases are rare; and that fact enables us to treat the passages on their own logical merits or demerits. I hope this point will become clearer as we proceed.

That is perhaps as much as I can usefully say in advance of discussing the particular passages (which I hope will make the criteria clearer as we go on). I do not, of course, claim that my conclusions on each passage are always correct, if only because different interpretations are sometimes finely balanced. But I do claim that these (and perhaps other) passages deserve this kind of attention.

PART 1

COMMENTS ON THE ILIAD

2. 291-98

ἦ μὴν καὶ πόνος ἐστὶν ἀνιηθέντα νέεσθαι·
καὶ γάρ τίς θ' ἕνα μῆνα μένων ἀπὸ ἧς ἀλόχοιο
ἀσχαλάᾳ σὺν νηὶ πολυζύγῳ, ὅν περ ἄελλαι
χειμέριαι εἰλέωσιν ὀρινομένη τε θάλασσα·
ἡμῖν δ' εἴνατός ἐστι περιτροπέων ἐνιαυτὸς
ἐνθάδε μιμνόντεσσι· τῶ οὐ νεμεσίζομ' Ἀχαιοὺς
ἀσχαλάαν παρὰ νηυσὶ κορωνίσιν· ἀλλὰ καὶ ἔμπης
αἰσχρόν τοι δηρόν τε μένειν κενεόν τε νέεσθαι.

Indeed it is a burden for us to go home without having accomplished anything. For a man who stays away from his wife for a single month chafes when he is with his many-benched ship, which the winter storms and the rising sea hem in; and for us the ninth revolving year has come, as we stay here. So I am not indignant that the Achaeans should chafe by their beaked ships. Yet even so it is disgraceful to stay long and return empty-handed.

Kirk does his best for this passage: 'Going home in frustration would be as bad as toiling on the battlefield, because, although even a month's delay away from home is bad...it is nevertheless disgraceful...', with the γάρ ('for') in 292 looking forwards (redressed by ἀλλὰ καὶ ἔμπης ('Yet even so') in 297). But that still does not really make sense of πόνος, which must mean something like 'toil' or 'labour': it would not be toil or labour for them to go home in frustration, and the disgrace would not make it so. The alternative (Leaf) 'truly here is toil to make a man return disheartened' can hardly be got out of the Greek. A borderline case at best, if not positively incoherent.

2. 356 (= 590)

τείσασθαι δ' Ἑλένης ὁρμήματά τε στοναχάς τε.

To avenge the struggles and groans over Helen

All commentators take ὁρμήματά τε στοναχάς τε as 'struggles and groans', either (1) Helen's struggles and groans (whilst being abducted and held captive) or (2) those of the Greeks in fighting to recover her. The objection to (1) is that Helen went with Paris voluntarily and was in general well-treated in Troy: to (2) that what the Greeks are trying to avenge is surely Helen's rape, not their own efforts to recover her - those efforts are part of their 'trying to avenge', not what they are trying to avenge. In any case, ὁρμήματά does not normally mean 'struggles' in the required sense: it refers rather to some kind of attack, or rush towards something, or initiative taken against something or somebody; 'to avenge the attacks we have made (are making) on Helen's behalf' does not seem very good sense. The connection with the idea of ravishing some Trojan's wife (355), and of Menelaus being especially keen on this vengeance (μάλιστα δε ἴετο ('and he particularly desired'), 589), might suggest (3) a specifically sexual connotation for ὁρμήματά and στοναχάς), which would make more sense of the notion of vengeance. But that is somewhat fanciful, and as it stands the line is obscure: perhaps a borderline case.

4. 297-309

ἱππῆας μὲν πρῶτα σὺν ἵπποισιν καὶ ὄχεσφι,
πεζοὺς δ' ἐξόπιθε στῆσεν πολέας τε καὶ ἐσθλούς,
ἕρκος ἔμεν πολέμοιο· κακοὺς δ' ἐς μέσσον ἔλασσεν,
ὄφρα καὶ οὐκ ἐθέλων τις ἀναγκαίῃ πολεμίζοι.
ἱππεῦσιν μὲν πρῶτ' ἐπετέλλετο· τοὺς γὰρ ἀνώγει
σφοὺς ἵππους ἐχέμεν μηδὲ κλονέεσθαι ὁμίλῳ·
" μηδέ τις ἱπποσύνῃ τε καὶ ἠνορέηφι πεποιθὼς
οἶος πρόσθ' ἄλλων μεμάτω Τρώεσσι μάχεσθαι,
μηδ' ἀναχωρείτω· ἀλαπαδνότεροι γὰρ ἔσεσθε.
ὃς δέ κ' ἀνὴρ ἀπὸ ὧν ὀχέων ἕτερ' ἅρμαθ' ἵκηται,
ἔγχει ὀρεξάσθω, ἐπεὶ ἦ πολὺ φέρτερον οὕτω.
ὧδε καὶ οἱ πρότεροι πόλεας καὶ τείχε' ἐπόρθεον,
τόνδε νόον καὶ θυμὸν ἐνὶ στήθεσσιν ἔχοντες."

First he arranged the horsemen, with their horses and chariots; and behind them the foot-soldiers, many and excellent, to be a bastion in the war. He forced the inferior troops into the middle, so that each man might fight by necessity even if he did not wish to. First he gave instructions to the horsemen: he told them to hold their horses back and not rush wildly in the conflict. "Let noone, trusting in his horsemanship and courage, set forth alone to fight with the Trojans in front of the others, nor let him retreat: for in that way you will be weaker. And whatever man from his own chariot comes up against another chariot; let him strike out with his spear, since that will be much better. In this way men of old time sacked cities and fortifications, having this intent and spirit within their hearts".

5

Commentators have discussed this at length (see Kirk for an excellent summary), but with regard to its content rather than its coherence. The content is indeed odd, but not actually incoherent; it is a tolerably clear account of mass chariot fighting, where the chariots are supposed to stay in line (303-05), and warriors in the chariots to thrust with their spears at close quarters (306-07). ἕρκος ("It is tempting to look to ἕρκος ἔμεν πολεμιο for some kind of sense", Kirk) seems to mean something like 'a tower of strength', a fortress or bastion, something which the enemy could not easily pass (as in 1.284 of Achilles): but it is not clear whether this refers only to the infantry or to the infantry and chariots together (in contrast to the κακους ('inferior troops', 'cowards'). In any case ἕρκος is the 'solid part', as one might say, of the battle-array.

But there are some logical incoherencies. μεν ('on the one hand') and πρωτα ('first') in 301 lead us to expect that Nestor will address the infantry later, and γαρ ('for') does not seem to have any obvious sense. The sudden lapse into direct speech would also leave the reader/hearer surprised and confused. I think this must count as incoherent.

5. 134-43

Τυδείδης δ' ἐξαῦτις ἰὼν προμάχοισιν ἐμίχθη,
καὶ πρίν περ θυμῷ μεμαὼς Τρώεσσι μάχεσθαι·
δὴ τότε μιν τρὶς τόσσον ἕλεν μένος, ὥς τε λέοντα,
ὅν ῥά τε ποιμὴν ἀγρῷ ἐπ' εἰροπόκοις ὀίεσσι
χραύσῃ μέν τ' αὐλῆς ὑπεράλμενον οὐδὲ δαμάσσῃ·
τοῦ μέν τε σθένος ὦρσεν, ἔπειτα δέ τ' οὐ προσαμύνει,
ἀλλὰ κατὰ σταθμοὺς δύεται, τὰ δ' ἐρῆμα φοβεῖται·
αἱ μέν τ' ἀγχιστῖναι ἐπ' ἀλλήλῃσι κέχυνται,
αὐτὰρ ὁ ἐμμεμαὼς βαθέης ἐξάλλεται αὐλῆς·
ὣς μεμαὼς Τρώεσσι μίγη κρατερὸς Διομήδης.

Then again the son of Tydeus went and mixed with the champions, though even before he was eager in his heart to fight the Trojans. At that time indeed thrice as much strength entered into him, as into a lion which a shepherd in the country, near to his fleecy sheep, wounds lightly as it jumps over the sheepfold, but does not kill it. He has aroused its strength, but then has no defence against it: he lurks amongst the steadings and shuns in fear the open places; and the sheep are piled up in heaps on each other. Then it jumps furiously out of the deep fold. Just so did strong Diomede mix eagerly with the Trojans.

Kirk's note on this is extremely clear and full, giving all the possible meanings for this admittedly obscure passage. I agree that the most plausible meaning for 140 is 'but he [sc. the shepherd] slips among the steadings and shuns in fear the empty [i.e. open] places': to take τα δ'ἐρημα ('the empty places') as 'the sheep, deserted, flee in panic' is too harsh. I also agree that 141 is likely to refer to the corpses of the sheep which the lion has killed, since 'some mention of a victim or victims might be expected'. But 142-43 is rather more difficult. The point is not, or not just, that 'the conjunction of ἐμμεμαως ('eager') and ἐξαλλεται ('jumps out'), viz. of increased courage and implied retreat, is odd'; it is rather that by 142 the lion must have made his kill, whereas Diomede (in this general context, anyway) is going to make his, as he does in 144 95.: yet the parallel of ἐμμεμαως in 142 with μεμαως in 143 seems to tie the lion's position fairly closely to Diomede's.

I do not deny that this is somewhat awkward or obscure, but we have to remember that Homeric similes are rarely parallel at all or even most points. Perhaps it is enough that the lion is lightly wounded, and that this only spurs on his rage. 'Incoherence' is here too strong a term.

5. 181-91

Τυδείδη μιν ἔγωγε δαΐφρονι πάντα ἐΐσκω,
ἀσπίδι γιγνώσκων αὐλώπιδί τε τρυφαλείῃ,
ἵππους τ' εἰσορόων· σάφα δ' οὐκ οἶδ' εἰ θεός ἐστιν.
εἰ δ' ὅ γ' ἀνὴρ ὅν φημι, δαΐφρων Τυδέος υἱός,
οὐχ ὅ γ' ἄνευθε θεοῦ τάδε μαίνεται, ἀλλά τις ἄγχι
ἕστηκ' ἀθανάτων, νεφέλῃ εἰλυμένος ὤμους,
ὅς τούτου βέλος ὠκὺ κιχήμενον ἔτραπεν ἄλλῃ.
ἤδη γάρ οἱ ἐφῆκα βέλος, καί μιν βάλον ὦμον
δεξιὸν ἀντικρὺ διὰ θώρηκος γυάλοιο·
καί μιν ἔγωγ' ἐφάμην Ἀϊδωνῆϊ προϊάψειν,
ἔμπης δ' οὐκ ἐδάμασσα· θεός νύ τίς ἐστι κοτήεις.

I think him like the warlike Diomede in every way, recognising him by his shield and his tubed helmet, and looking at his horses; but I do not know for certain whether it may be a god. If it is the man whom I say, the warlike son of Tydeus, then he does not fight furiously like this without a god - some one of the immortals stands by him, wrapped in a cloud about his shoulders, who turns away from him the sharp missile directed at him. For I have already sent a missile at him, and I struck his right shoulder, and it went right through his breastplate: and I thought I had sent him down to Hades, yet nevertheless I did not kill him. There must, then, be some angry god.

The first part of this passage is acceptable if we take ἐισκω ('I liken him to') in 181 literally: "I think him in every way like Diomede, but I'm not absolutely sure whether it might not be a god. If it is a man, Diomede, then there must be a concealed god nearby (ἀγχι ('near'), 185) who has made my shot ineffective". But then comes (191 θεος νυ τις ἐσσι κοτηεις which seems to mean "So it must be some angry god". It is natural to take this, with Leaf, as 'some wrathful god, then, is it': that is, it is not Diomede at all but a god. But that is directly contrary to 185 ff, the logic of which is "There must be some disguised god around, for (γαρ ('for'), 188) I wounded him all right, but didn't kill him, so - "; and we now expect "some god must be helping him". Can it mean "So there must be some angry god around", sc. to have made my shot ineffective? That is just possible, though 'angry' is a little odd - one would have expected some adjective to mean 'protective' or 'favouring him'. If it was actually a god who had been hit, not Diomede, the anger is more intelligible. It looks as if Pandaros, or the poet, has in 191 reverted to the idea of it being not Diomede but a god: and this is inconsistent with 185 ff. I think we must count this as a case of incoherence.

5. 885-87

ἀλλά μ' ὑπήνεικαν ταχέες πόδες· ἦ τέ κε δηρὸν
αὐτοῦ πήματ' ἔπασχον ἐν αἰνῇσιν νεκάδεσσιν,
ἤ κε ζὼς ἀμενηνὸς ἔα χαλκοῖο τυπῇσι."

But my swift feet carried me away. Otherwise for a long time I would have suffered woes there amongst the dreadful corpses; or else, alive, I would have been strengthless through the blows of bronze.

The passage has been much criticised, but the question of coherency is more complex than most commentators have thought. Kirk says "Does it make sense to say 'I would long have suffered woes among the piles of dead there, <u>or I would have been alive but devoid of strength, through blows of bronze</u>'? Surely not: either this god is thoroughly confused... or the composer of this v. must have taken ἐν αἰνῃσιν νεκάδεσσιν ('amongst the dreadful corpses') to imply 'among the dead in Hades'... - but that is specifically excluded by 886 " (his italics). We can perhaps forget about the god being confused (which would not excuse incoherence on the poet's part), and face the basic logical difficulty, which is this: either (1) the contrast between 885-86 and 887 is a contrast between Ares being killed and his remaining alive (ζωὸς ('alive'), 887), or (2) there is no such contrast. If (1), we face the problem of an immortal god being killed, and also a problem about δηρὸν in 885. If (2), it is not clear that there is <u>any</u> contrast at all, so that ζωὸς in 887 makes no sense (and ἀμενηνός ('strengthless') will also seem pointless). Thus the objection in Kirk's translation above is that the alternatives are not real ones: 'suffering woes among the piles of dead', is consistent with being 'alive' but 'devoid of strength through blows of bronze': that, I take it, is why Kirk thinks it makes no sense. This is a case of (2). So then Kirk considers taking 886 as "I would have suffered amongst the dead in Hades": i.e. Ares would have been killed, the contrast (1) is preserved; but 'in Hades' is excluded by αὐτοῦ ('there'), which must mean 'there on the battlefield'. And there remains the problem of Ares' immortality.

It seems clear from ζωὸς ('alive') (887) that the only hope of coherence lies in (1). We could escape Kirk's objection by taking αὐτοῦ not as referring to Ares' suffering among the dead in Hades, but as referring to his suffering the pain of death or destruction there on the battlefield amongst the corpses. Nor is the point about immortality absolutely insuperable: in 5. 388 we are told that Ares might or could have been 'destroyed' (ἀπόλοιτο), and the exact ontological status of Homeric gods and/or the bodies or *personae* they take on is obscure. The real objection lies in δηρὸν (885), which must mean 'for a long time' and makes no sense if we take πήματ' ἔπασχον ('I would have suffered woes') as, in effect, "I would have been killed". So 887, at least (which is odd in other than semantic ways, see Kirk), is incoherent in this context: perhaps a later addition.

7. 115-19, 173-74

ἀλλὰ σὺ μὲν νῦν ἷζευ ἰὼν μετὰ ἔθνος ἑταίρων,
τούτῳ δὲ πρόμον ἄλλον ἀναστήσουσιν Ἀχαιοί.
εἴ περ ἀδειής τ' ἐστὶ καὶ εἰ μόθου ἔστ' ἀκόρητος,
φημί μιν ἀσπασίως γόνυ κάμψειν, αἴ κε φύγῃσι
δηΐου ἐκ πολέμοιο καὶ αἰνῆς δηϊοτῆτος. . . .

καὶ δ' αὐτὸς ὃν θυμὸν ὀνήσεται, αἴ κε φύγῃσι
δηΐου ἐκ πολέμοιο καὶ αἰνῆς δηϊοτῆτος.

But do you now go and sit down with the gathering of your comrades, and the Achaeans will put up another champion against this man. Even if he is fearless and can never have enough of toil, I believe that he will be pleased to bend his knees and rest, if indeed he escapes from the fierce combat and dreadful strife...
...and he will profit in his own spirit, if he escapes from the fierce combat and dreadful strife.

This passage reads strangely. Commentators (see Kirk) have noted the (surely harsh) change of subject in 117 (to Hector), and the doubling of δηΐου ('hostile') and δηϊοτῆτος ('hostility'). But I do not think the strangeness lies in either of these: it is rather that 117-19 refer more naturally to someone who escapes from the war and battle in general, not from a one-to-one duel - as in Achilles' threat (19.71 ff.), where the same phrases are used (ἀσπασίως...γόνυ κάμψειν, ὅς κε φύγῃσι, κτλ. ('gladly...bend the knee, whoever flees, etc')). Certainly the passage starts with that implication: 'even if he is fearless and insatiable in respect of the moil of battle' (Kirk's phrase for μόθου ('toil')). And πολέμοιο ('war') is an odd word to use of a duel (it is not used in the earlier duel between Paris and Menelaus), even though it appears in 232.

The repetition of the phrase in 173-74 does not help with this difficulty. Indeed it might there be taken as meaning 'if he escapes from the war in general'. Moreover, the idea (in either passage) one of the duellists <u>escaping</u> from the duel is strange: Hector's terms (77 ff.) make it clear that it is to be a fight to the death. Of course (in 116 ff.) Hector would escape from it by <u>winning</u> the duel; but it seems rather feeble or pessimistic for Agamemnon to say "Even if Hector is fearless and insatiable of battle, he will at least have a hard time of it and be pleased to take a rest (when he wins)".

So I think the reader/hearer would find the addition of these three lines (and also 172-74) baffling and out of place, though not perhaps positively incoherent. I suspect that the formulas have been dragged from their normal context (of war and battle in general) and inappropriately used of the duel. At best a borderline case.

7. 312

εἰς Ἀγαμέμνονα δῖον ἄγον, κεχαρηότα νίκῃ.

Brought him to noble Agamemnon, rejoicing in his victory.

This is careless to the point of incoherence: the duel (see 273 ff.) is clearly a draw. Kirk's "Aias is rejoicing in the victory that was his by rights" does not fit the facts.

7. 332-43

αὐτοὶ δ' ἀγρόμενοι κυκλήσομεν ἐνθάδε νεκροὺς
βουσὶ καὶ ἡμιόνοισιν· ἀτὰρ κατακήομεν αὐτοὺς
τυτθὸν ἀποπρὸ νεῶν, ὥς κ' ὀστέα παισὶν ἕκαστος
οἴκαδ' ἄγῃ, ὅτ' ἂν αὖτε νεώμεθα πατρίδα γαῖαν.
τύμβον δ' ἀμφὶ πυρὴν ἕνα χεύομεν ἐξαγαγόντες
ἄκριτον ἐκ πεδίου· ποτὶ δ' αὐτὸν δείμομεν ὦκα
πύργους ὑψηλούς, εἶλαρ νηῶν τε καὶ αὐτῶν.
ἐν δ' αὐτοῖσι πύλας ποιήσομεν εὖ ἀραρυίας,
ὄφρα δι' αὐτάων ἱππηλασίη ὁδὸς εἴη·

> ἔκτοσθεν δὲ βαθεῖαν ὀρύξομεν ἐγγύθι τάφρον,
> ἥ χ' ἵππον καὶ λαὸν ἐρυκάκοι ἀμφὶς ἐοῦσα,
> μή ποτ' ἐπιβρίσῃ πόλεμος Τρώων ἀγερώχων.

We ourselves will assemble and bring the corpses here with oxen and mules; and we will burn them a little distance from the ships, so that each man may carry the bones back to his children, when we return again to our native land. We will pile up a single tomb around the pyre, raising up a common barrow from the plain; and onto that swiftly build high fortifications, as a defence for the ships and for ourselves. In them we will make well-fitting gates, so that there may be a way through them for driving chariots. And outside we will dig a deep trench close to it, which as a separate defence will keep back horse and foot-soldiers, in case ever the warfare of the proud Trojans weighs heavy on us.

There are several difficulties here, and at least one major incoherence. (Kirk's notes give most of the relevant points, but I differ in some of what follows.) The major incoherence is in 333-35. Commentators from Aristarchus onwards have regarded 334-35 as interpolated, the obvious difficulties being (1) that the common (ἕνα ('one') in 336 and probably ἄκριτον ('unseparated') in 337) pyre would make it impossible to identify the individual bones, and (2) that the idea of each man (ἕκαστος) bringing his own bones home to his children is absurd. But the trouble goes deeper, since if we excise these two lines ἀτὰρ κατακήομεν αὐτούς ('and we shall burn them') ends the sentence not just, as Kirk says, 'a little abruptly', but in a way which seems to me stylistically and syntactically intolerable. Indeed it is worse than that: Nestor ought to say something about the pyre before going on to talk about the tomb, but in fact mentions the pyre only *en passant* (336). This difficulty does not arise when the Greeks actually follow his advice in 420 ff.: that passage reads much more naturally, partly because the burning of the corpses on the pyre is adequately described in 427-32. So it seems that the whole passage from 333 onwards is at least confused.

How far onwards? I take 336-37 as intelligible enough in the sense of "let us heap up a common (ἄκριτον) tomb, raising it up (ἐξαγαγόντες) in the plain" (ἐκ πεδίου: or 'from the plain', it makes no matter): though other interpretations (see Kirk) are also possible. But ποτι here and also in 436 is difficult: it is not clear whether this means 'onto it', 'on it', 'attached to it', or (probably best) 'in front of it'. πύργους in 338 is not as bad as Kirk supposes ("Nestor mentions only towers here"), since it can certainly mean 'battlements' - that is, walls (not just individual towers), as in Od. 6.262-63 (ἣν περὶ πύργος ὑψηλός ('around which is a high fortification')). It is nevertheless odd - as it were, too <u>hurried</u> - in comparison with 437-38 where the πύργος is specifically mentioned. Finally ἀμφὶς ἐοῦσα ('being apart') in 342 is at least mysterious, particularly in view of ἐγγύθι ('near') in 341: Kirk says that "'being all round' the camp is acceptable", but if we press that too hard it runs into topographical difficulties (was the wall built with its two ends finishing at the seashore, or right round the whole camp, or what?)

I think that the whole of this passage represents a (rare) case in the Iliad (less rare in the Odyssey), where quite a lot of the text - ten lines or so - cannot be seen as a finished product but represents something more like 'work in progress' (see later under my Conclusions). At least it contains one or more incoherences, and much evidence of haste or carelessness.

7. 345-46

> Τρώων αὖτ' ἀγορὴ γένετ' Ἰλίου ἐν πόλει ἄκρῃ,
> δεινὴ τετρηχυῖα. παρὰ Πριάμοιο θύρῃσι·

There took place an assembly of the Trojans in the acropolis of Ilium, alarmingly tumultuous, by Priam's doors.

Kirk says "...how can an assembly or gathering be 'terrible', for the term can mean little less?" That it should be 'disturbed' is not problematic: at 2.95 τετρήχει δ'ἀγορή ('the assembly made a loud noise') (of the Achaean assembly). δεινή ('terrible') might fairly mean something like 'alarming'; but the absence of a copula between δεινη and τετρηχυια ('making a noise') suggests that δεινη is adverbial, the phrase meaning 'alarmingly tumultuous'. It reads naturally enough.

7. 351-53

> νῦν δ' ὅρκια πιστὰ
> ψευσάμενοι μαχόμεσθα· τῶ οὔ νύ τι κέρδιον ἡμῖν
> ἔλπομαι ἐκτελέεσθαι, ἵνα μὴ ῥέξομεν ὧδε.

But now we fight after having cheated on sincere oaths: so that I do not expect things will turn out at all to our advantage, wherefore we should not act thus.

Here on the other hand there is incoherence. The reference to 'cheating over the oaths' must refer back to Book 3 (the oaths taken for the duel between Paris and Menelaus) - quite a long way for the reader/hearer to remember. That is not intolerable, but τω οὐ νύ τι κέρδιον ἡμῖν ('therefore it will not be all profitable for us') is harder. We cannot excise the line, because the ending ἵνα μη ῥέξομεν ὧδε ('so that we ought not to do thus') would then make little sense. It would have to mean "So nothing now is advantageous for us": that is harsh in itself, and also the Trojans are in fact doing quite well (which is one reason why Nestor thinks it necessary to build the wall). The addition of τω gives the kind of sense we want ("things will not now turn out well for us, because we are morally in the wrong"); but then ἵνα μη ῥεξομεν ὧδε remains unexplained. Kirk thinks ἵνα is acceptable in the sense of 'where': "therefore I do not expect any beneficial result for us where we do not act as I suggest". But (1) it is doubtful whether ἵνα can bear this sense, and (2) even if it can, it must suggest that the Trojans could at some points act as he suggests and at other points not: but in fact either they give Helen back or they do not - it is a yes-or-no decision. That, together with the 'miserable piece of prosody' in the line (see Kirk), suggests incoherence: arising perhaps, as often in this book, from excessive compression or haste.

7. 434

> τῆμος ἄρ' ἀμφὶ πυρὴν κριτὸς ἔγρετο λαὸς Ἀχαιῶν,

Then a selected band of the Achaeans stood up round the pyre.

κριτος is odd (see Kirk): who is this specially chosen λαός ('people') that also builds the tomb and the walls *(435 ff.)*? Not absolutely incoherent but surely baffling to the reader/hearer.

7. 446-51, 456-58

Ζεῦ πάτερ, ἦ ῥά τίς ἐστι βροτῶν ἐπ' ἀπείρονα γαῖαν
ὅς τις ἔτ' ἀθανάτοισι νόον καὶ μῆτιν ἐνίψει;
οὐχ ὁράᾳς ὅτι δὴ αὖτε κάρη κομόωντες Ἀχαιοὶ
τεῖχος ἐτειχίσσαντο νεῶν ὕπερ, ἀμφὶ δὲ τάφρον
ἤλασαν, οὐδὲ θεοῖσι δόσαν κλειτὰς ἑκατόμβας;
τοῦ δ' ἤτοι κλέος ἔσται ὅσον τ' ἐπικίδναται ἠώς· . . . .

ἄλλος κέν τις τοῦτο θεῶν δείσειε νόημα,
ὃς σέο πολλὸν ἀφαυρότερος χεῖράς τε μένος τε·
σὸν δ' ἤτοι κλέος ἔσται ὅσον τ' ἐπικίδναται ἠώς.

Father Zeus, is there any mortal over the boundless earth who will still tell the immortals his intentions and plans? Do you not see that the long-haired Achaeans have built a fortification over their ships, and driven a trench round it, and have not given fair hecatombs to the gods? Indeed the fame of the fortification will reach as far as the dawn scatters its light...
Some other one of the gods might fear this plan of theirs, some one who is much weaker than you in his arms and strength: but your fame will extend as far as the dawn scatters its light.

ἐνίψει in 447 is odd: it must be intended as a future of ἐνέπειν and mean 'tell', but it does not really square with Poseidon's objection. The objection is partly that the Greeks have not sacrificed to the gods before building the wall, but chiefly (451 ff.) that their wall will outdo the wall that Poseidon had made earlier in Trojan history. Neither of these seems to have much to do with the Greeks telling the gods what they intend. The virtual repetition of 451 in 458 is also strange, and 458 does not really fit in with Zeus argument. His argument is to the effect that Poseidon is so strong (457) that he need not worry - he can break down the wall, cover the beach with sand, and thus blot it out altogether (461-63). All this is some way short of incoherence, but I think the reader/hearer would feel some unease about it. A borderline case.

8. 166-71

ἄξεις ἐν νήεσσι· πάρος τοι δαίμονα δώσω."
Ὣς φάτο, Τυδεΐδης δὲ διάνδιχα μερμήριξεν,
ἵππους τε στρέψαι καὶ ἐναντίβιον μαχέσασθαι.
τρὶς μὲν μερμήριξε κατὰ φρένα καὶ κατὰ θυμόν,
τρὶς δ' ἄρ' ἀπ' Ἰδαίων ὀρέων κτύπε μητίετα Ζεὺς
σῆμα τιθεὶς Τρώεσσι, μάχης ἑτεραλκέα νίκην.

"...will not carry off [the women] in our ships. Before that, I will bring your fate upon you." So he spoke; and the son of Tydeus was in two minds, and pondered whether to turn round his horses and fight face to face. Three times he pondered in his heart and his spirit, and three times Zeus the planner thundered from the mountains of Ida, establishing a sign for the Trojans, a victory won by alien strength.

There seems no doubt that this passage is difficult (even Kirk thinks it 'typical of this composer at his hastiest'). One difficult feature is δαίμονα δώσω ('I will give fate'): even if δαίμων could in Homer mean 'destiny' or 'fate', which it cannot, "I will give Destiny to you" is still highly unnatural. The lack of alternatives after μερμήριξεν ('pondered') in 167 is also odd, though the construction is found in the Odyssey (admittedly without διάνδιχα ('in two minds'), which makes 166-67 harder), and in the context the reader/hearer, though perhaps initially a bit surprised at the lack of alternatives, would fairly easily take it to mean something like "He was in two minds (διάνδιχα) and wondered whether to turn his horses", etc.

The sense and syntax of 171 appear much harder to judge. We would like to have a line which meant 'giving the Trojans the sign of (some kind of) victory in battle'; but that is not the line we have, nor can it be plausibly amended to read like that. So commentators have thought themselves forced to take σημα ('a sign') 'in apposition' to νίκην ('victory'), or 'as a zeugma' (both rather unclear phrases). But that will not do, because it is hard to see how the σημα can be a νίκη ('in apposition'); and almost as hard to see how producing (making, setting up, establishing, etc.) a σημα can also involve producing a νίκη ('as a zeugma'). The basic trouble is that νίκην must mean actual victory: Leaf says 'making a sign for the Trojans and a turning of the tide of battle', and of course that will make sense of σημα - by thundering, Zeus produces both a sign and a 'turning of the tide', the turning being supposed to start at once. But that will not do for νίκην. To make sense of τιθεις ('establishing'), we should have to translate it along the lines of 'setting up the initial conditions for' or 'laying the foundations for': but that sense will now not do for σημα. τιθεις σημα must mean simply 'giving them a sign'.

Some readers will think this over-fussy: why should the line not mean simply 'granting the Trojans a sign, and granting them victory in battle'? That the victory is prospective rather than immediate may be no objection. But the asyndeton is still worrying for any zeugma (that, presumably, is why the idea of 'apposition' has had a wider appeal). Yet 'apposition' fares no better: 'granting them a sign - that is, a victory' makes no sense. It is tempting here to take τιθεις firmly with νίκην, put the comma after σημα rather than after Τρώεσσι ('Trojans'), and take κτύπε ('thundered') with σημα: "Zeus thundered to them as a sign, granting the Trojans victory". That gets round the syntactical problems, but I do not think it reads naturally enough to be convincing. A borderline case at best.

8. 186-90

νῦν μοι τὴν κομιδὴν ἀποτίνετον, ἥν μάλα πολλὴν
Ἀνδρομάχη θυγάτηρ μεγαλήτορος Ἠετίωνος
ὑμῖν πὰρ προτέροισι μελίφρονα πυρὸν ἔθηκεν
οἶνόν τ' ἐγκεράσασα πιεῖν, ὅτε θυμὸς ἀνώγοι,
ἢ ἐμοί, ὅς πέρ οἱ θαλερὸς πόσις εὔχομαι εἶναι.

Now pay back to me the cost of the care, the very great care which Andromache daughter of great-hearted Eëtion gave you: she put down before you honey-hearted corn, and mixed wine for you to drink, whenever your spirit bade you - even before me, who claim to be her fine husband.

I note this only because many commentators have, as Kirk says, 'made heavy weather' of it. Kirk's note shows how it makes perfectly good sense, and I need not repeat here what he says (though I think the θυμος in 189 is the horses' θυμος and not Andromache's).

8. 213

> ὅσον ἐκ νηῶν ἀπὸ πύργου τάφρος ἔεργε,

As far as the trench, from the direction of the ships, enclosed a space away from the fortifications.

So too with this line, which Kirk also explains. ἐκ νηων ('from the ships') is at worst a bit vague, certainly not incoherent. Kirk says 'away from the ships', an appropriately vague phrase. I think the line is, so to speak, deliberately topographical: the reader/hearer is invited to start from (the direction of) the ships and then attend to the space between the trench and the wall. It is perhaps compressed, but not in any way confused.

8. 231-32

> ἔσθοντες κρέα πολλὰ βοῶν ὀρθοκραιράων,
> πίνοντες κρητῆρας ἐπιστεφέας οἴνοιο,

eating much flesh from straight-horned oxen, and drinking bowls to the brim with wine.

Here however Kirk seems to me somewhat fussy or alarmist. ὀρθοκραιράων ('with straight horns') is not 'comically grandiose' but simply formular (formulaic epithets are commonly applied without regard for the context). And 232 is not 'strictly nonsensical'. "...whereas setting up mixing-bowls...makes sense, <u>drinking</u> them, or even <u>from</u> them, does not (and drinking the whole of their contents is not a possible meaning)" (his italics); but we can say in English "They drank whole hogsheads" (or whatever) "of wine". There seems nothing amiss here.

8. 530-41

> πρῶϊ δ' ὑπηοῖοι σὺν τεύχεσι θωρηχθέντες
> νηυσὶν ἔπι γλαφυρῇσιν ἐγείρομεν ὀξὺν Ἄρηα.
> εἴσομαι εἴ κέ μ' ὁ Τυδείδης κρατερὸς Διομήδης
> πὰρ νηῶν πρὸς τεῖχος ἀπώσεται, ἢ κεν ἐγὼ τὸν
> χαλκῷ δῃώσας ἔναρα βροτόεντα φέρωμαι.
> αὔριον ἣν ἀρετὴν διαείσεται, εἴ κ' ἐμὸν ἔγχος
> μείνῃ ἐπερχόμενον· ἀλλ' ἐν πρώτοισιν, ὀίω,
> κείσεται οὐτηθείς, πολέες δ' ἀμφ' αὐτὸν ἑταῖροι,
> ἠελίου ἀνιόντος ἐς αὔριον· εἰ γὰρ ἐγὼν ὣς
> εἴην ἀθάνατος καὶ ἀγήρως ἤματα πάντα,
> τιοίμην δ' ὡς τίετ' Ἀθηναίη καὶ Ἀπόλλων,
> ὣς νῦν ἡμέρη ἥδε κακὸν φέρει Ἀργείοισιν."

And early at the first light of dawn, having armed ourselves with our gear, we shall rouse up fierce war by the hollow ships. I shall learn whether Tydeus' son, strong Diomedes, will push me back to the wall away from the ships, or whether I will kill him with the bronze and carry off his bloody arms. Tomorrow he will discern his own courage, if he stands up to my spear as I come upon him. But, I believe, he will lie wounded in the forefront of the battle, and many of his comrades round him, when the sun comes up for tomorrow. Would that I might be so deathless and ageless for all time, and be honoured as Athene and Apollo are honoured, as I am now sure that this day brings evil to the Argives.

See Kirk's notes on this passage and on Book 8 generally: there are many possible cases of interpolation, misplaced lines, borrowings or adaptations from other passages, and so on. Our concern is of course only with possible incoherence in the text as it stands.

533 has passed muster with all commentators, but I think it at least suspect. Kirk says "The τεῖχος ('wall') is of course that of Troy". That seems to me unnatural in the context, and unparalleled elsewhere. Hector is talking about fighting <u>at</u> the ships, as παρ νηων ('from the ships') implies (531) and he may well be looking forward to when he has broken through the Greek wall (as happens in Book 13). In that case τεῖχος is the Greek wall, and the question is whether Diomede will push him away from the ships back to that wall. There is, I believe, enough uncertainty here at least for the reader/hearer to be confused.

538, on the other hand, seems to me weak and repetitive, but not incoherent. 'Meaningless' (Kirk) is too strong for ἐς ('into') in ἐς αὔριον ('into the morrow'): it may mean "when the sun comes up for the morrow" or into the morrow", not exactly paralleled but intelligible. The real difficulty is that Hector seems to have got the days mixed up. ἥδε ('this') in 541 must surely mean 'this very day', νυν, with the present tense φέρει ('brings'), which conflicts with 'tomorrow'. This is certainly incoherent.

8. 558

> οὐρανόθεν δ' ἄρ' ὑπερράγη ἄσπετος αἰθήρ,

And the illimitable upper air, then, has been broken open down from the heavens.

Most commentators have thought this line to be acceptable in its other context (16.297 ff.), where the air seems to be 'broken' because Zeus has moved away the clouds (κινήσῃ νεφέλην ('moves the cloud'), 16.298); but not here, where there are no clouds. Thus Kirk: "The break in the clouds is a sudden event.... The description of this sudden break in the clouds is out of place". If that were right, this would surely count as an incoherence.

However, things are not quite as clear as that. It is misleading to talk of 'a break in the <u>clouds</u>'. since the subject is actually the upper air, αἰθήρ: <u>that</u> is what is 'broken'. But how, strictly or literally speaking, can the αἰθήρ be 'broken'? ὑπερράγη must mean something like 'broken <u>open</u>' or 'laid open' (by some breach), as perhaps a house may be 'broken open' or 'laid open' if the doors and windows are removed. The upper air is laid open, from heaven downwards (οὐρανόθεν). And now this seems intelligible enough for the present passage, particularly with ἄρ' ('so, then', 'as it seems'): "for, as it appears, the limitless air has been laid open from heaven downwards". It has been laid open by a previous removal of clouds or mist, and the passage is not a 'description' of a 'sudden break in the clouds' at all. There is no incoherence here.

9.182 ff.

Τὼ δὲ βάτην παρὰ θῖνα πολυφλοίσβοιο θαλάσσης

These two men went along the shore of the noisy sea.

The problem presented by the mixture of duals and plurals (from here up to 669) is notorious. I need not repeat Hainsworth's excellent note. It seems clear that, as he says, 'The duals survive from an archetype in which they were grammatically appropriate". He may also be right in saying that the confusion would be "quietly tolerated, for the acceptability of a text depends on its *auctoritas* as much as on its intelligibility", if that means only that the text (whether written or recited) would be accepted as 'Homeric'. But there also seems no doubt that the reader/hear would, at first sight/hearing, find it confusing and incoherent.

10.408-11

πῶς δ' αἱ τῶν ἄλλων Τρώων φυλακαί τε καὶ εὐναί;
ἄσσα τε μητιόωσι μετὰ σφίσιν, ἢ μεμάασιν
αὖθι μένειν παρὰ νηυσὶν ἀπόπροθεν, ἦε πόλινδε
ἄψ ἀναχωρήσουσιν, ἐπεὶ δαμάσαντό γ' Ἀχαιούς.

How about the guard-posts and sleeping-places of the other Trojans? What things do they plan with themselves - do they desire to stay where they are a little way off by the ships, or will they go back to the city, since they have defeated the Achaeans?

409 -11 are difficult. In 208-10 they make sense after πύθοιτο ('learn') in 207 ("...learn what sort of plans they are making - whether they intend .... or..."). But here, after 408, we should have to take ἄσσα ('what') as a direct interrogative ("What plans are they making?"); and even that sits badly with ἤ in 409 and ἦε in 410, which would normally mean 'either'... 'or'.... We might punctuate with a question-mark after σφίσιν, and a new question (introduced by ἤ) thereafter. That seems extremely difficult: the lines seem to have been transferred from 208-10 in a way which produces a kind of incoherence.

10. 496-97

ἀσθμαίνοντα· κακὸν γὰρ ὄναρ κεφαλῆφιν ἐπέστη
τὴν νύκτ', Οἰνείδαο πάϊς, διὰ μῆτιν Ἀθήνης.

...panting: for an evil dream stood over his head during the night - the offspring of Oeneus, by means of Athene's plan.

Hainsworth allows either (a) the sense of Diomede being the subject of Rhesos' evil dream (though 'concise to the point of obscurity'), or (b) "the bad dream was Diomedes, sword in hand, not of Diomedes" (his italics) - that is, in effect, 'stood over him as (like) an evil dream'. But νύκτ' ('during the night') is difficult in either case: more so with (b). It might just mean 'for the whole length of that night', a long-lasting nightmare: that is why Rhesos was ἀσθμαίνοντα ('panting'). A borderline case.

10.498 ff.: 527-29

τόφρα δ' ἄρ' ὁ τλήμων Ὀδυσσεὺς λύε μώνυχας ἵππους,
σὺν δ' ἤειρεν ἱμᾶσι καὶ ἐξήλαυνεν ὁμίλου
τόξῳ ἐπιπλήσσων, ἐπεὶ οὐ μάστιγα φαεινὴν
ποικίλου ἐκ δίφροιο νοήσατο χερσὶν ἑλέσθαι·

ἔνθ' Ὀδυσσεὺς μὲν ἔρυξε Διῒ φίλος ὠκέας ἵππους,
Τυδείδης δὲ χαμᾶζε θορὼν ἔναρα βροτόεντα
ἐν χείρεσσ' Ὀδυσῆϊ τίθει, ἐπεβήσετο δ' ἵππων·

Then the enduring Odysseus released the single-hoofed horses: he bound them together with thongs, and drove them out of the ruck, striking them with his bow - since he did not have the thought of taking up in his hands the shining whip from the decorated chariot.

Then Odysseus, beloved of Zeus, restrained the swift horses; and Diomede, jumping to the ground, placed the bloody arms in Odysseus' hands, and mounted the horses.

Much ink (see Hainsworth) has been expended on whether Odysseus and Diomede are using the chariot or just the horses. But it must be the latter: 503-13 make it clear that Diomede does not take up any of the options in 504-06, but at once obeys Athene's command, so that the chariot stays where it was. Odysseus unties the horses which had been tied to the chariot (475), ropes them together (499), and goads them on with his bow, since he did not have in mind (νοήσατο ('intended') must mean this) to take up the whip from the chariot (500-01). The real trouble is that this ride, with two horses (still roped together?), is not clearly conceived by the poet. Diomede is said to 'get on the horses', in the plural, in 513 and 529, when he can in fact only mount one horse; only Odysseus controls the horses in 513 and 527, though Diomede is the natural subject of μάστιξεν ('whipped') in 530. Hainsworth says that "It is hardly believable that the poet intended" the idea of the two horses being still roped together: but in that case it should not be Odysseus alone who controls them. No doubt the poet is using formulas normally used for chariot-driving; but that is no excuse. The picture is incoherent.

11. 47-52

Ἡνιόχῳ μὲν ἔπειτα ἑῷ ἐπέτελλεν ἕκαστος
ἵππους εὖ κατὰ κόσμον ἐρυκέμεν αὖθ' ἐπὶ τάφρῳ,
αὐτοὶ δὲ πρυλέες σὺν τεύχεσι θωρηχθέντες
ῥώοντ'· ἄσβεστος δὲ βοὴ γένετ' ἠῶθι πρό.
φθὰν δὲ μέγ' ἱππήων ἐπὶ τάφρῳ κοσμηθέντες,
ἱππῆες δ' ὀλίγον μετεκίαθον·

Then each man ordered his charioteer to restrain the horses, and keep them well-controlled there at the trench; and they themselves clad in their armour advanced on foot; and an unquenchable noise went up before the dawn. They ordered themselves at the trench long before the charioteers; and then the charioteers moved forward a little way behind them.

Hainsworth's note seems correct here (the πρυλέες ('soldiers') in 49 are the fighting-men from the chariots, who tell their charioteers in 47-48 to halt the chariots at the trench, and themselves proceed on foot: the ἱππήων ('charioteers') in 51 are the charioteers again). But he does not take up Leaf's difficulty with 51-52: Leaf says "It is hard to see how μέγα ('greatly', 'a lot') in this line is to be reconciled with ὀλίγον ('a little') in the next". We may however avoid incoherence by taking the first as referring to time and the second as referring to space: the men on foot are ready long before the chariots (which might have difficulty in negotiating the trench), and when all is ready the chariots move forward a little way behind the men on foot. That is slightly compressed, but not incoherent.

11. 100

στήθεσι παμφαίνοντας, ἐπεὶ περίδυσε χιτῶνας·

With their breasts gleaming, since he had stripped them of their tunics.

Hainsworth correctly says that "if περίδυσε (normally 'clad', 'put on') is right the only possible sense is that Agamemnon stripped the corpses". (It ought to mean the opposite, and no doubt we could emend to some more plausible compound of δύω.) But the true difficulties are (1) nothing is said about his removing their armour first (that thought perhaps underlines what Hainsworth calls the 'banal' alternative ἐπεὶ κλυτὰ τεύχε᾽ ἀπηύρα ('since he had taken away their bright armour')); and, more importantly, (2) the fact that Agamemnon should actually remove their tunics. What for? The parallel which Hainsworth adduces (2.416) of Agamemnon praying that he may do this to Hector does not lessen the oddity, for Hector is a special case. Admittedly Agamemnon is in a savage mood (he cuts off Hippolochos' head and arms, 146); but the idea of just removing a dead enemy's tunic as a mark of savagery is strange. In the case of Hector, he wants χιτῶνα...δαΐξαι ('to rend his tunic apart'): not, surely, to remove it but to tear it apart (by driving a sword or spear through it), so that the parallel is not a true one. In 100 there is no question of tearing their tunics apart in this sense - or at least not Oileus' tunic, since Agamemnon has struck him in the head (95 ff.). I take this line to be mysterious to the point of incoherence, and it is hard to see what textual emendations would improve it.

11. 127-29

εἰν ἑνὶ δίφρῳ ἐόντε, ὁμοῦ δ᾽ ἔχον ὠκέας ἵππους·
ἐκ γάρ σφεας χειρῶν φύγον ἡνία σιγαλόεντα,
τὼ δὲ κυκηθήτην.

Both being in one chariot, and they guided their swift horses both together; for the shining reins had slipped from their hands, and both of them were bowled over.

Most commentators (including Leaf and Hainsworth) accept this passage with only a mild query directed at σφεας ('them'): thus Leaf 'the reins had slipped from their hands' is not strictly accurate, since only the driver had dropped them" (his italics). But then ὁμοῦ δ᾽ ἔχον ὠκέας ἵππους ('both together they guided the swift horses') makes little sense. Leaf says "were both trying to drive" but how? Was one using the whip whilst the other pulled the horses' tails? The thing becomes absurd. We could try "Both in one chariot, and they had to deal with their swift horses both together" (because they had lost the reins, and the horses were in a state of chaos); but ἔχον can hardly translate in this way. At best a borderline case.

13. 71-72

ἴχνια γὰρ μετόπισθε ποδῶν ἠδὲ κνημάων
ῥεῖ᾽ ἔγνων ἀπιόντος· ἀρίγνωτοι δὲ θεοί περ·

For I easily recognised the prints of his feet and shins behind him as he went away: gods are easy to recognise.

In 62-65 Poseidon darts away from the Ajaxes (ἤιξε ('darted away'), 65) like a hawk, or as swiftly as a hawk: the simile makes it plain that he does not actually take the shape of a hawk (and if he had, it is not likely that there were any footprints left behind, *pace* Pollard in Janko). So what are the ἴχνια ποδῶν ἠδὲ κνημάων ('the prints of his feet and shins') by which one of the Ajaxes recognises him? Janko says "If he is known from his 'footprints', why mention his shins?"; but there is also a problem about why he should be recognisable from his footprints at all. Are the footprints particularly light or far apart (indicating a god's speed), or particularly heavy (indicating a god's weight), or what? No suggestion seems at all convincing.

It might seem possible to take ἴχνια in a more abstract sense than actual footprints: roughly as the impressions ('traces') which Poseidon left behind him, in their minds, by moving his feet and shins so quickly. That would make sense of the addition of the shins. But that is not convincing, in view of the usual sense of ἴχνια and particularly in view of μετόπισθε ('behind'), which seems to suggest something more concrete.

It is not easy to see here what the poet had in mind (perhaps he had nothing clear in mind); a borderline case at best.

13. 363

πέφνε γὰρ Ὀθρυονῆα Καβησόθεν ἔνδον ἐόντα,

For he killed Othryoneus from Kapesos, who was present indoors.

As Janko says, ἔνδον ἐόντα ('being inside') is a 'misused formula': it is here incoherent.

13. 423

νῆας ἔπι γλαφυρὰς φερέτην βαρέα στενάχοντα.

They carried him, as he groaned deeply, to the hollow ships.

This is almost universally thought to be an incoherence. Janko says "Since Hupsenor is stone dead (402-23n), his groans troubled the ancients ... had Homer used writing to better his poem, he would surely have erased this error". But he is not stone dead. Deiphobos has indeed 'loosed his limbs' (γούνατ᾽ ἔλυσε, 412); but Antilochos took care of his companion and covered him with his shield (419-20), which surely implies that he still lives, and can be carried off groaning in 423. Of course he dies later, and counts as one of the three slain (τρεῖς...πεφάσθαι ('to have killed three'), 447).

There is a parallel in 650 ff., where Harpalion is hit: his friends attend him (ἀμφεπένοντο ('attended'), 656) and take him to Troy in a chariot: he dies later (659-60).

13. 775-77

Ἕκτορ, ἐπεί τοι θυμὸς ἀναίτιον αἰτιάασθαι,
ἄλλοτε δή ποτε μᾶλλον ἐρωῆσαι πολέμοιο
μέλλω, ἐπεὶ οὐδ' ἐμὲ πάμπαν ἀνάλκιδα γείνατο μήτηρ·

"Hector, since it is in your heart to lay blame on one who is blameless, it is at another time indeed that I am likely to run away from the war, since my mother bore me as a son not totally without valour".

Difficult, but perhaps not quite incoherent. "At another time, rather, I am likely to draw back from the battle, since my mother bore me as a son not totally without valour" is hardly logical as it stands. I suppose we have to understand: "It is not at this time (*sc*. of crisis) that I am likely to draw back from the battle, since my mother bore me as a son not totally without valour, but at some other time". He goes on to say that he and his associates have been fighting the Greeks νωλεμέως, constantly (780). A borderline case at worst.

14. 484-85

τῶ καί τίς τ' εὔχεται ἀνὴρ
γνωτὸν ἐνὶ μεγάροισιν ἄρης ἀλκτῆρα λιπέσθαι."

So that a man may claim that there is a kinsman left at home to ward off harm.

There are some minor textual difficulties here which can be overcome (see Janko's note). But the obvious problem is that Akamas' taking vengeance for his brother's death on the battlefield does not square with the idea of a kinsman being left at home (ἐνὶ μεγάροισιν ('in the house')) as an ἄρεως ('of war') ἀλκτῆρα (ἄρεως is the standard reading). ἀλκτῆρα must mean 'one who wards off (the dangers of) war' or 'a defender in battle', and somebody left at home could not do that. If with Zenodotos we read ἄρης for ἄρεως, that would still most naturally mean 'one who wards off harm', which is equally inconsequential. Janko says that the avenger 'wards off the <u>harm</u> of being unrevenged' (his italics). That is an unnatural or forced interpretation in itself, and still leaves the idea of the avenger being left at home somewhat inappropriate: though it could just be taken as a gnomic remark about the possibility and desirability of vengeance by home-dwelling relatives. But it is more plausible to regard the passage as incoherent.

15. 668-73

τοῖσι δ' ἀπ' ὀφθαλμῶν νέφος ἀχλύος ὦσεν Ἀθήνη
θεσπέσιον· μάλα δέ σφι φόως γένετ' ἀμφοτέρωθεν,
ἠμὲν πρὸς νηῶν καὶ ὁμοιΐου πολέμοιο.
Ἕκτορα δὲ φράσσαντο βοὴν ἀγαθὸν καὶ ἑταίρους,
ἠμὲν ὅσοι μετόπισθεν ἀφέστασαν οὐδὲ μάχοντο,
ἠδ' ὅσσοι παρὰ νηυσὶ μάχην ἐμάχοντο θοῇσιν.

From their eyes Athene drove away the miraculous cloud of mist: the light shone out to them strongly from both directions - both from the ships and from the equally-poised battle. And they observed Hector of the powerful war-cry and his comrades: both those who stood behind and away and did not fight, and those who fought by the swift ships.

This passage does not present a clear or coherent picture of where everybody is, or what is the effect of Athene removing the mist. In 653-57 the poet unequivocally says that the Greeks retreated from the first line of ships (i.e. from the Trojan viewpoint, the nearest line), and stayed all together (ἀθρόοι ('together'), 657) by the huts (which must be conceived as behind this line). Athene removes the mist so that there is light on both sides or in two directions (ἀμφοτέρωθεν ('from two directions'), 669); and 670 looks as if it must mean 'both in the direction of the ships and in the direction of the impartial battle'. But, since the Greeks have retreated, this will be <u>same</u> direction.

The Greeks then can observe Hector and his comrades (671). Most commentators take the division in 672-73 as a division between the Greeks themselves, but that will not do, since according to 655 ff. <u>all</u> the Greeks (except for Aiax, 674 ff.) have retreated in a body. Can it refer to the Trojans - that is, to Hector's ἑταίρους ('comrades')? That is possible, but we have not been told that some of them are hanging back.

The whole passage (not least 670 and the obscure division in 672-73) is, I think, muddled and incoherent. It may be a case, rare in the Iliad, of 'work in progress': certainly not a finished product.

16. 367-83

Ἕκτορα δ' ἵπποι
ἔκφερον ὠκύποδες σὺν τεύχεσι, λεῖπε δὲ λαὸν
Τρωϊκόν, οὓς ἀέκοντας ὀρυκτὴ τάφρος ἔρυκε.
πολλοὶ δ' ἐν τάφρῳ ἐρυσάρματες ὠκέες ἵπποι
ἄξαντ' ἐν πρώτῳ ῥυμῷ λίπον ἅρματ' ἀνάκτων,
Πάτροκλος δ' ἕπετο σφεδανὸν Δαναοῖσι κελεύων,
Τρωσὶ κακὰ φρονέων· οἱ δὲ ἰαχῇ τε φόβῳ τε
πάσας πλῆσαν ὁδούς, ἐπεὶ ἂρ τμάγεν· ὕψι δ' ἀέλλη
σκίδναθ' ὑπὸ νεφέων, τανύοντο δὲ μώνυχες ἵπποι
ἄψορρον προτὶ ἄστυ νεῶν ἄπο καὶ κλισιάων.
Πάτροκλος δ' ᾗ πλεῖστον ὀρινόμενον ἴδε λαόν,
τῇ ῥ' ἔχ' ὁμοκλήσας· ὑπὸ δ' ἄξοσι φῶτες ἔπιπτον
πρηνέες ἐξ ὀχέων, δίφροι δ' ἀνακυμβαλίαζον.
ἀντικρὺ δ' ἄρα τάφρον ὑπέρθορον ὠκέες ἵπποι
ἄμβροτοι, οὓς Πηλῆϊ θεοὶ δόσαν ἀγλαὰ δῶρα,
πρόσσω ἱέμενοι, ἐπὶ δ' Ἕκτορι κέκλετο θυμός·
ἵετο γὰρ βαλέειν· τὸν δ' ἔκφερον ὠκέες ἵπποι.

The swift-footed horses carried off Hector along with his gear, and he left behind the Trojan host, which the dug trench held back against their will. Many swift horses that drew the chariots left behind in the trench the chariots of their masters, having broken their poles at the root. And Patroclus followed after, giving vehement orders to the Danaans and boding ill for the Trojans. The Trojans with screams and terror filled up all the paths, for they were cut off. A cloud of dust rose high beneath the clouds, and the single-hoofed horses went at full stretch back towards the city, away from the ships and the huts. Patroclus shouted, and made for the place where he saw the greatest number of people in tumult. Men fell headlong from their chariots beneath his axle-wheels, and the chariots were overturned. But his own immortal swift horses, the noble gifts which the gods had given Peleus, jumped directly over the trench, eagerly going forward. His spirit cried out towards Hector, for he wished to smite him; and the swift horses bore him out and away.

There is perhaps no single point at which this passage is demonstrably and wholly incoherent, but there are a number of items which suggest that it is unfinished or unrevised or sufficiently confused to baffle the reader/hearer. I will list these, though it is hardly worth while analysing each in detail:
(1) 370-71 shows that there were many Trojan chariots on the Greek side of the trench, now struggling to get out: we have not been told of these earlier.
(2) ἀξαντ᾽ ('breaking') in 371, normally taken as a dual going with the plural ἵπποι ('horses'), is odd (and it would be equally odd to take it as intransitive in sense with ἅρματ᾽ ('chariot').
(3) 374 is doubly mysterious. (a) What and where are the ὁδούς ('ways', 'paths')?
(b) τμάγεν ('were cut') is compressed to the point of unintelligibility.
(4) In 376 κλισιάων ('huts') (if we take that literally) is odd: the Trojan chariots had hardly got as far as the huts.
(5) In 378-79 the poet reverts from Patroclus' chariot to the Trojan chariots, then goes back again in 380 to Patroclus (unless ἄξοσι ('axles') in 378 refers to Patroclus' chariot, in which case the plural is strange): this is at least awkward.
(6) In 382 ἐπι... θυμός ('at...his spirit') is also compressed and not immediately intelligible.

This is, I think, enough to show that the passage needs revision: perhaps a borderline case.

16. 507

ἱεμένους φοβέεσθαι, ἐπεὶ λίπον ἅρματ᾽ ἀνάκτων.

Desiring to run away, since they had left the chariot of their masters.

Normally taken as 'a minor slip' (Janko), since 'the horses cannot have left the vehicle'. It may perhaps be saved by translating 'since the chariot lacked its masters', but λίπον ἅρματ᾽ is used in 371 with the horses as subject, and a different sense here is unlikely. It must be taken as a minor incoherence.

16. 659-61

ἔνθ᾽ οὐδ᾽ ἴφθιμοι Λύκιοι μένον, ἀλλὰ φόβηθεν
πάντες, ἐπεὶ βασιλῆα ἴδον βεβλαμμένον ἦτορ,
κείμενον ἐν νεκύων ἀγύρει·

Then not even the noble Lycians stood, but they all fled when they saw their king struck to the heart, lying in the heap of corpses.

Taken as 'difficult' by Janko: "If 'all' means 'the Lycians' and the 'king' is Sarpedon ... why is 'harmed in his heart' so weak an expression for 'dead', how can they see him if he is buried under corpses, and why do they react to his death only now and not at 532, when Glaukos told them of it?" But (1) βεβλαμμένον ἦτορ ('struck to the heart') can mean something like 'struck down at heart' or 'mortally wounded'; (2) Sarpedon may still be recognisable even with corpses on top of him; and (3) in 532 Glaukos only urges on the Lycians (we are not told how they responded) - here, perhaps because they see the body for the first time, and certainly because Hector flees and calls on the other Trojans to flee (656-58), their natural response is flight. The passage is coherent enough.

16. 614-15

αἰχμὴ δ᾽ Αἰνείαο κραδαινομένη κατὰ γαίης
ᾤχετ᾽, ἐπεί ῥ᾽ ἅλιον στιβαρῆς ἀπὸ χειρὸς ὄρουσεν.

And the spear of Aeneas flew off and quivered in the ground, since it sped vainly from his strong hand.

Generally acknowledged as an interpolation (though printed in most texts). It is obviously incoherent as it stands, since what happened to Aeneas' spear has already been dealt with in 611-13.

17. 91-105

" ὤ μοι ἐγών, εἰ μέν κε λίπω κάτα τεύχεα καλὰ
Πάτροκλόν θ᾽, ὃς κεῖται ἐμῆς ἕνεκ᾽ ἐνθάδε τιμῆς,
μή τίς μοι Δαναῶν νεμεσήσεται, ὅς κεν ἴδηται.
εἰ δέ κεν Ἕκτορι μοῦνος ἐὼν καὶ Τρωσὶ μάχωμαι
αἰδεσθείς, μή πώς με περιστήωσ᾽ ἕνα πολλοί·
Τρῶας δ᾽ ἐνθάδε πάντας ἄγει κορυθαίολος Ἕκτωρ.
ἀλλὰ τίη μοι ταῦτα φίλος διελέξατο θυμός;
ὁππότ᾽ ἀνὴρ ἐθέλῃ πρὸς δαίμονα φωτὶ μάχεσθαι
ὅν κε θεὸς τιμᾷ, τάχα οἱ μέγα πῆμα κυλίσθη.
τῶ μ᾽ οὔ τις Δαναῶν νεμεσήσεται, ὅς κεν ἴδηται
Ἕκτορι χωρήσαντ᾽, ἐπεὶ ἐκ θεόφιν πολεμίζει.
εἰ δέ που Αἴαντός γε βοὴν ἀγαθοῖο πυθοίμην,
ἄμφω κ᾽ αὖτις ἰόντες ἐπιμνησαίμεθα χάρμης
καὶ πρὸς δαίμονά περ, εἴ πως ἐρυσαίμεθα νεκρὸν
Πηλεΐδῃ Ἀχιλῆϊ· κακῶν δέ κε φέρτατον εἴη."

O, alas for me, if I leave behind the beautiful armour and Patroclus, who lies there for the sake of my honour - I fear that some one of the Danaans may be indignant, whoever may see it: yet I hesitate lest, if I fight by myself against Hector and the Trojans, I shall be alone and surrounded by many men: and Hector of the shining helmet is bringing all the Trojans here. But why does my own dear heart debate all these things? Whenever a man, against the will of a god, sets out to fight with another man whom the god honours, then soon a great evil comes upon him; so none of the Danaans will be indignant with me, if one were to see me giving ground to Hector, since he fights with the god's backing. But perhaps I could find out from Aias of the powerful war-cry; and then we could both go together, our minds full of battle-fury, even against god's will, to see if perhaps we could drag back the corpse for Achilles son of Peleus: that would be the best course amongst our evils.

There is nothing obscure or incoherent until κακων....εἴη ('of evils...would be') in the last line; but the passage as a whole does, I think, make that phrase difficult to understand. Up to 101 the logic is clear. It is a typical 'reflection' or 'pondering' speech. "If I allow the Trojans to get Patroclus' corpse and his armour, the Greeks will hold it against me" (91-93). "If on the other hand I fight alone against Hector and his troops, I shall be at a hopeless disadvantage" (94-96). "But why am I debating this? Anyone who fights against a god's will invites destruction, so the Greeks will not hold it against me if I do not fight Hector, since the god is on his side" (97-101). Then, we suppose, a quite new thought strikes him: to get Ajax' help. 102 is somewhat difficult: does πυθοίμην ('learn', 'find out') mean 'find out where Ajax is' (in 115 he looks around for him, παπταίνων) or 'find out from Ajax whether he will help me', or what? In any case the idea is that together they can continue the fight even against the god's will (προς δαίμονα, 104).

The phrase κακων....εἴη cannot of course mean 'that would be the greatest of evils', since that is what he actually chooses to do. It must presumably mean 'that would be the best [i.e. in effect the least] of evils'. But that is in itself oddly expressed: why does the poet not use a more readily intelligible formula? He must have the idea that all the three possible courses of action are 'evil'. But that is also odd, since 97-101 suggest that he can in fact retreat and keep his honour: there seems nothing 'evil' about that course. And *a fortiori* with the third course: why is that seen as an 'evil' at all? It may be because they will have to fight προς δαίμονα. Nevertheless both the phrase itself, and its application to the situation, are far from clear: perhaps a borderline case of incoherence.

17. 327-32

" Αἰνεία, πῶς ἂν καὶ ὑπὲρ θεὸν εἰρύσσαισθε
Ἴλιον αἰπεινήν; ὡς δὴ ἴδον ἀνέρας ἄλλους
κάρτεΐ τε σθένεΐ τε πεποιθότας ἠνορέῃ τε
πλήθεΐ τε σφετέρῳ, καὶ ὑπερδέα δῆμον ἔχοντας·
ἡμῖν δὲ Ζεὺς μὲν πολὺ βούλεται ἢ Δαναοῖσι
νίκην· ἀλλ' αὐτοὶ τρεῖτ' ἄσπετον οὐδὲ μάχεσθε."

"Aeneas, how could you protect the steep city of Ilium even against a god? Indeed I have seen other men who trusted in their might and strength and courage, and in their numbers and their undaunted host. But Zeus wants victory for us much more than for the Danaans: yet you are in great fear and do not fight"

There seems no way in which Apollo's speech to Aeneas can be seen as having a coherent logic. It starts off "How can you possibly protect Troy against the will of the god?" This fits a context of his persuading Aeneas not to fight: and it continues, initially at least, in the same vein: "Indeed, I have seen other cases of men who trusted in their own strength", etc. We naturally expect something like "...and they came to grief too". But we do not get this, in fact we get nothing at all. Then he says "But in fact Zeus is on our side, so go and fight bravely". Even if we interpreted it along the lines of "Of course you couldn't protect Troy against god's will - other men have tried this and come to grief - but now the god is on our side", the initial mention of ἀνέρας ἄλλους ('other men') is still odd, as is the omission of the way in which other fighters against god's will came to grief.

It is this which prompted the emendation of ὑπερδέα ('dauntless') to ὑπὲρ Δία ('against Zeus') which would certainly ease the strain in itself (the other men are fighting against Zeus). But the emendation is hopeless: it leaves no serious sense for δημον ('host', 'people'), and the καὶ ('and') which precedes it is illogical - we need some adversative particle. It is not true (*pace* Edwards) that "the sense 'inferior in number'... fits well with the rest of the sentence": the parallels with κάρτει ('might'), σθένει ('strength'), ἠνορέῃ ('courage') and πληθει ('numbers') show that this must be something on which such men could reasonably rely. Eustathius' sense of 'undaunted' is much more plausible. Something like that alone would give the passage a coherence which it would otherwise lack.

19. 221-25

αἰψά τε φυλόπιδος πέλεται κόρος ἀνθρώποισιν,
ἧς τε πλείστην μὲν καλάμην χθονὶ χαλκὸς ἔχευεν,
ἄμητος δ' ὀλίγιστος, ἐπὴν κλίνῃσι τάλαντα
Ζεύς, ὅς τ' ἀνθρώπων ταμίης πολέμοιο τέτυκται.
γαστέρι δ' οὔ πως ἔστι νέκυν πενθῆσαι Ἀχαιούς·

Soon men become satiated with war, in which the bronze cuts down many corn-stalks, but the crop is very small when once Zeus has inclined his scales - Zeus who is the overseer of war for men. But it is not at all possible for the Achaeans to mourn for the corpse with empty bellies.

The very many different interpretations of 221-23, particularly of ἄμητος δ' ὀλίγιστος ('the crop is very small') (see Edwards), suggest at least obscurity if not incoherence. The best interpretation is Edwards' (following Leaf *et al.*), who takes the phrase to mean 'but the crop is very small', so that we can translate on the lines of "...battle, in which the bronze cuts down a great deal of corn-stalks, but the crop is very small", i.e. there is not much harvest gained. The idea is that a lot of trouble and effort goes on (perhaps that a lot of people lose their lives, being cut down by bronze weapons as the com-stalks are by the bronze sickle), but not much positive gain. I do not think we need be worried by what kind of gain is in question (booty? glory? survival? victory?). What is more worrying is (1) that the exegetical scholia, and other commentators, take ἄμητος differently, to mean 'harvest-time'; and καλάμην to mean 'straw' (after threshing), which leaves one wondering where the grain or harvest is supposed to come from. (If it meant 'corn-stalks', it would come from them - only not much of it.) And (2), more seriously, the metaphor is introduced much too suddenly to be readily intelligible.

It is also not clear whether ἐπὴν...Ζεύς 'when Zeus inclines his scales', refers to just any battle (when Zeus' scales incline one way or another), or specifically to a battle in which the scales are inclined against the warriors concerned (in this case the Greeks). And finally, γαστέρι ('belly') hardly makes sense in 225: it is not at all possible for the Achacans to lament the corpse - with an empty belly? Because of the state of their bellies? All these difficulties amount, I think, to general incoherence: this may be a case of 'work in progress'.

18. 470-73

φῦσαι δ' ἐν χοάνοισιν ἐείκοσι πᾶσαι ἐφύσων,
παντοίην εὔπρηστον ἀϋτμὴν ἐξανιεῖσαι,
ἄλλοτε μὲν σπεύδοντι παρέμμεναι, ἄλλοτε δ' αὖτε,
ὅππως Ἥφαιστός τ' ἐθέλοι καὶ ἔργον ἄνοιτο.

And twenty bellows in all blew in their funnels, sending out well-made blasts of air of all kinds: they were on hand for him as he busied about, at one time or another, as Hephaestos wished it and completed his work.

Edwards does his best for this: the bellows are "on hand for the busy smith (σπεύδοντι παρέμμεναι ('to be present to him as he busied about')) as he time and again requires their blast (ἄλλοτε μεν...('at one time'))". ἄλλοτε δ'αὖτε means 'at another time again', not 'on the contrary' as Leaf and Willcock take it (i.e. ceasing to blow)". But the real trouble (with either interpretation) is with παρεμμεναι ('to be present'). For the bellows are <u>there</u> all the time, not sometimes there and sometimes not. Hephaistos may indeed 'require their blast' and use them from time to time, but that is another matter. We might just save this by claiming that it means 'are there to his hurrying hand', i.e. that the phrase implies both the presence (permanent) of the bellows <u>and</u> the presence (occasional) of Hephaistos. But I think this difficulty, and the general obscurity and compression of the line, displays something close to incoherence. A borderline case at best.

18. 498-506

λαοὶ δ' εἰν ἀγορῇ ἔσαν ἀθρόοι· ἔνθα δὲ νεῖκος
ὠρώρει, δύο δ' ἄνδρες ἐνείκεον εἵνεκα ποινῆς
ἀνδρὸς ἀποφθιμένου· ὁ μὲν εὔχετο πάντ' ἀποδοῦναι
δήμῳ πιφαύσκων, ὁ δ' ἀναίνετο μηδὲν ἑλέσθαι·
ἄμφω δ' ἱέσθην ἐπὶ ἴστορι πεῖραρ ἑλέσθαι.
λαοὶ δ' ἀμφοτέροισιν ἐπήπυον, ἀμφὶς ἀρωγοί·
κήρυκες δ' ἄρα λαὸν ἐρήτυον· οἱ δὲ γέροντες
ἥατ' ἐπὶ ξεστοῖσι λίθοις ἱερῷ ἐνὶ κύκλῳ,
σκῆπτρα δὲ κηρύκων ἐν χέρσ' ἔχον ἠεροφώνων·
τοῖσιν ἔπειτ' ἤϊσσον, ἀμοιβηδὶς δὲ δίκαζον.

The people were there all together in an assembly. Then a dispute arose: two men disputed about the penalty concerning a man who had been killed. One claimed that he had given everything back, demonstrating this to the people; the other denied it, and said that he had nothing. They both wished the judge to set the penalty. The people spoke for both sides, and supported both, and the heralds restrained them. The elders sat upon polished stones in a sacred circle, and had the rods of clear-voiced heralds in their hands. To them they dashed, and they judged in turn.

Most of the obscurities here do not amount to incoherence; the poet's audience may (probably would) have had a sufficiently clear picture of this kind of legal battle to give a clear sense to the words and phrases in 499-501, even if they are not entirely clear to us. That may even apply to 505, though it is hard to see why the elders should <u>all</u> have heralds' staffs in their hands (if that is what it means). But 506 is even harder. "The elders leapt to their feet with their staffs" is quite unconvincing. Edwards' "It may be better to take the litigants as subject 'To these elders then they dashed'", with a change of subject for δίκαζον ('to judge') (the elders do the judging), is even more so. Perhaps some textual emendation is required. At best a borderline case, saved only by the assumption that the text describes a scene totally familiar to the audience.

18. 509-16

Τὴν δ' ἑτέρην πόλιν ἀμφὶ δύω στρατοὶ ἥατο λαῶν
τεύχεσι λαμπόμενοι· δίχα δέ σφισιν ἥνδανε βουλή,
ἠὲ διαπραθέειν ἢ ἄνδιχα πάντα δάσασθαι,
κτῆσιν ὅσην πτολίεθρον ἐπήρατον ἐντὸς ἔεργεν·
οἱ δ' οὔ πω πείθοντο, λόχῳ δ' ὑπεθωρήσσοντο.
τεῖχος μέν ῥ' ἄλοχοί τε φίλαι καὶ νήπια τέκνα
ῥύατ' ἐφεσταότες, μετὰ δ' ἀνέρες οὓς ἔχε γῆρας·
οἱ δ' ἴσαν· ἦρχε δ' ἄρα σφιν Ἄρης καὶ Παλλὰς Ἀθήνη,

Around the other city two armies of people were encamped, shining in their armour. Two plans seemed to please them: either to sack the city or to divide everything into two parts - all that the lovely city contained inside it. But they were not yet persuaded, and armed themselves for an ambush. Their dear wives and young children manned the wall and guarded it, and with them the men whom old age had overtaken; the other men issued forth, and Ares and Pallas Athene led them.

I do not think we can save this from incoherence. The two στρατοι ('armies') are both on the same side, against the city (as their divided βουλή ('plan', 'counsel') in 511-12 shows). The two ideas are either to sack the city or to divide up its treasures. But divide them between whom? The most immediately natural interpretation (1) is between the two στρατοι; but does that not require a sack in the first place? We can get out of this by saying that διαπραθέειν ('to sack') means either just destroying the city and its treasures, or some free-for-all rather than an equal division of the spoils. But then πείθοντο ('they were persuaded') in 513 is odd: οἱ δ' ('and they') as the following lines make plain, must refer to the citizens, who then arm for an ambush and carry it out. What are they not 'persuaded' <u>about</u>? That suggests (2) the idea of a deal whereby the division is between the citizens and the attacking armies. The armies suggest this deal, but the citizens οὐ πω πείθοντο ('were not yet persuaded') to accept it. But then 510-11 are intolerably compressed, even though the idea of such a deal is well-known (Hector wonders whether to offer it to the Greeks, 22.111 ff).

The subsequent lines are, in my judgement, fairly clear. The οἱ δ' in 516 and 520 are the citizens, as are the τοισι ('them') in 523: they are ambushing the cattle. In 526-27 the subjects are the ambushed men and the cattle: the οἱ μέν ('they on the one hand') in 527 are the citizens again. Then the οἱ δ' ('they on the other hand') in 530 refers to the attacking army. But it is evidently not clear to all readers. Edwards says that the poet may have meant 'the seizing of the <u>besiegers</u>' cattle by the <u>townsmen</u>, though the reverse would seem a more likely event' (his italics). That seems to me to make nonsense of the whole passage, since the townsmen are setting the ambush: 'the reverse' is impossible. But if a respectable editor can interpret it thus, perhaps even these lines are more obscure or incoherent than I suppose!

COMMENTS ON THE ILIAD

21. 200 ff.

Ἦ ῥα, καὶ ἐκ κοημνοῖο ἐρύσσατο χάλκεον ἔγχος, κτλ.

He spoke, and drew his bronze spear out from the cliff.

There are some problems in this part of the book about where Achilles actually is in relation to the river: the text seems at least obscure and perhaps self-contradictory, if not positively incoherent. It may be worth going into this in more detail; at least we may see if the poet had any clear and consistent picture in mind.

In 200-04 Achilles leaves Asteropaios in the river; and in 205 he goes after the Paionians, who παρ ποταμον πεφοβήατο (206). This probably means 'were flying along the river' (i.e. in the river, not alongside it), since it is only after Achilles kills some of them (209-10) that the river complains to him- about being choked with bodies: Achilles is in the river, and kills them there. ἀνέρι εἰσάμενος ('in the likeness of a man') in 213 is absurd (one might say, pictorially incoherent: are we to picture a man shaped Xanthos, visible but speaking 'out of a deep current', or what?) Xanthos tells Achilles to wreak his havoc on the Trojans in the plain, away from the river (πεδίον κάτα ('over the plain'), 217); and Achilles agrees to this in 223 (ἔσται ταυτα (it shall be thus'), κτλ). So when ἐπέσσυτο ('he dashed') in 227 we assume that he is now operating on the plain. However, it is clear from 240-46 that Achilles is in fact still in the river (so that we should translate 233-34, ἔνθορε...ἀπαΐξας (he jumped in ... darting away'), as 'jumped in the middle of the river, darting away from the bank': not, as we might otherwise be tempted to do, as 'rushed into the midst of the Trojans', *sc.* on the plain). He does not leave the river until 246-47 (ἐκ δίνης...ἤϊξεν πεδίοιο ('out of the current ... he darted over the plain')). So there is an inconsistency here.

22. 126-27

οὐ μέν πως νῦν ἔστιν ἀπὸ δρυὸς οὐδ' ἀπὸ πέτρης
τῷ ὀαριζέμεναι, ἅ τε παρθένος ἠΐθεός τε,

For it is not now possible to dally with this man 'from an oak or a rock', like a maiden and a young man.

The phrase ἀπο δρυος οὐδ' ἀπο πέτρης ('from an oak nor from a rock') has always baffled commentators (see Richardson's note), and its sense in *Od.* 19.163 does not help here. But we cannot accuse the poet of incoherence or nonsense, since it seems to be a cliché whose sense is now lost to us. It may have meant, for instance, something like 'from nowhere in particular' or 'against no specific background' or 'in no particular context'. Then the Odyssey passage would mean 'for you are not from nowhere' (i.e. you must come from some particular background); and in this passage Hector is saying that he cannot negotiate or 'dally' (ὀαριζέμεναι) with Achilles without taking the particular context into account, i.e. their mutual enmity. He cannot converse with him from scratch, so to speak.

22. 194-98

ὁσσάκι δ' ὁρμήσειε πυλάων Δαρδανιάων
ἀντίον ἀΐξασθαι ἐϋδμήτους ὑπὸ πύργους,
εἴ πώς οἱ καθύπερθεν ἀλάλκοιεν βελέεσσι,
τοσσάκι μιν προπάροιθεν ἀποστρέψασκε παραφθὰς
πρὸς πεδίον· αὐτὸς δὲ ποτὶ πτόλιος πέτετ' αἰεί.

As often as he made an attempt to dart directly opposite the Dardanian gates, to beneath the shelter of the well-built fortifications, so that perhaps those on top might defend him with their missiles, so often did Achilles anticipate him and turn him away in advance towards the plain, whilst he himself flew on always on the side of the city.

Richardson says that Achilles 'must be keeping on the inside of Hector, which is hard to reconcile with their both being on the waggon-track (146)'; adding 'but we should not stop to reflect on such details here'. The addition is a little too blithe: not only is this a crucial scene, but it is clearly envisaged by the poet, as this (somewhat elaborate) sentence shows.

We are to suppose that the city is at least partially surrounded by the Greeks (whom Achilles prevents from attacking Hector, 205-6), so that Hector cannot safely turn away from the city. But on the other hand he cannot safely turn nearer to the city since such a turn would shorten the (already dangerously short) distance between him and Achilles. (Achilles could make straight for the Dardanian Gate, narrowing the distance as Hector turned towards it: having, as it were, to cover only one side of a triangle whilst Hector covered two sides.) So Hector could with safety only run straight on, along the waggon-track and past the springs. That was the general route for both runners. But sometimes Hector did make an attempt to dart, or begin to dart (ὁρμήσειε ... πύργους ('dart...fortifications')) towards the gates: and then Achilles prevented this route 'in advance' (παραφθὰς ('anticipating')) by always running 'on the city side' (ποτι πτόλιος) - that is, swerving towards the city so as to cut him off.

This is one of the cases where the poet is exact in envisaging the scenes: worth a comment, if only because it contrasts with the cases where he is not.

23. 103-04

" ὢ πόποι, ἦ ῥά τίς ἐστι καὶ εἰν Ἀΐδαο δόμοισι
ψυχὴ καὶ εἴδωλον, ἀτὰρ φρένες οὐκ ἔνι πάμπαν·

"Great heavens! - so there is then some soul or image even in the house of Hades, though there are no wits at all therein"

A well-known crux (see Richardson's note). None of the suggested solutions will do. (1) "So, then, it is true that there survives a soul and an image even in the house of Hades" must go with "but there are no φρένες ('wits', 'intellligence') at all in it", both being the conclusions Achilles draws from his experience, as the γαρ ('for') in 105 shows. It can hardly mean, as Aristarchus thought, "So, then,....but of course in general after their owners have been buried they have no φρένες (though Patroclus, being unburied, does have some)".

(2) The suggestion that Patroclus does not have φρένες or not completely (πάμπαν), is even more fatuous: what Patroclus says in 69-92 shows enough φρενες for anyone. (3) φρένες can indeed mean 'midriff', a particular part of the body, but hardly refer to the whole body: it must mean 'wits' or 'intelligence', as in Od.10.492 ff., and elsewhere. If it meant 'body' or 'physical existence', Achilles would have gone on to say, not only that Patroclus' ghost appeared to him, but also that he tried to clutch it but failed. But he does not say this. We are forced to assume that ἀταρ ...... πάμπαν was thoughtlessly (and, in this context, incoherently) added.

23. 323-25

αἰεὶ τέρμ᾽ ὁρόων στρέφει ἐγγύθεν, οὐδέ ἑ λήθει
ὅππως τὸ πρῶτον τανύσῃ βοέοισιν ἱμᾶσιν,
ἀλλ᾽ ἔχει ἀσφαλέως καὶ τὸν προύχοντα δοκεύει.

He looks always towards the turning-post and turns near to it, and he remembers how from the first to keep the horses taut with the oxhide reins: he holds them firmly, and looks at the man in front of him

Leaf may be wrong to describe 'the whole passage', i.e. the whole of Nestor's speech, as 'hopelessly obscure'; but these particular lines are far from clear.

The beginning of 323 must mean "he always keeps his eye on the turning-point, and turns close to it", and what immediately follows most naturally refers (1) only to this part of the race, not to the race in general, so that the following lines have to make sense in that light. Alternatively, if less naturally, (2) the general structure is of the form "He always keeps his eye on the turning-point ... and (throughout the race) remembers to..."; and that demands a different kind of sense for what follows.

Richardson (without argument) assumes (2), and translates "Always keeping his eye on the turning-post wheels close to it, and he does not forget how from the start [το πρωτον 'at first', 'at the start', *sc.* presumably from the start of the whole race] to keep (his horses) taut with the ox-hide reins, but he holds them steadily in hand, and fixes his gaze on the competitor in the lead". The trouble with this is partly that το πρωτον does not naturally mean 'from the start', but also that it is far from certain that τανύσῃ means 'keep taut'. Thus in 16.375 the Trojans, whose horses τανύοντο, are fleeing in panic; presumably their horses were not 'kept taut', but given their heads. τανύοντο might mean just 'ran under control' or 'were stretched out in their harness', as it seems to do in 16.475 (ἐν ῥυτῆρσι τ.). It would then be a general injunction to keep the horses under control throughout the race, contrasted with the foolish charioteer who ἀφραδέως...ἑλίσσεται / ἵπποι δὲ πλανόωνται ('swerves thoughtlessly, and the horses wander') (320-21). If we adopt this interpretation, it seems better to take ἱμασιν as 'traces' or 'harness' rather than 'reins', since it is the traces rather than the reins which keep the horses 'stretched out'. But then, if the injunction applies throughout the race, το πρωτον makes little sense: and there may also be some inconsistency between το πρωτον and τον προυχοντα δοκέυει ('he keeps his eye on the leader').

(1) is more attractive, taking οὐδέ ἑ λήθει ('nor does it escape him') ff. to refer to what happens <u>after</u> the turning-point. Thus Rieu translates: "He is not caught napping when the time comes [i.e. for the first time, πρωτον] to use the ox-hide reins [or, perhaps better here, the whip] and stretch his horses". That does justice to πρωτον; and also to τανύσῃ, which most probably means 'make them go full out'. That is what seems to happen in the actual race, when during the πύματον δρόμον (373) ἵπποισι τάθη δρόμος ('the horses ran at full stretch') (374-75). Then we should translate 325 rather differently: "he stretches them out to the full with the whip, but still keeps them safely under control, and [*sc.* <u>after</u> he has passed the turning-point] watches the leader". But I do not think this sense for τανύσῃ reads naturally, and the idea of always watching the leader fits more naturally with the earlier part of the race (Nestor seems to think in 344 ff. that if Antilochos does what he should at the turning-point, he will be the leader and there will be no one to keep his eye on).

A third possibility (3) is that the injunction refers only to the <u>first</u> part of the race (not throughout it). That does justice to το πρωτον though we have to interpret τανύσῃ in Richardson's sense of 'keep taut' or 'keep under control' (with the reins or in the harness). And the back-tracking to the beginning of the race (after having spoken of the turning-point) will be odder than (2).

All this is certainly obscure. Whether or not we regard it as incoherent depends on whether the reader/hearer could naturally assume one or another of (1), (2) or (3) to be <u>the</u> sense of the passage. I am frankly unsure about this, chiefly because I suspect that the modem reader is not clear (despite its numerous uses) about what exactly τανύσῃ would normally be taken to mean by the poet's readers/hearers. It may, as Richardson says, have had a well-known meaning in 'the technical language of racing', in which case there might be no doubt. In view of this we cannot assume incoherence.

23. 638-9

οἴοισίν μ᾽ ἵπποισι παρήλασαν Ἀκτορίωνε,
πλήθει πρόσθε βαλόντες, ἀγασσάμενοι περὶ νίκης,

With their horses alone did the Aktorione drive past me, pressing in front because of their numbers, being eager for victory.

Richardson says that 'forging ahead through their superior numbers ... seems the simplest explanation of the phrase' (πληθει...('numbers, 'throng')), there being two Aktonione to one Nestor. That is not convincing, particularly since in 641-2 Nestor does not give their double-act as a <u>reason</u> for their winning. Other explanations (see Richardson) are worse still. Perhaps 'forging ahead in the mêlée' (*sc.* of chariots) is the least implausible. But I doubt if the reader/hearer could assign any clear sense to the phrase. At least a borderline case.

23. 874-9

ὕψι δ' ὑπὸ νεφέων εἶδε τρήρωνα πέλειαν·
τῇ ῥ' ὅ γε δινεύουσαν ὑπὸ πτέρυγος βάλε μέσσην,
ἀντικρὺ δὲ διῆλθε βέλος· τὸ μὲν ἂψ ἐπὶ γαίῃ
πρόσθεν Μηριόναο πάγη ποδός· αὐτὰρ ἡ ὄρνις
ἱστῷ ἐφεζομένη νηὸς κυανοπρῴροιο
αὐχέν' ἀπεκρέμασεν, σὺν δὲ πτερὰ πυκνὰ λίασθεν.

He saw the tender dove high below the clouds: as it wheeled there he shot it through its middle, and the shaft pierced it right through: it fell back to earth and was fixed in front of Meriones' foot. The bird itself sitting on the mast of the dark-prowed ship bent its head, and its thick wings drooped.

See Richardson. It is certainly incoherent that Meriones' arrow should have fallen at his feet after hitting the dove and that the dove should then be sitting on the mast far away. The poet has no clear picture in mind.

24. 53-54

μὴ ἀγαθῷ περ ἐόντι νεμεσσηθέωμέν οἱ ἡμεῖς·
κωφὴν γὰρ δὴ γαῖαν ἀεικίζει μενεαίνων.

Lest we should be indignant with him, good man though he is: for it is only dumb earth that he insults in his fury.

It is difficult not to see the γαρ ('for') in 54 as logically incoherent: why should the fact that Hector's body is just 'mute clay' or 'dumb earth' be a reason for the gods' indignation? κωφην γαρ δη ('for indeed [it is] dumb...') is strongly emphatic, as most translators acknowledge (e.g. Rieu "What is he doing in his fury but insulting senseless clay?").

There are three possibilities. (1) We can take 54 as summarising the reason for the gods' possible indignation, and play down κωφην γαιαν: 'for he is doing shameful things to this mute clay in his fury', with the stress on ἀεικίζει ('insult', 'violate'). Those who pay serious attention to γαρ must take this line: the trouble is that the idea of the body as 'mute clay' is not really a Homeric one (despite 7.99, quoted by Richardson), and that Hector's body is not really seen in this light at all. (2) would involve attaching the gods' indignation precisely to the fact that it is just 'mute clay', and that Achilles is therefore mad or deranged in insulting it: the gods' displeasure is directed against Achilles for his madness or derangement. That is possible, but involves taking κωφην γαιαν in a fairly wide sense, and one not really consonant with Apollo's earlier remarks (35 ff.), which blame Achilles for not returning the (important) corpse to Priam. It might also be just possible (3) to take γαιαν literally: Achilles is insulting the (sacred but dumb) earth itself by dragging the corpse on it: but that is somewhat fanciful, and again does not square with Apollo's speech in general.

I incline to (1) or (2), but it seems to be at least a borderline case of incoherence.

24. 139

τῇδ' εἴη· ὅς ἄποινα φέροι καὶ νεκρὸν ἄγοιτο,

Let it be so: let him bring the ransom and take away the corpse.

See Richardson's note; but neither (1) "Let it be so: let he who brings the ransom also carry away the corpse", nor (2) (without the colon after εἴη ('be')) "Let the man who brings the ransom and carries away the corpse be present here" is at all plausible (Richardson's 'rather awkward' is too weak): whilst (3) taking εἴη as a form of εἶμι ('I will go') (*ibo*) is implausible in itself and does not really help with the general sense. A fourth possibility, not canvassed in the literature, is to take ὅς ('he' or 'who') as demonstrative rather than relative: "Let it be so: let him (*sc.* Priam) bring the ransom and take away the corpse" - but Priam has not been mentioned in Thetis' speech to Achilles. I suspect the line is corrupt, or that other lines have been omitted (Achilles' speech is curiously brief): certainly it does not read coherently.

PART 2

COMMENTS ON THE ODYSSEY

1. 358-59

> μῦθος δ' ἄνδρεσσι μελήσει
> πᾶσι, μάλιστα δ' ἐμοί· τοῦ γὰρ κράτος ἔστ' ἐνὶ οἴκῳ.'

Talk shall be concern of men - all men, especially me: for mine is the power in the house.

This (rather feeble) attempt to re-use the structure of Il. 6.490-93 (Hector to Andromache, with μυθος instead of πολέμος ('war')) lands the poet with some obscurity, at least verging on the incoherent. All commentators take μυθος ('talk') in its normal Homeric meaning of 'speech' or 'talk'; but the whole of Telemachus' remarks are only about what the bard is to sing of (345 ff.), not about speech or talk in general. So Telemachus' final remark is not only harsh but irrelevant: "Why do you object to the bard singing of this? There is no harm in it, Zeus is ultimately to blame, people always like hearing the latest songs, other people besides Odysseus had a bad time of it, etc.: so just you go about your woman's business, and leave any talking to men, especially to me" - hardly coherent logic. It also fails to square with the fact that Penelope talks quite a lot later on in the Odyssey, without Telemachus or anyone else raising any objection.

It is tempting to suggest that μυθος here means 'story-telling' and is a substitute for ἀοιδη ('singing', 'recitation') (which would present metrical difficulties in this formulaic context). But that is contrary to all other Homeric usage, and it is better just to accept this as, at best, a borderline case of incoherence.

1. 386-98

> μή σέ γ' ἐν ἀμφιάλῳ Ἰθάκῃ βασιλῆα Κρονίων
> ποιήσειεν, ὅ τοι γενεῇ πατρώϊόν ἐστιν."
> Τὸν δ' αὖ Τηλέμαχος πεπνυμένος ἀντίον ηὔδα·
> " Ἀντίνο', εἴ πέρ μοι καὶ ἀγάσσεαι ὅττι κεν εἴπω,
> καί κεν τοῦτ' ἐθέλοιμι Διός γε διδόντος ἀρέσθαι.
> ἦ φῂς τοῦτο κάκιστον ἐν ἀνθρώποισι τετύχθαι;
> οὐ μὲν γάρ τι κακὸν βασιλευέμεν· αἶψά τέ οἱ δῶ
> ἀφνειὸν πέλεται καὶ τιμηέστερος αὐτός.
> ἀλλ' ἦ τοι βασιλῆες Ἀχαιῶν εἰσὶ καὶ ἄλλοι
> πολλοὶ ἐν ἀμφιάλῳ Ἰθάκῃ, νέοι ἠδὲ παλαιοί,
> τῶν κέν τις τόδ' ἔχῃσιν, ἐπεὶ θάνε δῖος Ὀδυσσεύς·
> αὐτὰρ ἐγὼν οἴκοιο ἄναξ ἔσομ' ἡμετέροιο
> καὶ δμώων, οὕς μοι ληίσσατο δῖος Ὀδυσσεύς."

"Take care that the son of Kronos does not make you a king in sea-girt Ithaca, which is your ancestral right". Then wise Telemachus spoke back to him again: "Antinoos, even if you are amazed at what I might say, that too I would be willing to take up, if Zeus granted it. Do you think that is the worst thing to happen amongst men? No, it is not at all a bad thing to be a king: at once a man's house becomes wealthy, and he himself is more honoured. But indeed there are other kings too of the Achaeans, many of them, young and old, in sea-girt Ithaca; so let one of them have this honour, since godlike Odysseus has died. Then I will simply be the lord of my own house and of the slaves which godlike Odysseus has acquired as booty for me.

It is remarkable that the straight contradiction in this passage has not attracted more comment. The logical form is:

(1) "Perhaps Zeus may make you an X, Telemachus" (386-87)
(2) "Well, I'd be quite happy to be an X: (390)
(3) But there are plenty of other Xes in Ithaca: (394-95)
(4) So let one of them have this privilege (*sc.* being an X)." (396).

The contradiction is obvious, whatever value we assign to X (i.e. whatever βασιλευς ('king', 'lord') may mean): how can someone who is already an X (3) come to get the privilege of being an X (4)?

Short of whole-scale emendation, there seem to be only two ways of trying to resolve this:

(a) We may violently repunctuate 394-95, so as to create another class of people who are not βασιληες: perhaps with a comma after εἰσι ('are'), so that we could (just) translate "But the Achaians already have some βασιληες, and there are many other people in sea-girt Ithaca, young and old, one of whom might acquire this privilege". That reads very unnaturally.

(b) We may translate βασιλευεμεν ('to be a king') as referring not just to being a βασιλευς *sans phrase* but rather to the particular overlordship or status of Odysseus (τοδ' ἔχῃσιν...Ὀδυσσεύς ('have this [honour]...Odysseus')): "there are plenty of other - let one of them enjoy this particular lordship". That is not impossible, but it also is very unnatural: βασιλευεμεν naturally refers to simply 'being a βασιλευς', as described in 391-93.

So the poet is seriously confused: more than simply careless, since there is no easy way in which the passage can be emended to make sense. Why does he mention the other βασιληες at all? There seems to be a confused collation of the two thoughts (i) there are plenty of βασιληες in Ithaca already, and (ii) let someone else (not I) become a βασιλευς in Odysseus' stead. The second of these is the predominant idea, as 397-98 make plain: someone else can be βασιλευς in Odysseus' stead, and I will just be master of my own house. There is also a further confusion caused by the latent thought 'being the βασιλευς', the supreme ruler, like Odysseus. This is Telemachus' birthright (πατρώιον, 387), and in 400-01 Eurymachus seems to have this in mind (ὅς τις ἐν ἀμφιάλῳ Ἰθάκῃ βασιλεύσει Ἀχαιων ('who shall be king of the Achaeans in sea-girt Ithaca')), where βασιλεύσει probably means (if it means anything clear at all) 'be the king'. An extended case of incoherence.

2. 240-51

ἦσθ' ἄνεω, ἀτὰρ οὔ τι καθαπτόμενοι ἐπέεσσι
παύρους μνηστῆρας κατερύκετε πολλοὶ ἐόντες."
Τὸν δ' Εὐηνορίδης Ληόκριτος ἀντίον ηὔδα·
" Μέντορ ἀταρτηρέ, φρένας ἠλεέ, ποῖον ἔειπες
ἡμέας ὀτρύνων καταπαυέμεν. ἀργαλέον δὲ
ἀνδράσι καὶ πλεόνεσσι μαχήσασθαι περὶ δαιτί.
εἴ περ γάρ κ' Ὀδυσεὺς Ἰθακήσιος αὐτὸς ἐπελθὼν
δαινυμένους κατὰ δῶμα ἑὸν μνηστῆρας ἀγαυοὺς
ἐξελάσαι μεγάροιο μενοινήσει' ἐνὶ θυμῷ,
οὔ κέν οἱ κεχάροιτο γυνή, μάλα περ χατέουσα,
ἐλθόντ', ἀλλά κεν αὐτοῦ ἀεικέα πότμον ἐπίσποι,
εἰ πλεόνεσσι μάχοιτο· σὺ δ' οὐ κατὰ μοῖραν ἔειπες.

"You sit silent, and do not at all fasten upon the suitors with your words and restrain them, though they are few and you many". Leocritos son of Euenor spoke back to him: "Mentor, you mischief-maker, madman! What a thing to say, urging them on to put a stop to this! But it is difficult even for men with superior numbers to start a fight about feasting. For even if Odysseus of Ithaca himself were to come, and desired in his heart to drive out the proud suitors from this hall, as they were feasting in his house, then his wife would have no joy of him when he came, much though she might miss him; rather would he then in that place meet a terrible fate, if he fought against greater numbers. So you did not speak sensibly."

This is a good example of the text's confusion. Commentators (e.g. West) invite us to choose between the two alternatives for 245: (1) it is hard even for men with a numerical advantage to fight about feasting, (2) it is hard to fight about feasting against men with a numerical advantage (i.e. the suitors). The trouble is that neither works. 241 deliberately stresses the numerical advantage of the Ithacans generally over the suitors, so that (2) is impossible, and (1) seems the obvious sense (καὶ reads naturally as 'even'). But 246 ff. must have the logic: "for (γάρ) even if Odysseus himself were to try it, he would fail because of our superior numbers" (εἰ πλεόνεσσι μάχοιτο ('if he fought with more men')). There is no way of satisfying both demands: the text has been put together casually.

2. 312-16

ἢ οὐχ ἅλις ὡς τὸ πάροιθεν ἐκείρετε πολλὰ καὶ ἐσθλὰ
κτήματ' ἐμά, μνηστῆρες, ἐγὼ δ' ἔτι νήπιος ἦα;
νῦν δ' ὅτε δὴ μέγας εἰμὶ καὶ ἄλλων μῦθον ἀκούων
πυνθάνομαι, καὶ δή μοι ἀέξεται ἔνδοθι θυμός,
πειρήσω ὥς κ' ὔμμι κακὰς ἐπὶ κῆρας ἰήλω,

Is it not enough that before this you wasted my many fine possessions, you suitors, and I was as yet still a child? But now indeed I am full-grown, and I learn by listening to the words of others, and my anger rises inside me, and I will try to fasten evil fates upon you.

Most commentators take 314-15 as "But now I am grown up, and learn (*sc.* about the true state of affairs) by listening to the words of others..." What others? West says "Telemachus means Mentes, despite the generalising pl." But the real problem is, what does he learn? Neither Mentes nor anyone else actually tells Telemachus anything about the suitors which he does not already know. Indeed Mentes asks the questions and Telemachus gives the answers, not *vice versa*. It is hard to see how Telemachus could fail to know anything relevant.

This might be saved by supposing that it is just the suitors' behaviour when he was a child that Telemachus learns about, by hearing of it from others. The snag is that neither Mentes nor anyone else in the text tells Telemachus that the suitors' bad behaviour has been going on ever since he was a child, and there is no indication that this particular piece of knowledge is important: none of Telemachus' (very frequent) complaints refer to the past in this way.

Another interpretation might be "Now that I am grown up, and listen to other people, and have the wit to understand" (i.e. a rather extended way of saying he is now adult). But πυνθάνομαι ('learn', 'find out') can hardly bear this sense. Alternatively, Telemachus may refer by πυνθάνομαι not to a knowledge of the facts - he knows these quite well - but to an understanding, by listening to other people (like Mentes), of what he could or ought to do about it. That fits better with what Mentes actually says (he gives moral or political or prudential advice rather than factual information). We might translate "Now that I am grown up, and appreciate the position by having listened to other people..."

This last is perhaps the best (of a bad job); but the text does not really make it clear. A borderline case at best.

3. 230-38

" Τηλέμαχε, ποῖόν σε ἔπος φύγεν ἕρκος ὀδόντων.
ῥεῖα θεός γ' ἐθέλων καὶ τηλόθεν ἄνδρα σαώσαι.
βουλοίμην δ' ἂν ἐγώ γε καὶ ἄλγεα πολλὰ μογήσας
οἴκαδέ τ' ἐλθέμεναι καὶ νόστιμον ἦμαρ ἰδέσθαι,
ἢ ἐλθὼν ἀπολέσθαι ἐφέστιος, ὡς Ἀγαμέμνων
ὤλεθ' ὑπ' Αἰγίσθοιο δόλῳ καὶ ἧς ἀλόχοιο.
ἀλλ' ἦ τοι θάνατον μὲν ὁμοίιον οὐδὲ θεοί περ
καὶ φίλῳ ἀνδρὶ δύνανται ἀλαλκέμεν, ὁππότε κεν δὴ
μοῖρ' ὀλοὴ καθέλῃσι τανηλεγέος θανάτοιο."

"Telemachus, what a word has escaped the barrier of your teeth! A god, if he wishes, can easily save a man even from far off. I would prefer for my part to come home and see my day of returning even after suffering many pains, rather than come and be killed by my own hearth, in the way that Agamemnon perished by the trickery of Aigisthus and of his own wife. But indeed death is common to all, nor can the gods protect even one dear to them from it, whenever in fact the dire fate of death that lays a man low overtakes him.

This is a case of commentators claiming problems where there are none. West says that 231 "admits two interpretations: (1) a god, if he will, can easily bring a man home even from a distant land; (2) a god, if he will, can even at a distance save a man", adding, "it may be wrong to ask which the poet really meant" (Why?). On (1), "231 is quite irrelevant to what Telemachus has just said": on (2) (Aristarchus' preference) 232-35 do not 'follow on logically from what had been said' and 236-38 are 'inconsistent with 231'.

Nestor has just said (216 ff.) words to the effect of "Maybe Odysseus will come home after all and take his vengeance". Telemachus replies (226-28) "No, that's impossible, I couldn't hope for that even if the gods wanted it". So what is in question is whether the gods can bring a man home to safety. We have to choose, not between (1) and (2), alternatives which imply different kinds of 'saving' (bringing home safely on the one hand, and - presumably - saving his life on the other), but rather between (a) τηλόθεν ('from afar') implying that the god is at a distance, or (b) τηλόθεν implying that the man is at a distance. But I am not sure that these are real alternatives:

τηλόθεν seems to mean just, as it were, 'by remote control': the two parties are at a distance from each other. Strictly we must take τηλόθεν with the verb σαῶσαι ('to save'), not with ἄνδρα ('a man'); so insofar as the choice is real, we must prefer (a): the god can, operating from a distance, bring the man to safety.

Then the logic is: "And this is worth doing, because it is better to come home even after difficulties (ἄλγεα πολλά ('many pains')) than to get home easily and then be killed like Agamemnon". Then Athene turns to a different kind of 'saving', saving from death: "As for death, not even the gods can stop that, even for a favourite of the gods, if it is fated".

4. 244-49

αὐτόν μιν πληγῇσιν ἀεικελίῃσι δαμάσσας,
σπεῖρα κάκ' ἀμφ' ὤμοισι βαλών, οἰκῆϊ ἐοικώς,
ἀνδρῶν δυσμενέων κατέδυ πόλιν εὐρυάγυιαν·
ἄλλῳ δ' αὐτὸν φωτὶ κατακρύπτων ἤϊσκε
δέκτῃ, ὃς οὐδὲν τοῖος ἔην ἐπὶ νηυσὶν Ἀχαιῶν.
τῷ ἴκελος κατέδυ Τρώων πόλιν.

He inflicted an unsightly beating upon himself, and put foul rags round his shoulders, like a servant; and then he entered the broad-wayed city of his enemies. By hiding himself he made himself seem like a different person, a beggar - and was not at all the sort of person he was by the ships of the Achaeans. Looking like that, he entered the city of the Trojans.

Another example of a non-problem. δέκτῃ (pace many commentators) can hardly be a proper name. It is not just that the relative clause which follows is 'clumsy and perplexing' (West), but that there is no apparent reason why Odysseus should want to look like an identifiable Greek (the text here says nothing of the story of Odysseus representing himself as a Greek who has turned against his masters: the πληγῇσι ('blows') of 244 is not enough). It is only the apparent inconsistency of δέκτῃ with the earlier οἰκῆϊ ('servant') that really causes any trouble.

One possibility is that δέκτῃ (otherwise unknown) means something which is not inconsistent with οἰκῆϊ: for instance, 'someone who receives his food from other people', 'a slave', 'a dependant'. But we may also accept Aristarchus' translation ('beggar') and take οἰκῆϊ as referring only to the σπεῖρα κάκα ('evil rags'). The sense would be "He put on a menial's clothes and thus entered the city: in fact he disguised himself as a different kind of person, a beggar - not at all like what he was by the Greek ships. That was what he was like when he entered the city, and everyone..." In other words, it seems to me over-precise to claim any inconsistency here. (As one might say: "He put on working-class clothes, and disguised himself as a beggar".)

4. 795-837

Ἔνθ' αὖτ' ἄλλ' ἐνόησε θεὰ γλαυκῶπις Ἀθήνη·
εἴδωλον ποίησε, δέμας δ' ἤϊκτο γυναικί,
Ἰφθίμῃ, κούρῃ μεγαλήτορος Ἰκαρίοιο,
τὴν Εὔμηλος ὄπυιε, Φερῇς ἔνι οἰκία ναίων.
πέμπε δέ μιν πρὸς δώματ' Ὀδυσσῆος θείοιο,
ἧος Πηνελόπειαν ὀδυρομένην, γοόωσαν,
παύσειε κλαυθμοῖο γόοιό τε δακρυόεντος.
ἐς θάλαμον δ' εἰσῆλθε παρὰ κληῖδος ἱμάντα,
στῆ δ' ἄρ' ὑπὲρ κεφαλῆς, καί μιν πρὸς μῦθον ἔειπεν·
" Εὕδεις, Πηνελόπεια, φίλον τετιημένη ἦτορ;
οὐ μέν σ' οὐδὲ ἐῶσι θεοὶ ῥεῖα ζώοντες
κλαίειν οὐδ' ἀκάχησθαι, ἐπεί ῥ' ἔτι νόστιμός ἐστι
σὸς πάϊς· οὐ μὲν γάρ τι θεοῖς ἀλιτήμενός ἐστι."
Τὴν δ' ἠμείβετ' ἔπειτα περίφρων Πηνελόπεια,
ἡδὺ μάλα κνώσσουσ' ἐν ὀνειρείῃσι πύλῃσιν·
" Τίπτε, κασιγνήτη, δεῦρ' ἤλυθες; οὔ τι πάρος γε
πωλέαι, ἐπεὶ μάλα πολλὸν ἀπόπροθι δώματα ναίεις·
καί με κέλεαι παύσασθαι ὀϊζύος ἠδ' ὀδυνάων
πολλέων, αἵ μ' ἐρέθουσι κατὰ φρένα καὶ κατὰ θυμόν,
ἣ πρὶν μὲν πόσιν ἐσθλὸν ἀπώλεσα θυμολέοντα,
παντοίῃς ἀρετῇσι κεκασμένον ἐν Δαναοῖσιν,
ἐσθλόν, τοῦ κλέος εὐρὺ καθ' Ἑλλάδα καὶ μέσον Ἄργος.
νῦν αὖ παῖς ἀγαπητὸς ἔβη κοίλης ἐπὶ νηός,
νήπιος, οὔτε πόνων εὖ εἰδὼς οὔτ' ἀγοράων.
τοῦ δὴ ἐγὼ καὶ μᾶλλον ὀδύρομαι ἤ περ ἐκείνου.
τοῦ δ' ἀμφιτρομέω καὶ δείδια μή τι πάθῃσιν,
ἢ ὅ γε τῶν ἐνὶ δήμῳ, ἵν' οἴχεται, ἢ ἐνὶ πόντῳ·
δυσμενέες γὰρ πολλοὶ ἐπ' αὐτῷ μηχανόωνται,
ἱέμενοι κτεῖναι, πρὶν πατρίδα γαῖαν ἱκέσθαι."
Τὴν δ' ἀπαμειβόμενον προσέφη εἴδωλον ἀμαυρόν·
" θάρσει, μηδέ τι πάγχυ μετὰ φρεσὶ δείδιθι λίην·
τοίη γάρ οἱ πομπὸς ἅμ' ἔρχεται, ἥν τε καὶ ἄλλοι
ἀνέρες ἠρήσαντο παρεστάμεναι, δύναται γάρ,

SENSE AND NONSENSE IN HOMER

Παλλὰς Ἀθηναίη· σὲ δ' ὀδυρομένην ἐλεαίρει·
ἥ νῦν με προέηκε τεῒν τάδε μυθήσασθαι.'

Τὴν δ' αὖτε προσέειπε περίφρων Πηνελόπεια·
' εἰ μὲν δὴ θεός ἐσσι, θεοῖό τε ἔκλυες αὐδῆς,
εἰ δ' ἄγε μοι καὶ κεῖνον ὀϊζυρὸν κατάλεξον,
ἤ που ἔτι ζώει καὶ ὁρᾷ φάος ἠελίοιο,
ἦ ἤδη τέθνηκε καὶ εἰν Ἀΐδαο δόμοισι.'

Τὴν δ' ἀπαμειβόμενον προσέφη εἴδωλον ἀμαυρόν·
' οὐ μέν τοι κεῖνόν γε διηνεκέως ἀγορεύσω,
ζώει ὅ γ', ἦ τέθνηκε· κακὸν δ' ἀνεμώλια βάζειν.'

Then the goddess grey-eyed Athenes had another thought. She made a ghost-figure and in form it was like a woman, Iphthime, the daughter of great-hearted Icarius: Eumelos had married her, who lived in Pherai. Athene sent this ghost to the house of divine Odysseus, so as to stop Penelope, who was lamenting and weeping, from her tears and sad weeping. It slipped into her chamber by the thong of the bolt; it stood above her head and spoke a word to her: "Are you asleep, Penelope, you who are so sad in your dear heart? But the gods who live at ease do not allow you to weep or be sorrowful, since your son is still returning: for he is not at all a sinner in the eyes of the gods". Then the prudent Penelope answered her, as she slumbered very sweetly at the dream-gates: "Sister, why have you come here? Before this you have never used to come, since you live far distant from here. And now you bid me stop my suffering and my many sorrows, which trouble me in my heart and my spirit. Before this I have lost my fine, lion-hearted husband, outstanding in all kinds of excellence among the Danaans - a fine man, whose fame spreads wide over Greece and the midst of Argos. And now my beloved son has gone on a hollow ship - he is young, and inexperienced in labours and speech-making: and him I lament even more than my husband. I tremble for him and fear that he may be suffering something: either from the people of the country where he has gone to, or on the sea. For many enemies plot against him, desiring to kill him, before he reaches his native land". Answering her then spoke the shadowy ghost: "Have courage, and do not at all fear anything too much in your heart. For he has such a good escort along with him, she whom other men also have prayed to stand by them - for she has the power to do so: that is, Pallas Athene. She takes pity on your lamentation, and now she has sent me forth to tell you these things". Answering her prudent Penelope spoke: "If indeed you are a god, and have heard the voice of a god, come, tell me about that wretched man - whether he is still alive and sees the light of the sun, or is already dead and in the house of Hades". Answering her spoke the shadowy ghost: "I will not tell you directly about that man, whether he is alive or dead: and it is wrong to babble empty words".

An extremely baffling passage. The difficulties begin with νόστιμός (806): does this mean 'still able to return', 'liable to return' - i.e. he still has a (good?) chance of returning -, or 'still going to return, or 'already (ἔτι) returning'? Either of the last two should carry more comfort and conviction to Penelope than it evidently does. That difficulty is comparatively trivial: the problems really begin with Penelope's reply in 810 ff., which reads almost as if the ghost had not spoken (despite 812). She asks why the ghost has come: but the ghost has already told her that, and given her some assurance about Telemachus.

Penelope then sets out her twin troubles, about Odysseus (814-16) and Telemachus (817-23). The ghost gives a clear reply: Athene will look after Telemachus, and Athene has sent the ghost to tell her so. Then we have the strange line 831, which as it stands must mean "If indeed you are a god and have heard the voice of a god": to which commentators understandably object that the ghost is not a god. Understandably but wrongly, and the strangeness is more apparent than real. We know (from 795 ff.) that the ghost is a ghost and not a god, but Penelope does not have this information. She begins (810) by thinking that it is actually her sister (and why has she come from such a distance to visit her?). The ghost does not confirm or deny this, but just says "Athene has sent me" (829). Penelope is, after all, more or less asleep (ἐν ὀνείρειησι πύλησιν ('at the gates of dreams'), 809) and may well be baffled by the speaker's ontological status. It is a distinct possibility that the speaker is some kind of divine power or god, sent by another god (as Hermes was sent by Zeus in 5. 28 ff.). So she says "if indeed - that is, only if - you are a god ...."

The choice between MSS readings ἔκλυες ('you have heard') and ἔκλυον ('I have heard') does not much affect this matter. The former would mean "If indeed you are a god and have heard what (another) god has said to you", i.e. what Athene has told you: the latter "If indeed you are a god, and it is a god's voice I have (just) heard". Both seem quite acceptable, the latter slightly to be preferred. (West's objection that this makes it 'merely tautological' is ill-founded: Homer is littered with such tautologies.)

So far, perhaps so good. But now comes trouble. 833 must surely refer to Odysseus: Penelope wants to know about him too (κεῖνον ('that man') referring back to ἐκείνου ('that man') in 819). The ghost says (836-37) I will not speak of him διηνεκέως, whether he lives or is dead". διηνεκέως normally means 'at length', 'continuously', 'from start to finish': and the obvious objection here is that the ghost does not say anything about Odysseus at all. It is not clear that this objection is really much diminished by taking διηνεκέως as 'positively' or 'explicitly' (which would be a unique sense for the word), because the ghost does not say anything even non-positively or inexplicitly. We might try to find (invent) a meaning for it along the lines of 'directly; or 'immediately; ("I won't tell you straightaway", with the implication that Penelope may be told later): but that is scraping the bottom of the barrel.

It is better to begin, at least, by sticking to the normal meaning of διηνεκέως so that 835 means something like " I will not give you a blow-by-blow account of him". We then have a choice between the orthodox interpretation (a) " I will not tell you whether he is alive or dead", and the possible interpretation (b) "Whether in fact he is alive or dead, I will not give you a full account of him". That bears somewhat on the sense of κακον ... βάζειν ('a bad thing...to babble') (837 = 11.464), where Odysseus excuses himself from answering Agamemnon's enquiry about whether his son Orestes is alive by saying "I don't know at all whether he is alive or dead, κακον ... βάζειν; that is, presumably, something like "so anything I say on this point would be ἀνεμώλια ('windy', 'vain', 'empty') (just so much hot air, one might say), and it's not good to talk hot air".

West says "It is absurd that the dream-figure should thus allege lack of reliable information as grounds for its refusal":

but (a) the ghost does not allege anything of the kind, and (b) if it did, that would be good grounds - just the same grounds as Odysseus alleges (11.463). That is not the problem: the problem is the opposite, that the ghost does not say that it does not know, it just says that it is not going to tell. Probably ζώει ... τέθνηκε ('is alive...has died') is best taken in the orthodox way, "I shall not tell you whether he is alive or dead"; but either interpretation sits badly with διηνεκέως " I shall not give you a full account", because the implication of that is that the ghost does know something. And it also sits badly with κακον ... βάζειν, since it would not (certainly not for Penelope) be ἀνεμώλια.

So we have to say, I think, not just that familiar formulae have been carelessly used in 836 and 837, but rather that the poet has just not bothered to make sense of the ghost's answer to Penelope about Odysseus at all. Indeed the whole passage would read much better without 830-37: then after the encouraging 825-29 the ghost would depart leaving Penelope feeling happier (φίλον ... ἦτορ ἰάνθη ('her dear...heart was warmed'), 840): something she might well not have felt after the ghost's dismissive remarks about Odysseus. Nevertheless Penelope's enquiry about Odysseus follows naturally enough from her list of complaints in which Odysseus figures (814-16 and 819), so that the excision of the passage is not justified, even if we were to permit ourselves such dramatic measures. It seems that the poet has, so to speak, lost heart or lost interest in the ghost's reply, and hence produced nonsense. An extended case of incoherence.

5. 140-44

πέμψω δέ μιν οὔ πη ἐγώ γε·
οὐ γάρ μοι πάρα νῆες ἐπήρετμοι καὶ ἑταῖροι,
οἵ κέν μιν πέμποιεν ἐπ' εὐρέα νῶτα θαλάσσης.
αὐτάρ οἱ πρόφρων ὑποθήσομαι, οὐδ' ἐπικεύσω,
ὥς κε μάλ' ἀσκηθὴς ἣν πατρίδα γαῖαν ἵκηται."

But I myself will not at all give him an escort. For I have with me no oared ships or comrades who could escort him over the broad back of the sea. But willingly will I suggest things to him, nor hide anything, so that quite unscathed he may come to his native country.

This is at least careless. Hainsworth says "πέμψω ('send', 'escort') implies the provision of means as well as permission", but that hardly helps. She does provide him with means by helping him build the boat; but in any case 140 contradicts not only Hermes in 146, οὕτω νυν ἀπόπεμπε ('thus now send him off'), but more directly πομπήν ('an escort') in 233, and πέμπ' in 263.

The contradiction is not really helped by any interpretation of 143. That appears to mean something like "But I will willingly suggest things to him" (or perhaps "give him some materials, *sc.* the tools and timber and so on)" and "I will not hide anything from him" (*sc.* either the materials and/or the message from Zeus: but in fact she does conceal the latter). 143 is actually rather a baffling line in itself.

In any case the text reads strangely. 137-40 suggest that Calypso's attitude is essentially "Well, Zeus has ordered it, so let him damned well go" (ἐρρέτω ('let him go'), 139) "but I'm not in any way going to arrange/facilitate his going". Then she softens and says "I'll make helpful suggestions to him and not hide anything from him" (143) "so that he can get home safely"(144); and Hermes accepts this, οὕτω ... ἀπόπεμπε, (146). Then she seems in practice to go further, and devises arrangements for his going (πομπήν, 233), and actually sends him off under the aegis of such arrangements (πέμπ', 263). Some such changes of heart are required if πέμπω and πόμπη are to retain any single sense, because of the contradictions between 140, 146, 233 and 263. The alternative is to take 140 in a different sense from the rest, to mean "I won't give him a proper escort (with ships, rowers, etc.)" - in itself a bit odd: one would have expected "I can't give him a proper escort"; and this sharp difference in sense seems highly improbable. So unless we assume the relevant changes of heart on the part of Calypso (changes which are not explicitly marked in the text), we have to accept that the text as it stands is contradictory ('nonsensical' is too strong here).

10.17 ff. do not really help with this incoherence, but nevertheless shed some (rather faint) light. In 16-17 Odysseus asks Aeolus for πόμπη and gets it (τευχε δε πομπήν ('he provided an escort')). All we are told that Aeolus does is to give him a bag of winds (19 ff.) and then raise up a west wind to take Odysseus home (25 ff.): the latter is clearly useful, and perhaps the former should be conceived as useful inasmuch as tying down the winds in a bag might be taken as preventing the winds from spoiling Odysseus' voyage (as they certainly do when the bag is opened, 47 ff.). On Odysseus' return to Aeolus, the latter just tells him to go away (ἐρρ', 72) and they have a hard time rowing, because there is no longer any πομπή (οὐκέτι ... πομπή, 79). So πομπη does indeed imply more than just permission to go (Aeolus is only too anxious to get rid of him): it implies at least some kind of help. A full-scale πομπή is what the Phaiecians promise and provide (e.g. as used in 7.317 and elsewhere): a ship and rowers.

Some of the confusion in the Calypso scene may be caused simply by the fact that πέμπω and ἀπόπεμπω - but probably not πομπή - can also be used in (as it were) quite general and non-technical senses, meaning just 'to send off or 'dismiss': as indeed in 10.76 where Aeolus dismisses Odysseus indignantly (ἀπέπεμπε), though three lines later Odysseus says that he was given no πομπή. Thus in 5.146 Hermes may mean simply "All right, then, let him go/dismiss him under those conditions - have respect for the anger of Zeus", stressing just the idea of letting him go. This is what the gods are keen on, not the provision of assistance for his going. Zeus tells Hermes earlier to arrange ὡς κε νέηται ... οὔτε θεῶν πομπη οὔτε...('so that he may go, neither with any escort of the gods nor...') (5.31-32): it is only when he gets to the land of the Phaiecians that he is to get a πομπή (37).

That distinction, between ἀπόπεμπω or πέμπω and πομπη, slightly mitigates the confusion in the Calypso passage. It is reinforced by Odysseus' remark in 5.173, after Calypso has told him to build a raft and that she will provide him with food and garments and a following wind (162 ff.). He says in effect "It's not really a πομπή that you're planning" (ἀλλὸ ... οὐδέ τι πομπήν ('something else,...and not at all an escort')). Here at least, and no doubt elsewhere, πομπή implies not just (a) permission to leave, or (b) the provision of some assistance (Calypso has promised that), but also (c) some sort of honest intention to further the interests of the person concerned. The confusion is caused by the fact that some or all of these criteria may be used for special ('technical') senses of πέμπω, and πομπή. But that still leaves the contradiction of πέμψω (140) with other uses.

5. 154-55

ἀλλ' ἦ τοι νύκτας μὲν ἰαύεσκεν καὶ ἀνάγκῃ
ἐν σπέσσι γλαφυροῖσι παρ' οὐκ ἐθέλων ἐθελούσῃ·

But indeed during the nights he slept with her under compulsion in the hollow cave; she was willing but he was not.

The text is mysterious about Odysseus' attitude towards sleeping with Calypso, to say the least: indeed it is contradictory. Here he does it ἀνάγκῃ ('by necessity'); in 226-27 however τερπέσθην φιλότητι ('they delighted in love-making'), which does not look like any form of compulsion. Are we to suppose that (a) Odysseus was frightened of what Calypso might do if he did not comply, or (b) that Calypso (after all some kind of goddess) exercised a sort of magic power over him, or simply (c) that there was nowhere else he could reasonably sleep? None of these seem at all convincing. Nor is there anything in previous descriptions of Odysseus' position (e.g. in 1.14 ff. or 56 ff.) which helps at all. If we try to guess about the gory sexual details, we have to say that Odysseus seems to have been potent (τερπέσθην) even though he did it οὐκ ἐθέλων and ἀνάγκῃ (154-55). Imagination boggles: so does the text. A borderline case.

6. 119-26

"Ὤ μοι ἐγώ, τέων αὖτε βροτῶν ἐς γαῖαν ἱκάνω;
ἦ ῥ' οἵ γ' ὑβρισταί τε καὶ ἄγριοι οὐδὲ δίκαιοι,
ἦε φιλόξεινοι, καί σφιν νόος ἐστὶ θεουδής;
ὥς τέ με κουράων ἀμφήλυθε θῆλυς ἀυτή,
νυμφάων, αἳ ἔχουσ' ὀρέων αἰπεινὰ κάρηνα
καὶ πηγὰς ποταμῶν καὶ πίσεα ποιήεντα.
ἦ νύ που ἀνθρώπων εἰμὶ σχεδὸν αὐδηέντων;
ἀλλ' ἄγ', ἐγὼν αὐτὸς πειρήσομαι ἠδὲ ἴδωμαι."

O, alas, to the land of what mortals have I come? Are they overbearing and savage and not righteous, or are they hospitable, and is their mind god-fearing? For a female cry of young women came about me - of nymphs, who occupy the steep peaks of mountains and the springs of rivers and the grassy glades. Am I now near human beings who speak? But come, I myself will try and see.

This passage is odd: not exactly nonsense, but hardly coherent sense either. It starts with a formulaic enquiry (119-21), which Odysseus also uses both when he came to the land of the Cyclops and on arriving in Ithaca. That implies that he knows he has arrived in the land of some mortals (and indeed, if he believes what Leucothea told him in 5.344, he ought to know what he is in the land of the Phaiecians: but Odysseus is not a trusting character, and this hardly carries weight). Then his evidence or reason for this (122) is that he has heard the female cry of young women (θῆλυς ἀυτή ('a female cry')) - that offers a perfectly good reason, and is the natural translation. So far so good.

But then we have the mention of nymphs. This is difficult (a) because the phrase κουράων νυμφάων ('of young women nymphs') is not Homeric, and it is not clear just what it can mean. Nymphs (and other quasi-divinities) can be called κοῦραι in the sense of 'daughters' (of Zeus or whoever), but that will not work here. 'Of young female creatures, i.e. nymphs' is also not convincing: we would have to translate 'of young nymphs' -, possible but not Homeric. Then (b) why should the voices of nymphs be a reason for thinking that there are mortals present? And (c) how are we to translate 125: as a statement, "I must be near people with human speech"? But that raises the difficulty in (b) again - unless we are to suppose that nymphs only operate in human territory (unconvincing). Taking 125 as a question (as in the Oxford text), 'Am I near people with human speech?", is not much better.

It is just possible to save both the nymphs and the logic with some repunctuation, and taking ἦ in 125 as 'or': "A female voice of young feminine creatures came over me - was it of nymphs, who or am I now near to people of human speech?" But that is not convincing, if only because ἦ is much more likely just to introduce a statement or question rather than to offer an alternative. I think we have to accept some degree of incoherency here.

6. 263-65

καλὸς δὲ λιμὴν ἑκάτερθε πόληος,
λεπτὴ δ' εἰσίθμη· νῆες δ' ὁδὸν ἀμφιέλισσαι
εἰρύαται· πᾶσιν γὰρ ἐπίστιόν ἐστιν ἑκάστῳ.

There is a fine harbour on either side of the city, and a narrow entrance. The curved ships are drawn up about the road: for everyone has a dock for himself.

It is not really clear whether this is a coherent topographical description or not: the individual phrases are comprehensible enough, but the whole picture is somewhat obscure.

There is a good harbour on each side of the city: that is, two harbours (λιμένας ('harbours'), 7.43). The phrase λεπτὴ εἰσίθμη ('a narrow entrance'), coming as it does between the remark about the harbours and the remark about the ships, might be taken as referring to the harbour(s), on the analogy of ἀραιὴ δ'εἴσοδος ('a narrow way in') in 10.90, which refers to a harbour. But that will hardly make sense, and understandably it has normally been taken as referring to some sort of narrow road or causeway leading to the city, though this is not paralleled. So far, more or less, so good. Then νῆες δ' ὁδὸν ... εἰρύαται, which must mean "the ships are drawn up on (beside? along? next to?) the road", though the absence of a preposition is odd. (It cannot mean "the ships protect the road", since ships do not protect roads.) So then we have the picture represented in the sketches of some editors (e.g. Merry), which shows a peninsula with a city on the end of it, reached by a narrow causeway (presumably the εἰσίθμη ('entrance')), which forms part of each harbour, with the ships drawn up along either side of the causeway. What remains odd is πασιν ἐπίστιόν ἐστιν ἑκάστω ('there is for all, for each man, a boathouse (?)'). Pace Aristarchus, ἐπίστιον cannot be the same as ἐφέστιον i.e. a household: it makes no sense to say "For everyone has his own household". Nor is it easy to accept the scholiast's sense (anyway unparalleled) of a slipway or boathouse.

That there is some kind of muddle here seems clear: just what kind it seems impossible to say.

6. 278-84

ἦ τινά που πλαγχθέντα κομίσσατο ἧς ἀπὸ νηὸς
ἀνδρῶν τηλεδαπῶν, ἐπεὶ οὔ τινες ἐγγύθεν εἰσίν·
ἤ τίς οἱ εὐξαμένῃ πολυάρητος θεὸς ἦλθεν
οὐρανόθεν καταβάς, ἕξει δέ μιν ἤματα πάντα.
βέλτερον, εἰ καὐτή περ ἐποιχομένη πόσιν εὗρεν
ἄλλοθεν· ἦ γὰρ τούσδε γ' ἀτιμάζει κατὰ δῆμον
Φαίηκας, τοί μιν μνῶνται πολέες τε καὶ ἐσθλοί."

Indeed she has taken in some foreigner, some wanderer, from his ship - since there are none who live near to us. Or perhaps she has prayed much to some god, and the god has come down from heaven to answer the prayer, and will be her master for ever. It would have been better if she herself had gone abroad and found a husband from elsewhere: for indeed she despises all the Phaiecians here in this country, though many fine men woo her.

Some but not all of the difficulty here is caused by the editors who (almost universally) take 282-83 as "Better so, if indeed she has gone and found a husband from elsewhere: for she despises ...". That would have to be taken as heavily sarcastic; but it also fails to do justice both to the (surely emphatic) καὐτή ('herself indeed') and to ἄλλοθεν ('from elsewhere', 'from foreign parts') which together must mean something like "if she herself had gone abroad and found a husband". There is no question of her having done this in 278-81: there she has either picked up a wrecked sailor (in her own land) or been picked up by a god (also in her own land).

So we should rather translate in the sense of "Rather than pick up a wrecked sailor here, or be picked up by a god here, it would have been better if she had herself gone abroad and found a husband from some other land". But there remains a difficulty about why this would have been better. That might be soluble: the point might be that Nausicaa would at least then have made a sensible choice, rather than relying on the accident of either a wrecked sailor or some divine intervention. But I do not find this very convincing: the text is intrinsically obscure. A borderline case.

7. 31-35

μηδέ τιν' ἀνθρώπων προτιόσσεο μηδ' ἐρέεινε.
οὐ γὰρ ξείνους οἶδε μάλ' ἀνθρώπους ἀνέχονται,
οὐδ' ἀγαπαζόμενοι φιλέουσ' ὅς κ' ἄλλοθεν ἔλθῃ.
νηυσὶ θοῇσιν τοί γε πεποιθότες ὠκείῃσι
λαῖτμα μέγ' ἐκπερόωσιν, ἐπεί σφισι δῶκ' ἐνοσίχθων·

Do not look at any person, nor question any. For the people here do not endure men who are strangers: they do not make them welcome, or befriend anyone who comes from abroad. They trust in their swift ships which are so speedy, and cross the great gulf of the sea, since the Earth-shaker has given them that power.

This is on any account a baffling passage. The first difficulty is that *prima facie* at least Athene seems to be saying that the Phaiecians behave unpleasantly to strangers - they do not tolerate them, welcome them, or befriend them (φιλέουσι). But this does not at all square with 8.31-33:

ἡμεῖς δ', ὡς τὸ πάρος περ, ἐποτρυνώμεθα πομπήν.
οὐδὲ γὰρ οὐδέ τις ἄλλος, ὅτις κ' ἐμὰ δώμαθ' ἵκηται,
ἐνθάδ' ὀδυρόμενος δηρὸν μένει εἵνεκα πομπῆς.

And we, as in the past, must hurry to arrange an escort. For nobody else, no other man who comes to my house, ever waits here in sorrow for a long time, for an escort.

Admittedly Alcinoos is speaking here only to the upper-class Phaiecians, ἡγήτορες ἠδὲ μέδοντες ('the leaders and counsellors') (26): but Phaiecia is generally represented in idealistic if not utopian terms, and the people listened to Alcinoos as to a god (θεου ὡς, 7.10), so that even the unfriendliness of lower-class Phaiecians would be strange. Moreover, this would be compounded by one interpretation of the second difficulty, which is the logical connection between 31-33 and 34-35. For a possible interpretation of this connection is that the Phaiecians do not actually get any visiting strangers, since they live so far away from other men (this is the ellipsis we are supposed to understand), and rely on their swift ships if they themselves want to go anywhere. But that, of course, puts 31-35 even more at odds with what Alcinoos says.

The second difficulty involves the internal coherence of the passage. There is no particle which connects 32-33 with 34-35 in such a way as to make the logic of any connection at all plain; and this is in itself rather strange. One would expect some such logic as "They don't deal" (or, "They don't deal in a friendly way") with strangers because they just keep themselves to themselves, live far off, and rely on their swift ships when they want to go anywhere", or "... but they just keep themselves to themselves", etc. Some such logic is just intelligible even without a connecting particle, as in English "They don't deal with strangers: they just keep themselves to themselves", etc.; and perhaps τοί γε in 34 may carry the force of 'just' ("They don't deal with strangers: what they do is just to keep themselves to themselves", etc.)

But on any account there is some logical ellipsis between (a) not dealing with strangers, and (b) trusting in swift ships. The natural reading of the Greek in 32-33 is that the Phaiecians do have experience of strangers, but do not behave with friendship towards them. But that makes the ellipsis very hard to fill in. We should have to envisage some such logic as "They are not friendly to strangers, because they don't get many of them and hence haven't developed the norms of friendly intercourse one might expect, and that's because they keep themselves to themselves and rely on their swift ships", etc. It is therefore tempting to interpret 32-33 in the sense of "They don't have the habit or don't ever engage in the practice of tolerating, welcoming and befriending strangers" (sc. because they never get any) "because they keep themselves to themselves and rely on their swift ships", etc.

That, I think, lessens the difficulty of the ellipsis, and therefore to some extent the internal incoherence. But it is an unnatural way to take the Greek, and runs up against 7.16-17

μή τις Φαιήκων μεγαθύμων ἀντιβολήσας
κερτομέοι ἐπέεσσι καὶ ἐξερέοιθ' ὅτις εἴη.

Lest one of the great-hearted Phaiecians should meet you and insult you with his words, and ask you who you are

where κερτομέοι ('insult', 'chide', 'rebuke') must imply unfriendliness; and it also, as I have said, makes a worse fit with Alcinoos' later remarks. So on any account the passage is not only inconsistent with what Alcinoos says, but internally incoherent.

7. 205-6

οὔ τι κατακρύπτουσιν, ἐπεί σφισιν ἐγγύθεν εἰμέν,
ὥς περ Κύκλωπές τε καὶ ἄγρια φῦλα Γιγάντων."

Nor do they hide anything away, since we are close to them, like the Cyclopes and the savage races of the Giants.

We have to take this together with 5.35

Φαιήκων ἐς γαῖαν, οἳ ἀγχίθεοι γεγάασιν,

To the land of the Phaiecians, who are close to the gods.

and perhaps 6.203, μάλα γαρ φίλοι αθανάτοισιν ('for we are very dear to the immortals'). I doubt if these and other passages present a coherent picture of the Phaiecians' relationship to the gods: it seems to be a borderline case.

(1) Most modern editors take the relationship to be, as it were, social or religious, rather than a relationship of geography or kinship (thus Hainsworth: "ἐγγυθεν... ('near to') refers to the Phaiecians' special relationship with the gods, rather than to their kinship"): that is, the gods especially favour the Phaiecians, or are on close terms with them. That will certainly not do, for many reasons. Most obviously (a), 7.201 ff. has the logic "The gods have always appeared visibly to us and mixed socially with us, because we are close to them (ἐπεί...εἰμέν ('for ... we are'), 205): that would be incoherent, being 'close to them' must have some other sense. Then (b), if 'being close to them' is taken to imply good relationships with the gods - they show the Phaiecians special favour because the Phaiecians are μάλα φίλοι ('very dear') (6.203) - this will not at all square with 7.206, since the Cyclopes and the Giants are not at all good candidates for such a relationship (indeed the Cyclopes take no account of the gods at all:

οὐ γὰρ Κύκλωπες Διὸς αἰγιόχου ἀλέγουσιν
οὐδὲ θεῶν μακάρων, ἐπεὶ ἦ πολὺ φέρτεροί εἰμεν.

for the Cyclopes pay no heed to aegis-bearing Zeus or the blesses gods, since indeed we are much stronger.

9.275-76). Nor (c) does the jealousy of Poseidon against the Phaiecians, and Zeus' agreement that Poseidon should turn the Phaiecian ship to stone and overshadow the Phaiecian city with a great mountain (indeed Zeus himself actually suggests that plan to Poseidon), at all suggest the gods' general beneficence towards the Phaiecians (13. 125 ff.). Certainly the utopian picture of the Phaiecian state suggests that they have enjoyed the gods' especial favour (cf. especially 7.132, θεων ἐσαν ἀγλαά δωρα ('they were the glorious gifts of the gods')); but (a) and (b) above are decisive.

(2) if ἐγγύθεν in 7.205 and ἀγχίθεοι ('close to the gods') in 5.35 are taken geographically, we face two difficulties. First, though there is some sort of indication that the Giants and the Cyclopes have a vague geographical connection with the Phaiecians (7.59 for Giants, 6.5 for Cyclopes), there is no supporting evidence that these two peoples were themselves geographically close to the gods (whatever indeed that might mean in cartographical terms). Second, the gods in Homer are invariably pictured as living far away from any people or tribe - particularly, in fact, from those to whom they showed especial favour or close intercourse, such as the Aethiopians (who lived far away, and were in any case divided into east and west Aethiopians: see 1.22-24). There is certainly no coherent geographical picture here.

(3) The most natural sense for ἀγχίθεοι in 5.35 is a kinship sense, and that fits also with the Cyclopes (Poseidon was the Cyclopes' father, 9.529), and (for all we know, and not implausibly) with the Giants. Like (2), this sense also gives a plausible logic to what Alcinoos says in 7.205 ff. - perhaps a better sense than (2): roughly, "they are on good social terms with us because they are near kin to us", as against "...because they live near us". But the problem here is that the Phaiecians are not all that near in kin to the gods: Nausithoos was the son of Poseidon, and Alcinoos only his grandson. Even compared with better-known and (as it were) more ordinary mortals in Homer (Achilles, Helen), the relationship is not outstanding.

(2) and/or (3) are perhaps the best of a bad job here; but there is no really convincing and coherent picture that would allow us to translate the relevant passages unequivocally. A borderline case.

8. 109 ff.

βὰν δ' ἴμεν εἰς ἀγορήν, ἅμα δ' ἕσπετο πουλὺς ὅμιλος,
μυρίοι· ἂν δ' ἵσταντο νέοι πολλοί τε καὶ ἐσθλοί.

They went off to go to the assembly-place, and a great crowd of people followed them, in thousands; and up stood many fine young men.

I mention the incoherence of this passage chiefly because it reinforces what I have argued to be the incoherence in 6.262 ff., where the city of the Phaiecians, its harbours, entrance, and location of its ships are described. In the present passage they go off to the agora (109); immediately many young men stand up to take part in athletics (110-19), and by 122 they are raising a dust in the plain (πεδίοιο). There is no plausible sense of ἀγορήν ('market-place', 'place of assembly')) which will accommodate this and other athletic events; and anyway we know where the Phaiecians' ἀγόρα is supposed to be - it is

καλὸν Ποσιδήιον ἀμφὶς,
ῥυτοῖσιν λάεσσι κατωρυχέεσσ᾽ ἀραρυῖα.

around the fair temple of Poseidon, fitted with stones dragged there and dug in. (6.266-67)

and near the ships   ἔνθα δὲ νηῶν ὅπλα   (268).

there is the equipment for the ships.

It is fair to describe this as incoherent rather than just casual or careless, because in 6.262 ff. the poet is clearly trying to give a serious description of the topographical layout. A reasonable parallel is with the location of Ithaca (9.20 ff.), where he is also trying to do this, and also does it incoherently; not with, say, the location of Circe's or Calypso's island, where he palpably does not care much about the topography.

8. 124-25

ὅσσον τ᾽ ἐν νειῷ οὖρον πέλει ἡμιόνοιϊν,
τόσσον ὑπεκπροθέων λαοὺς ἵκεθ᾽, οἱ δ᾽ ἐλίποντο.

As far as is the range of mules in a furrow, so far he ran out in front from the others and came to the crowd, and the rest were left behind.

I am not sure if the poet meant anything and coherent by 124, or whether what he meant is just mysterious to us. Commentators certainly find it hard to cope. Thus Merry "the ἡμιόνων-οὖρα, or 'mules' range', represents the distance by which a team of mules beats a team of oxen in ploughing", relying on Iliad 10.351-53

ἀλλ᾽ ὅτε δή ῥ᾽ ἀπέην ὅσσον τ᾽ ἐπὶ οὖρα πέλονται
ἡμιόνων, αἱ γάρ τε βοῶν προφερέστεραί εἰσιν
ἑλκέμεναι νειοῖο βαθείης πηκτὸν ἄροτρον.

But when he was as far away as is the range of mules, which are more efficient than oxen at dragging the wrought plough in the deep furrow.

But that passage does not specify the ἡμιόνων οὖρα as the distance <u>by which</u> mules beat oxen, only as the distance mules actually plough. How long are they supposed to be ploughing for? Butcher and Lang (p.119) say "The distance here indicated seems to be that which the mule goes in ploughing, without pausing to take breath" - hardly convincing. Hainsworth tangles with the Homeric land system, and claims that οὖρα are the limits ... i.e. the side-limits ... of a standard area of plough-land: hence 'distance', 'range'", which is barely comprehensible. I suppose if there was a standard <u>length</u> of plough-land we might arrive at a distance by knowing how much <u>width</u> of it mules could plough. Hainsworth adds blithely "The distance would be 20-30m.", but says nothing about the crucial question of how long the mules are supposed to be ploughing for. Perhaps a day? But if we know neither how long they plough, nor the standard length, we can reach no figure at all.

It may be that the Homeric audience was entirely familiar with the answers to these questions: or it may be, more simply, that they had in mind a standard time - how far mules could plough in, say, an hour. But it seems probable that the poet has here taken over an idea - the 'mules' range' - which he himself did not understand. The idea is not so much incoherent internally as lacking in content; not so much self-contradictory as vacuous, as one might say "As far as an eagle flies over the mountains (and eagles are much faster than sparrows)".

8. 167 ff.

οὕτως οὐ πάντεσσι θεοὶ χαρίεντα διδοῦσιν
ἀνδράσιν, οὔτε φυὴν οὔτ᾽ ἂρ φρένας οὔτ᾽ ἀγορητύν.
ἄλλος μὲν γὰρ εἶδος ἀκιδνότερος πέλει ἀνήρ,

Thus the gods do not give gracious gifts to all men, neither form nor intelligence nor eloquence. For one man is defective in his appearance...

This is another example where commentators make incoherence out of coherence. They are obsessed with the idea that, as Hainsworth puts it, "The thought is illogically expressed, since the sense required is 'the gods do not give all their gifts to anyone', not 'the gods do not give their gifts to everyone'"; and some dare to translate 167 with 168 as if it made sense, thus Merry "...not to all men do the Gods grant [all] graces, neither form, nor wisdom, nor eloquence". Not only does that not translate 167 as it is, but it makes nonsense of 168, where particular gifts are mentioned individually, and the sense is that none of these gifts are given to everyone. It does not pretend to be a list of <u>all</u> gifts, but a list of particular gifts which not all men have.

The sense of what follows in 169-75 is not (though I think this is what has bewitched the commentators) "Thus one may have all other gifts but still lack X": it is rather that "Thus one may lack X (a good appearance) - but fortunately this may be compensated by Y (skill in speaking): another may have X, but lack Y, so that there is no particular gift which is universally bestowed".

8. 192-93

ὁ δ᾽ ὑπέρπτατο σήματα πάντων
ῥίμφα θέων ἀπὸ χειρός· ἔθηκε δὲ τέρματ᾽ Ἀθήνη

It flew over the marks of all of them, as it sped swiftly from his hand; and Athene set down the marking-points.

It is not clear that commentators have even faced the difficulty here. Thus Merry is content to say that τέρματα ('end-points', 'limits') 'merely repeats σήματα' ('signs', 'marks'); Hainsworth that the τέρματα 'denote the point that defined his throw, presumably the point where the discus first hit the ground, which the umpire was charged to observe, and that the σήματα... mark the τέρματα'. But the obvious trouble is with ἔθηκε ('established', 'set down'): Athene seems to be putting something down or at least establishing something (not just observing something): ἔθηκε τήρματα can hardly mean 'fixed the landing-points'. σήματα seems clear enough: it is some kind of peg or visible mark, so that Athene goes on to say (195) that even a blind man could distinguish Odysseus' mark (σημα) because it is so far from the rest. So what are we to do with τέρματα.? Alternative readings (βήματα) suggest that this problem may have presented itself quite early in the history of the text, but no alternative seems at all convincing. Perhaps τέρματα are a kind of second-stage σήματα: the umpire notes where the discuses land and puts down a σήμα for each, then after everyone has thrown the umpire puts down τέρματα. These might be 'the final marking-points' (e.g. for first, second and third place) or else 'the extreme marking-points', i.e. the points which marked the best throws.

But that is highly speculative. Unless there is (was) some specialised sense of τέρματα which we do not know of, and which will make sense of the passage, we have to confess its obscurity. There may be something wrong with the text: or it may just be carelessly composed. But it is incoherent as it stands.

8. 278-81

ἀμφὶ δ' ἄρ' ἑρμῖσιν χέε δέσματα κύκλῳ ἁπάντῃ·
πολλὰ δὲ καὶ καθύπερθε μελαθρόφιν ἐξεκέχυντο,
ἠΰτ' ἀράχνια λεπτά, τά γ' οὔ κέ τις οὐδὲ ἴδοιτο,
οὐδὲ θεῶν μακάρων· πέρι γὰρ δολόεντα τέτυκτο.

And around the posts he put a mass of bonds, on every side in a circle; and there were many other bonds also coming down in profusion from the beams on high, like slender spiders' webs, which nobody could see, not even one of the blessed gods - so cunningly were they fashioned.

I am not entirely sure whether this is a case of coherence (or incoherence), since it may reasonably be asked how much coherence one expects of a tale of this kind - a kind of fairy-tale, as one might say. However, though one expects fairy-tales to contain magical devices and not to be plausible in realistic or naturalistic terms, they do have and obey their own logic; and after some consideration I count this as a case of incoherence.

One difficulty is the translation of 278. Hainsworth says that "The mechanics of Hephaistos' trap would be more intelligible if his bed were a four-poster, with curtains and canopy; but such a bed is unknown to the monuments", and that "the ἑρμινες ('posts' or 'props') are therefore 'legs' rather than 'posts'". But that does not sit well with other uses of ἑρμινες and we cannot rely on archaeology to give us a complete picture of all beds as Homer imagined them (particularly on Olympos, where Hephaistos is the originator of many strange devices). Moreover we do not need a full-scale four-poster for the 'mechanics', only some posts which rise above the level where the couple slept. In Hainsworth's view we should have to picture Hephaistos' net as attached to the legs and hence lying on the floor, presumably rising up to encircle the couple when they made love; an unnecessary implausibility. Of course I admit the whole thing is implausible - particularly in respect of why the nets should come down at the right time. We are told only that ἀμφι δε δεσμοι ... ἐχυντο ('the bonds came all down round about them') (296-297):, are we to suppose that when they began to make love it triggered off the nets?

It is hardly worthwhile pursuing this further; but we must note the major difficulty, which lies in the fact that not even a god could see these nets (οὐ κέ τις ... μακάρων ('not even one of the blessed'), 280-81), yet in 327 the gods do appear to see them, εἰσορόωσι ('they see'). Hephaistos has not <u>told</u> them that there are nets, yet Apollo and Hermes at least are clear about it (δεσμοις , 336: δεσμοι ('bonds') 340). That seems to me more than just careless, even in a fairy-story; but some will judge me to be afflicted here with a kind of Teutonic literal-mindedness. A borderline case.

8. 315-18

οὐ μέν σφεας ἔτ' ἔολπα μίνυνθά γε κείεμεν οὕτω,
καὶ μάλα περ φιλέοντε· τάχ' οὐκ ἐθελήσετον ἄμφω
εὕδειν· ἀλλά σφωε δόλος καὶ δεσμὸς ἐρύξει,
εἰς ὅ κέ μοι μάλα πάντα πατὴρ ἀποδῷσιν ἔεδνα,

I do not think they will lie thus for a little time still, even though they are so much in love: soon both of them will not wish to sleep there; but my trick and the bond will restrain them, until her father pays me back the full bride-price, all of it.

Commentators make this incoherent, but it is not. Almost all take the logic to be: "I don't expect they will want to lie there even a little time" (315), followed by "Soon they will both not want to sleep there" (316-17), and "But my device will keep them there till..." (317-18). The objections to this are (1) κειέμεν ('to lie') has to be taken as 'desire to lie' (or 'will desire to lie', which is how commentators normally translate: cf. Merry, p.97, though the future is unnecessary): but this use or sense is unknown, for all that Hainsworth says "The desiderative force is here clear" (p.368); (2) the second element of the logic, "Soon (τάχ') they will both not want to sleep there", is pointless and a bathos after the first element.

The coherent alternative is 'I don't think they will lie there just for a little time (μίνωνθά γε)", "Certainly they will soon not want to lie there", "But my device will jolly well keep them there until I get my money back". This takes κειέμεν in its usual sense, and makes sense of the passage as a whole.

8. 370-79

Ἀλκίνοος δ' Ἄλιον καὶ Λαοδάμαντα κέλευσε
μουνὰξ ὀρχήσασθαι, ἐπεί σφισιν οὔ τις ἔριζεν.
οἱ δ' ἐπεὶ οὖν σφαῖραν καλὴν μετὰ χερσὶν ἕλοντο,
πορφυρέην, τήν σφιν Πόλυβος ποίησε δαΐφρων,
τὴν ἕτερος ῥίπτασκε ποτὶ νέφεα σκιόεντα
ἰδνωθεὶς ὀπίσω· ὁ δ' ἀπὸ χθονὸς ὑψόσ' ἀερθεὶς
ῥηϊδίως μεθέλεσκε, πάρος ποσὶν οὐδας ἱκέσθαι.
αὐτὰρ ἐπεὶ δὴ σφαίρῃ ἀν' ἰθὺν πειρήσαντο,
ὀρχείσθην δὴ ἔπειτα ποτὶ χθονὶ πουλυβοτείρῃ
ταρφέ' ἀμειβομένω· κοῦροι δ' ἐπελήκεον ἄλλοι

COMMENTS ON THE ODYSSEY

Alcinoos ordered Halios and Laodamas to dance alone, since noone rivalled them. So then when they had taken the fair ball in their hands, the purple ball which clever Polybos had made for them, one of them would throw it up to the shadowy clouds, bending backwards: and the other would jump up high from the ground and catch it easily, before touching the ground with his feet. Then when they had tried their skill with the ball in every way indeed, then indeed they danced on the fertile earth, moving their limbs rapidly. The other young men applauded.

Commentators have seized on the difficulty of ἀν' ἰθυν ('with might and main', 'to the fullest extent') (377): this is indeed a difficulty, but relates to the passage as a whole. Most have assumed that they go on playing with the ball in 378 ff., and hence translate ταρφέ' ἀμειβομηένω ('changing rapidly') along the lines of 'passing the ball frequently from hand to hand': they are then left with the idea that "The sense required is 'up aloft', in contrast with ποτι χθονι ('on the ground')" (Hainsworth).

But that is surely wrong. Alcinous tells them to dance (371). Then when (ἐπει, 372) they have played with the ball, when indeed (ἐπει δη, 377) they have had their shot with the ball, then indeed they danced (ὀρχείσθην, 378). They danced on the fertile ground (χθονι πουλυβοτείρη) as against jumping in the air as they did before (ἀπο χθονος ὑψόσ' ἀερθεις ('raised high from the ground'), 375), ταρφέ' ἀμειβομένω which must mean something like 'moving their limbs rapidly in succession'.

So in a general way the structure of the passage makes sense (which it certainly would not on the earlier interpretation). We are left with ἀν' ἰθυν, but this is now at least manageable. I suppose it means, in consonance with what ἰθυς ('strength') usually means as a noun, something like Merry's "with might and main, like ἀνα κράτος ('with all their strength')": or perhaps 'according to their strength': or perhaps, taking ἀνα with πειρήσαντο ('made trial'), 'when they had made trial of their strength/skill with the ball'.

Where there is a suspicion of incoherence (but not more) is in fact in 374-76. The scenario is clear: one man tosses the ball, having bent himself backwards (ἰδνωθεις ὀπίσω), more or less vertically upwards: the other jumps up and catches it before he comes to earth again. One problem is, why does the first bend himself backwards? If he is throwing a fairly light and small ball - a cricket ball or baseball, for instance - using only one hand, it is just intelligible: one way of doing this is to bend (slightly) back, looking up to the sky, and throw it overarm. But the more natural way is just to stay more or less still and throw it upwards underarm. If he is throwing a heavy and large ball, like a medicine ball, bending backwards makes the former method more or less impossible: the thrower would naturally take the ball in both hands and throw it straight up. The other problem, which is neutral as regards what kind of ball is used, is why it should be thought particularly difficult to catch a ball while one's feet are off the ground. (Cricketers do this frequently.) I do not know what Hainsworth means by "Nothing quite matches the audacity of the performance here described". The reader should try it for himself: it is quite easy. Of course the first performer may have thrown the ball extraordinarily high, and/or the second made an extraordinarily high leap off the ground in catching it. But we are not told that. Certainly the passage is not clear enough to explain the merits of the performance; but that hardly amounts to logical incoherence.

8. 492

ἀλλ' ἄγε δὴ μετάβηθι καὶ ἵππου κόσμον ἄεισον

But come now, make a change and sing of the arrangement of the horse.

Another (rather subtle) case where editors create an incoherence, by taking κόσμον in the sense of 'making' or 'fashioning'. The difficulty is that Demodocos does not sing about this at all; and we are surely to suppose, both from Odysseus' emotional reaction (521 ff.) and from what we know of Demodocos' merits as a bard, that what he did sing fully met the requirements.

In fact Demodocos takes up his tale at exactly the right point. Odysseus goes through the preliminaries: he says (1) that Epeios made the horse, (2) Odysseus, having filled it with soldiers, got it into the Trojan citadel by a trick. Then Demodocos starts his recital at the point where (ἐνθεν ἑλων ('taking it up from the point where'), 500) the other Greeks had gone away and the soldiers were sitting with Odysseus in the horse, inside Troy (500-04). All that is entirely in order. So κόσμον has to mean something else if coherence is to be preserved.

I suspect the meaning approaches that of κατα κόσμον three lines earlier (489), where Odysseus says that Demodocos has sung of the Achaeans' deeds and sufferings κατα κόσμον. That must mean that he recited them in due order, that he gave a true historical account of them, 'as if he had been there himself (491). The κόσμον must, I think, mean something like 'the arrangements about the wooden horse', or 'the history of the wooden horse'. And that is exactly what Demodocos does, from the start of his recitation to its end in 520.

9. 21-26

ναιετάω δ' Ἰθάκην εὐδείελον· ἐν δ' ὄρος αὐτῇ,
Νήριτον εἰνοσίφυλλον ἀριπρεπές· ἀμφὶ δὲ νῆσοι
πολλαὶ ναιετάουσι μάλα σχεδὸν ἀλλήλῃσι,
Δουλίχιόν τε Σάμη τε καὶ ὑλήεσσα Ζάκυνθος.
αὐτὴ δὲ χθαμαλὴ πανυπερτάτη εἰν ἁλὶ κεῖται
πρὸς ζόφον, αἱ δέ τ' ἄνευθε πρὸς ἠῶ τ' ἠέλιόν τε,

I live in clear-seen Ithaca. There is a mountain in it, Neriton with shaking leaves, very conspicuous. And around it many islands are located, very close to each other, Dulichium and Same and wooded Zacynthos. But Ithaca itself lies low in the sea, towards the gloom, and the others are apart and face the dawn and the sun.

A *locus classicus*, the difficulties of which require only a brief statement.
(1) There is a flat contradiction between ἀμφι ... ἀλλήλῃσι ('around...to each other') and the statement that the other

islands lie ἄνευθε ('apart') (26).
(2) 24 does not square with πολλαι in 23 (three islands are not πολλαι).
(3) The islands in 24 are not in fact μαλα σχεδον ἀλλήλῃσι (very close to each other').
(4) The description of Ithaca in 25-26 does not square either with the facts about Ithaca or (more significantly) with Homer's other descriptions of it (particularly with the ὄρος ἀριπρεπες ('a conspicuous mountain') of 21-22). αὐτη χθαμαλη ... κειται ('but it itself lies low') seems to be formulaic (cf. its use in 10.196), and makes little sense here,

9. 482-86

κὰδ δ' ἔβαλε προπάροιθε νεὸς κυανοπρῴροιο
τυτθόν, ἐδεύησεν δ' οἰήιον ἄκρον ἱκέσθαι.
ἐκλύσθη δὲ θάλασσα κατερχομένης ὑπὸ πέτρης·
τὴν δ' αἶψ' ἤπειρόνδε παλιρρόθιον φέρε κῦμα,
πλημυρὶς ἐκ πόντοιο, θέμωσε δὲ χέρσον ἱκέσθαι.

And it fell down a little way in front of the dark-prowed ship, and came so close as to wet the end of the steering-oar. The sea was in a turmoil as the rock fell into it; and at once the back-washing wave, a surge out of the sea, carried the ship to the land, and drove it to reach the shore...

9. 539-42

κὰδ δ' ἔβαλεν μετόπισθε νεὸς κυανοπρῴροιο
τυτθόν, ἐδεύησεν δ' οἰήιον ἄκρον ἱκέσθαι.
ἐκλύσθη δὲ θάλασσα κατερχομένης ὑπὸ πέτρης·
τὴν δὲ πρόσω φέρε κῦμα, θέμωσε δὲ χέρσον ἱκέσθαι.

And it fell a little behind the dark-prowed ship, and came so close as to wet the end of the steering-oar. The sea was in a turmoil as the rock fell into it: the wave carried the ship forwards, and drove it to reach the shore.

These two passages have to be taken together for obvious reasons. The question of incoherency is not so clear. For it is not just (as most editors claim) that 483 produces the incoherence of a stone which in 482 falls in front of the ship only just missing the rudder at the back of it, so that if we deleted 483 everything would be all right. There is more to be said.

The first point is that in 482 ff. the poet has a tolerably clear idea of the danger of the ship being driven back on to the Cyclop's territory, so that Odysseus has to shove it off with a pole (487-88: λαβων περιημκεα κοντον / ὦσε παρεξ ('taking a long pole, he pushed it off and away')). θέμωσε...ἱκέσθαι must mean something like 'drove it onto the dry land' or at least 'drove it so that it reached the dry land'. But that will hardly do for the same phrase in 542, which is immediately followed in 543 by την νησον ἀφικόμεθ' ('we came to the island'), since this latter implies some further travel by the ship. So it looks as if θέμωσε κτλ. is in place in 486, the earlier passage, but not in 542.

Secondly, the sea seems to be doing something different in 484-86 from what it does in 541-42. Both in 484 and 541 (identical lines) the sea ἐκλυσθη which must mean something like 'was thrown into turmoil;, or 'was made to produce a deluge of water'. But in 543 the wave simply carries it forwards (πρόσω), whereas in 485-86 it seems (in my judgement at least) that the opposite happens: there is a πλημυρις εκ πόντοιο, i.e. a surge coming <u>out of</u> (from the direction of) the sea, and a wave which is παλιρρόθιον, surging <u>back</u> - that is, a kind of backwash. The poet has the picture (not so absurd as it may seem) of the rock upsetting the sea in such a way that the sea, as it were, sucks the boat back in the direction of where the rock fell.

If this latter is correct, then 483 can stand: the rock falls just short of the back of the ship, missing the rudder, and the sea sucks the ship back to the land. But now, what about προπάροιθε in 482? I think this can be saved: it does not have to mean 'in front of' in the sense of 'in front of the ship's bow' (which would of course make nonsense of 483). It can mean something like 'just before the place where the ship was', 'just short of the ship'. So that passage may be in itself coherent: and all the MSS read προπάροιθε. In 539 some MSS read προπάροιθε, though most read μετόπισθε ('behind'). If προπάροιθε is right, in the sense suggested of 'just short of the ship', then we have to accept that in this case the effect was to drive the ship forwards (πρόσω), though in the earlier case the effect was the opposite. But of course we would also have to accept this if we read μετόπισθε. In both cases the rock falls just short of the ship (just behind it); but the effect is different. It is easy to see how a poet, editor or transcriber who did not accept these different effects would have insisted on μετόπισθε for 539, contrasted with προπάροιθε in 482: he would have thought, naturally enough, that any rock falling behind a ship would drive it forwards rather than suck it backwards (as is indeed normally the case in real life). So, with these readings, it would seem that only 483 is a problem: and indeed that line was rejected very early, before Aristarchus.

Nevertheless, I doubt that the incoherence lies there. I think the first passage, 482 ff., is in fact coherent - chiefly because, as I have said, 485-86 strongly suggest a backwash rather than a driving forward. Something has gone wrong with the latter passage. I suspect that some poet (editor, transcriber, etc.) wanted - not untypically in our texts - to reduplicate the rock-throwing scene, perhaps in a stronger form (πολυ μείζονα λααν ('a much greater rock'), 537-38), repeated the formulaic lines 540-41 from 483-84, and also the formulaic θέμωσε...ἱκέσθαι from 486. But he thought that the sea had to carry the ship forwards, and hence put in πρόσω and established the reading μετόπισθε: but still leaving the awkwardness of the transition from 542-43. If that is correct, then the incoherence lies in the latter passage, and emerges chiefly in that awkwardness: the ship did not reach the χέρσον ('shore'). On the other hand, if we overlook that awkwardness and take the latter passage as satisfactory, we have either (a) to get rid of 483, so that the rock falls in front of the ship and the sea drives it back to the Cyclops' land (which fails to do justice to the backwash idea in 485-86), or else (b) translate προπάροιθε as 'just short of, keep 483, and keep the backwash - but this then makes the latter passage, 539 ff., problematic. I prefer (b): but the passage certainly contains some incoherence.

9. 501

ἀλλά μιν ἄψορρον προσέφην κεκοτηότι θυμῷ·

ἄψορρον ('back') must mean "I spoke back to him", I answered him": but in fact the last person to speak (not counting Odysseus' companions in 494 ff.) was not the Cyclops but Odysseus himself (475 ff.). So the Cyclops has said nothing for Odysseus to answer. the Cyclops has indeed done something, i.e. throw his rock (481). Can Odysseus be said to 'answer' or 'speak back' to this? I think not: it seems more likely that the poet has simply forgotten the order of events. It would make sense if ἄψορρον could mean 'again' rather than 'in return', but that is unparalleled. ἄψορρον is incoherent.

10. 1-27

Αἰολίην δ' ἐς νῆσον ἀφικόμεθ'· ἔνθα δ' ἔναιεν
Αἴολος Ἱπποτάδης, φίλος ἀθανάτοισι θεοῖσι,
πλωτῇ ἐνὶ νήσῳ· πᾶσαν δέ τέ μιν πέρι τεῖχος
χάλκεον ἄρρηκτον, λισσὴ δ' ἀναδέδρομε πέτρη.
τοῦ καὶ δώδεκα παῖδες ἐνὶ μεγάροις γεγάασιν,
ἓξ μὲν θυγατέρες, ἓξ δ' υἱέες ἡβώοντες.
ἔνθ' ὅ γε θυγατέρας πόρεν υἱάσιν εἶναι ἀκοίτις.
οἱ δ' αἰεὶ παρὰ πατρὶ φίλῳ καὶ μητέρι κεδνῇ
δαίνυνται· παρὰ δέ σφιν ὀνείατα μυρία κεῖται,
κνισῆεν δέ τε δῶμα περιστεναχίζεται αὐλῇ
ἤματα· νύκτας δ' αὖτε παρ' αἰδοίῃς ἀλόχοισιν
εὕδουσ' ἔν τε τάπησι καὶ ἐν τρητοῖσι λέχεσσι.
καὶ μὲν τῶν ἱκόμεσθα πόλιν καὶ δώματα καλά.
μῆνα δὲ πάντα φίλει με καὶ ἐξερέεινεν ἕκαστα,
Ἴλιον Ἀργείων τε νέας καὶ νόστον Ἀχαιῶν·
καὶ μὲν ἐγὼ τῷ πάντα κατὰ μοῖραν κατέλεξα.
ἀλλ' ὅτε δὴ καὶ ἐγὼ ὁδὸν ᾔτεον ἠδ' ἐκέλευον
πεμπέμεν, οὐδέ τι κεῖνος ἀνήνατο, τεῦχε δὲ πομπήν.
δῶκε δέ μ' ἐκδείρας ἀσκὸν βοὸς ἐννεώροιο,
ἔνθα δὲ βυκτάων ἀνέμων κατέδησε κέλευθα·
κεῖνον γὰρ ταμίην ἀνέμων ποίησε Κρονίων,
ἠμὲν παυέμεναι ἠδ' ὀρνύμεν ὅν κ' ἐθέλῃσι.
νηὶ δ' ἐνὶ γλαφυρῇ κατέδει μέρμιθι φαεινῇ
ἀργυρέῃ, ἵνα μή τι παραπνεύσει ὀλίγον περ·
αὐτὰρ ἐμοὶ πνοιὴν Ζεφύρου προέηκεν ἀῆναι,
ὄφρα φέροι νῆάς τε καὶ αὐτούς· οὐδ' ἄρ' ἔμελλεν
ἐκτελέειν· αὐτῶν γὰρ ἀπωλόμεθ' ἀφραδίῃσιν.

We came to the island of Aiolia. There Aiolos son of Hippotas lived, dear to the immortal gods, on the floating island. All about it an unbreakable bronze wall was built, and the smooth rock ran up to it. Twelve children had been born to him in his house, six daughters and six youthful sons; and he gave the daughters to be wives to his sons. They were always feasting with their dear father and noble mother, and a myriad good things were there for them; and the courtyard resounded about the sweet-smelling palace by day - and then by night they slept with their revered wives on rugs and in their pierced beds. Those were the people whose city and fine houses we came to. He entertained me for a whole month, and asked me about everything: about Ilion and the ships of the Argives and the Achaeans' return; and I told him everything rightly. But when indeed I myself asked him for a passage, and bade him give me an escort, he did not at all refuse but arranged an escort for me. He flayed a nine-year-old ox and gave me its skin, within which he tied down the paths of the blustering winds: for the son of Kronos had made him guardian of the winds, to hold back or rouse up whichever he wanted. He bound them down in the hollow ship with a bright silver thong, so that the wind should not blow even a little; then for my benefit he send forth the breath of Zephyros to blow, so that it might carry the ships and the men themselves. But that was not to be: for we perished by our own folly.

This passage is certainly written with excessive brevity and/or awkwardness and/or carelessness. Whether it involves positive incoherence is more difficult. There is one notorious crux in 10, on which see below. It will be best simply to go through the passage in the way that a hearer/reader might hear/read it, and note the difficulties.

There is nothing incoherent about the description of the island itself. A bronze wall runs all round it (4), and a smooth (that is, a sheer) cliff ἀνεδέδρομε (4), which might mean 'runs up to the wall' or just 'runs up', (sc. from the sea to the level of the island, which is conceived as a plateau). The description of what goes on in Aeolos', palace (5-12) is also acceptable. 13 presents a problem. The και μεν ('and on the one hand') is odd, as is its repetition in 16, but only grammatically so. What is more odd is the δώματα καλά. ('fine houses'). The των ('of them') must refer to Aeolos and his twelve children; but they live in the palace, so what can be meant by 'their city and fine houses'? Then in what (plausible) sense of πομπη ('escort', 'arrangements for a journey') did Aeolos τευχε πομπήν ('arranged an escort')? There are problems about just what a πομπή is, on which see my note on Calypso's πομπή (Book 4, ad loc.). We have either to say that his giving Odysseus the bag of winds constituted part of a πομπή at least, or that πομπή implies that he also made other arrangements not here mentioned (for instance, giving Odysseus food and water).

10 is a notorious crux, but I think not (by my definition) an incoherence; the difficulties. are grammatical/syntactical rather than logical. If the text is sound, it is clear that the poet wants to convey (a) that the palace is filled with the smoke or savour of cooked food, or perhaps of burnt offerings (κνισηεν ('smelling')), (b) that there is some sort of noise that resounds about (περιστεναχιζεται) and (c) that the courtyard (αὐλη) comes into the picture somehow; all this being the result of the perpetual (αἰει ('always')) feasting mentioned in 8-9. If we take δωμα to be the subject ('the palace resounds round about') then the nominative αὐλη is impossible. We then have the choice between (a) reading (with some MSS) αὐλη and translating 'the steaming/smoking palace resounds about with noise, in the courtyard' (sc. as one of the places where the noise may be heard): or (b) taking αὐλη as the subject and translating 'the courtyard resounds about the steaming/smoking palace'. Of these (b) seems to me quite satisfactory. Those who like neither of these propose various emendations (see Heubeck), none very convincing; and anyway, if they were, there would be no further difficulty or incoherence.

Then we have to make sense of 23-27. Aeolos ties the winds down so tightly that none of them can escape and blow even a little (ὀλιγόν περ): so when he sends a west wind to help

Odysseus on his way, this does not come from the bag. So far, so good. But then οὐδ' ἄρ ἐμελλεν / ἐκτελέειν ('he was not about to accomplish it'). We cannot intelligibly translate "He sent the west wind to blow, to carry us and our ships, but as it turned out he wasn't about to accomplish this or "... this wasn't about to be accomplished", because the wind did blow and (apparently) they sailed with it for nine days (28); and it makes no difference whether we take the subject of ἐμελλεν ('he was not about', or 'it was not about') as Aeolos or impersonally, though the latter seems preferable. But perhaps we can save this either by understanding something like 'all the way back home' after φέροι ('carry'), or by stressing' the prefix of ἐκτελέειν ('to accomplish fully'), 'this wasn't going to do its job right to the end'.

All this is certainly obscure in many places: at best a borderline case.

10. 190-97

ὦ φίλοι, οὐ γὰρ ἴδμεν ὅπῃ ζόφος οὐδ' ὅπῃ ἠώς,
οὐδ' ὅπῃ ἠέλιος φαεσίμβροτος εἶσ' ὑπὸ γαῖαν
οὐδ' ὅπῃ ἀννεῖται· ἀλλὰ φραζώμεθα θᾶσσον
εἴ τις ἔτ' ἔσται μῆτις· ἐγὼ δ' οὐκ οἴομαι εἶναι.
εἶδον γὰρ σκοπιὴν ἐς παιπαλόεσσαν ἀνελθὼν
νῆσον, τὴν πέρι πόντος ἀπείριτος ἐστεφάνωται.
αὐτὴ δὲ χθαμαλὴ κεῖται· καπνὸν δ' ἐνὶ μέσσῃ
ἔδρακον ὀφθαλμοῖσι διὰ δρυμὰ πυκνὰ καὶ ὕλην."

"Friends, we do not know where the gloom or the dawn is, nor where the sun which brings light to mortals goes below ground or where it rises; so let us take thought quickly, if indeed there is any good counsel - though I think there is none. For I went up to a look-out point on the crags, and saw an island which the boundless sea encircles. The island itself lies low; and I saw with my eyes in the midst of it smoke coming through the thick bushes and the wood".

There are two probable incoherences in this passage: -

1. It is ridiculous to suppose that (190-92) they do not know where the sun rises and sets, particularly since they have been in the same place for two days and noticed the dawn (144). One might try to save this by interpreting "we do not know where..." in the sense of their not knowing anything about the geography of 'where the dawn/sunset is': that is, they know the direction of east and west, but know nothing about what terrain actually lies east and west. They know that the sun rises over there, but they do not know (for instance) that 'there' is, say, in the direction of Ithaca or the mainland or anything else. We might translate 'We do not know over what territory the sun rises and sets". But that is highly unconvincing: it is much more plausible to suppose that this passage fits a picture of their being somewhere at which even the fixed points of dawn and dusk are unknown or unclear - as if they were in the Arctic Circle or worse, somewhere where the sun did not rise and set at fixed points at all. And that does not fit Odysseus' actual position.

2. 194-95 ought to mean "I went up to a look-out point and saw that we were on an island" but that is not what it says - what it says is "I saw an island". Then it goes on to say (196) "The island itself lies low". This fits a picture in which someone goes up to a high point and sees an island: not the island he is standing on, but another island which lies low (compared with where he is standing). The poet has forgotten that Odysseus is on the island: "I saw an island - it lies low" is hence incoherent, rather as "I saw a man" is incoherent if the man is oneself. αὐτη...κειται ('it...lies') is formulaic (as in 9.25, where Odysseus is describing Ithaca as viewed from far off), and (perhaps significantly) does not occur after 148, when Odysseus describes what he did: he goes up to a look-out point, but does not say that he 'saw an island' or that 'it lies low'. Here, 195-96 have been brought in incoherently.

The logic of the passage as a whole is in any case obscure. In 190 Odysseus begins to describe their problems (the γαρ ('for') must presumably be taken in the sense of "things look bad for us, for..."): the problems are essentially that they are hopelessly lost, and Odysseus says he has no plan to meet this situation (193). Then he says that he saw smoke coming up from an island (194-97), and this is what alarms his crew (198 ff.), not their being lost. It looks as if 190-93 have just been added without regard for the context.

10. 282-83

ἕταροι δέ τοι οἵδ' ἐνὶ Κίρκης
ἔρχαται,

My companions here are held in Circe's house.

A small but distinct inconsistency: οἵδε ('these men here') is normally deiktic, and should mean 'these here'. But Odysseus has to go some way to Circe's palace (309); his companions are not visible or near, and οἵδε inappropriate.

10. 403 (=423)

νῆα μὲν ἄρ πάμπρωτον ἐρύσσατε ἤπειρόνδε,

First of all, drag up your ship to land.

This is incoherent as it stands, because it must mean 'drag your ship to land'; ἠπειρόνδε cannot mean 'up into the land'. Thus 4.780, νηα .... ἔρυσσαν ('they dragged...the ship') means 'first of all they dragged their ship to the deep sea'. In other words, one can only drag a ship when it is on land. It is tempting to read here ἐρέσσατε, 'row'. (The ship has been put into a λιμένα ('harbour'), 141, which is consistent with the idea of rowing it to land.)

11. 142-44

ἡ δ' ἀκέουσ' ἧσται σχεδὸν αἵματος, οὐδ' ἑὸν υἱὸν
ἔτλη ἐσάντα ἰδεῖν οὐδὲ προτιμυθήσασθαι.
εἰπέ, ἄναξ, πῶς κέν με ἀναγνοίη τὸν ἐόντα;"

And she sat in silence near to the blood, but did not dare to look at her son in the face, nor to address him. Tell me, lord, how can she recognise me for who I am?

The difficulty here is with 143, particularly ἐτλη ('dared'). The line naturally means "She has not dared (had the courage or the endurance) to look on her son face to face, nor to address words to him", with the implication that she could do so if only she had the nerve. But in fact the problem is that she cannot <u>recognise</u> him until she has drunk the blood, as 144 makes plain ("How can she recognise me for who I am?"), and as is clear from 153 ("She came up and drank the black blood: and immediately she recognised me") and elsewhere (with Agamemnon's ghost in 390: "Straightaway he recognised me, when he had drunk the black blood": this is standard practice for these ghosts, although it is not always mentioned in the case of every ghost).

The difficulty is made slightly worse by the fact that Teiresias in his reply does not actually answer Odysseus' question: he says nothing about what is required for ghosts to recognise anyone, only that whatever ghost Odysseus allows to come near the blood will tell him the truth (νημερτὲς ἐνίψει, 148). And that fits with Teiresias' own initial appearance (90-99), where there is no problem about recognition: on the contrary, Teiresias recognises Odysseus (ἔγνω, 91) <u>before</u> he has drunk the blood. He asks Odysseus to let him drink the blood so that he may tell truth to Odysseus (96): he drinks the blood, and then speaks of Odysseus' destiny (98 ff.).

So there is, in any case, some incoherence about the necessity of drinking the blood: is it for recognition and/or for truth-telling? Teiresias' case might be thought exceptional, and indeed is said to be so in 10.493-95 by Circe ("...his intelligence is still valid: to him alone Persephone has granted, even though he is dead, his wits and the power of thought - the others just flit around as shadows"). (Though we might fairly ask here, if his intelligence is in place, why does he need to drink the blood at all?) There seem at least to be two ideas about the need for blood-drinking, which are not properly coordinated.

If we insist on consistency, along the lines of 'All ghosts have to drink the blood (except Teiresias') to recognise anyone, and all ghosts (including Teiresias') have to drink the blood in order to tell truth", we shall have to overlook Teiresias' failure to reply to Odysseus' question: and we shall have to do something about ἐτλη in 143. The latter is not totally impossible: what the blood gives the ghosts is <u>strength</u>, which may be thought necessary for recognition, and we might translate ἐτλη as 'she has not had the strength', which is perhaps not too far from the basic idea in the verb. But I think it more plausible to assume that the poet's ideas on this topic were incoherent and not properly thought out.

11. 156-58

χαλεπὸν δὲ τάδε ζωοῖσιν ὁράσθαι.
μέσσῳ γὰρ μεγάλοι ποταμοὶ καὶ δεινὰ ῥέεθρα,
Ὠκεανὸς μὲν πρῶτα, τὸν οὔ πως ἔστι περῆσαι

It is hard for living men to see these things. For in the midst are great rivers and fearsome streans - first of all Ocean, which it is not at all possible to cross.

χαλεπὸν in 156 must mean simply 'difficult' in practical terms (not psychologically 'hard' or 'grim'), since the γαρ ('for') in 157 leads into the reasons why it is difficult - i.e. there are large rivers in the way. What rivers? Some commentators take these to be ordinary rivers, not those of the underworld: that would entail taking πρῶτα ('first') to mean 'and chief of these, Oceanos', rather than 'and first of all, Oceanos', since on this account Oceanos would be the last (rather than the first) river that had to be crossed. That is just possible, but very unlikely: why should rivers be singled out as especially difficult? Only one or two rivers in Greece, at least, like the Acheloos, present any difficulty at all.

It seems thus virtually certain that the rivers are those of the underworld: that μέσσῳ ('in the middle') i.e. in between the traveller to the underworld and the underworld itself, lie 'great rivers and terrible torrents'. These will be those mentioned by Circe to Odysseus in 10.513-14, the Acheron, Pyriphlegethon, Kokytos; and Styx. But now we face some sort of incoherence, or at least a lack of clarity. It is clear that Odysseus has in fact reached the underworld, or at least that part of it which his mother says is hard to visit because of the rivers which are μέσσῳ; yet Odysseus does not in fact <u>cross</u> these rivers - or if he does, the text does not say so.

What Odysseus is instructed by Circe to do (10.513-29) is to go to the junction of Pyriphlegethon and Kokytos, stick to that point (χριμφθεὶς πέλας ('sticking close'), 516), and then dig his trench. He is to turn the heads of his sacrificial victims towards Erebos, which must be the inner or deeper part of Hades: the ghosts come up from out of Erebos (ὑπὲξ Ἐρέβευς ('up from out of Erebus') 11.37): he himself is to turn away from Erebos, ἀπονόσφι τραπέσθαι (10.529), which must include the idea of turning towards the rivers. What in fact he does is just to go alongside the stream of Ocean (παρὰ ῥόον Ὠκεανοῖο, 11.21) until he comes to the place of which Circe had told him (ὃν φράσε, 22). The rivers do not figure at all.

No doubt we should not expect topographical coherency in Homer's underworld: and it may not be worthwhile to attempt a coherent map. But the text itself is not coherent in terms of its own story: it is as if the author of 11 had forgotten the instructions of Circe in 10.

11. 313-16

οἵ ῥα καὶ ἀθανάτοισιν ἀπειλήτην ἐν Ὀλύμπῳ
φυλόπιδα στήσειν πολυάϊκος πολέμοιο.
Ὄσσαν ἐπ' Οὐλύμπῳ μέμασαν θέμεν, αὐτὰρ ἐπ' Ὄσσῃ
Πήλιον εἰνοσίφυλλον, ἵν' οὐρανὸς ἀμβατὸς εἴη.

They had sworn to set up the strife of much-darting war against the immortals in Olympus. They desired to set Ossa up against Olympus, and then set Pelion with its shaking leaves on Ossa, so that the heaven might be approachable.

It is not an adequate defence of this passage to say that the Homeric conception of where the gods live is 'vague' (Heubeck). Actually I doubt whether this is even true: the gods clearly live, as many phrases like Ὀλυμπία δώματ' ἔχοντες ('occupying Olympian houses') show, on Olympus, at the top of the mountain; and that puts them in the heavens. In other words, if one had asked 'Homer' "Do the gods live on Olympus or in the heavens?", I think he would have answered "Both".

I do not deny that there could be further logical pressure on this picture (as is very common with religious pictures of a quasi-empirical kind); but any 'vagueness' it has will not justify this passage. It must mean "They even threatened that they would set up the battle-din of furious war on Olympus: they desired to set Ossa on Olympus, and trembling-leaved Pelion on Ossa, so that the heaven might be able to be climbed"; and that of course makes us ask whether the battle is to take place on Olympus or in the οὐρανος ('heaven'), and whether the gods are thought of as living in the former or the latter place.

There are possible ways out, none convincing. (1) We can translate "They even threatened, to the gods on Olympus, that they would...": i.e. Olympus was where the threat was made, not the scene of the battle. The battle is to be in the οὐρανος, to reach which they pile Ossa on Olympus and Pelion on Ossa. But that still leaves the question of where the gods live: not, if this interpretation is to do any work, on Olympus but in the οὐρανος (which is against the usual Homeric picture). (2) We may translate the first ἐπ' in 315 as 'up against', and the second ἐπ' as 'on top of', and translate "They desired to put Ossa up against Olympus, and then pile Pelion on Ossa, so that they could climb up to the heaven" (i.e. to the top of Olympus). But this reads more or less impossibly: both cases of ἐπ' must surely bear the same sense. (3) We may assume that the battle was to be on Olympus <u>while</u> they were trying (but what for?) to reach the οὐρανος: as they try to pile Ossa on Olympus (and Pelion on Ossa) they fight with the gods. But that is even more unconvincing. The passage is internally incoherent.

11. 330-32

ἀλλὰ καὶ ὥρη
εὕδειν, ἢ ἐπὶ νῆα θοὴν ἐλθόντ ἐς ἑταίρους
ἢ αὐτοῦ· πομπὴ δὲ θεοῖς ὑμῖν τε μελήσει."

But now it is the time to sleep, going either to your swift ship and to your comrades, or here: the escort shall be the concern of the gods and yourselves.

Commentators (e.g. Merry) take 331 as referring to the ship which the Phaiecian young men have made ready for Odysseus' voyage in 8.48 ff. The ἑταίρους ('comrades') will then be the young men themselves, Odysseus' 'companions' on the voyage. But this is quite unconvincing. (1) 332 suggests that Odysseus is dissociating his πομπη ('escort') from his night's sleep: (2) the young men have in fact returned from the ship to Alcinoos' palace (8.56): and (3) ὑμιν ('to you') does not read at all naturally with this sense. It seems much more likely that the poet has, as it were, simply forgotten that Odysseus no longer has a ship or ἑταίροι of his own, and hence produced this piece of incoherence.

11. 363-66

" ὦ 'Οδυσεῦ, τὸ μὲν οὔ τί σ' ἐΐσκομεν εἰσορόωντες
ἠπεροπῆά τ' ἔμεν καὶ ἐπίκλοπον, οἷά τε πολλοὺς
βόσκει γαῖα μέλαινα πολυσπερέας ἀνθρώπους
ψεύδεά τ' ἀρτύνοντας, ὅθεν κέ τις οὐδὲ ἴδοιτο·

O Odysseus, as we look at you we do not at all imagine you to be a deceiver or a cheat, of the kind that the black earth fosters in large numbers, spread all over it - men who fashion falsehoods, and no one can detect from whence they come.

The problem is with 366: ὅθεν ... ἴδοιτο ('see...from whence'). Editors make various suggestions, e.g. Heubeck 'such lies that no one is able to see through them'. But neither this nor any other suggestion (that I have seen) comes anywhere near translating the text as it stands: in particular they fail to do justice to ὅθεν ('from whence'). As it stands the text appears incoherent, indeed unintelligible. One might envisage some lacuna after ἀρτύνοντας ('fashioning') which would make sense of ὅθεν κτλ. It may be possible to save the incoherence by translating 'and nobody can detect where they come from'; 'they' here being the men whom the black earth produces all over the place, not the ψεύδεα ('falsehoods'). That seems to fit the general thrust of the passage. But it is at least compressed to the point of incoherence.

11. 572-75

Τὸν δὲ μέτ' Ὠρίωνα πελώριον εἰσενόησα
θῆρας ὁμοῦ εἰλεῦντα κατ' ἀσφοδελὸν λειμῶνα,
τοὺς αὐτὸς κατέπεφνεν ἐν οἰοπόλοισιν ὄρεσσι,
χερσὶν ἔχων ῥόπαλον παγχάλκεον, αἰὲν ἀαγές.

After him I saw the mighty Orion, driving wild beasts together in the asphodel meadow, the beasts which he himself had killed on the lonely mountains, having in his hands a club all made of bronze, for ever unbreakable.

Commentators appear to glory in 573-74: e.g. "...Orion in Hades hunts the very same prey that he once pursued on earth" (Heubeck), "...driving the wild beasts together over the mead of asphodel, the very beasts that he himself had slain on the lonely hills..." (Butcher and Lang). It is not clear whether they mean by this (1) that Orion hunts in Hades the identical beasts that he hunted on the lonely mountains when he was alive, or (2) that in Hades he hunts the same kind of beasts. But neither will really work.

(1) does more justice to the text: τους...κατέπεφνεν must surely mean 'which he himself had killed'. But then 573 is strange: why is Orion represented as ὁμου ειλευντα these beasts? The phrase must mean something like 'driving together', 'penning together', referring to the well-known idea of driving or beating game, so as to prevent the game dispersing and make it easier to kill. But Orion has (on this account) already killed the beasts; so, if there is any special point in saying that these are the identical beasts, we should expect something like 'he was collecting them together', or

'he was flaying them', or something referring to a process after the killing. (It is tempting to take εἰλευντα as 'collecting them, i.e. the dead bodies, together', but this is not what the word seems to mean in Homer.)

(2) gets over this difficulty: Orion in Hades is driving game, the same kind of game that he used to kill when alive. But this hardly translates κατέπεφνε ('killed'); αὐτός ('he himself') is out of place: and other uses of κατέπεφνε in Homer are not imperfect but aorist in sense (e.g. Od. 3.252, 4.534). An imperfect sense is necessary for this translation to work.

So there is an incoherence. It arises perhaps from the fact that the poet can hardly represent Orion as killing the beasts in Hades (anything in Hades is already dead), hence has to represent him as hunting them: yet he also wants to say that they are the same beasts as those he has already killed.

12. 50-51

δησάντων σ' ἐν νηὶ θοῇ χεῖράς τε πόδας τε
ὀρθὸν ἐν ἱστοπέδῃ, ἐκ δ' αὐτοῦ πείρατ' ἀνήφθω,

Let them bind you hand and foot in the swift ship, upright in the mast-socket; and from you yourself let ropes be fastened.

This is a very difficult passage: I am not sure whether it involves an incoherency or not. It is certainly incoherent or otherwise unintelligible in the way that most commentators take it.

Heubeck takes ἀνήφθω as 'You should remain bound'. That will obviously not do (apart from any strictly grammatical considerations), (1) because in 179 we have πείρατ' ἀνῆπτον which must mean 'they fastened cables' and thus calls into question any plausible construction for 51 ("You should remain bound in respect of cables" is not convincing, 'by a cable' still less so): and more decisively because (2) 51 reappears in 162, where Odysseus is giving instructions to his crew, so that 'you should remain bound' makes no sense at all. So ἀνήφθω must have the sense of 'let there be fastened'; not 'let them fasten', which will also make no sense as addressed to the crew in 162.

Most commentators translate ἐκ δ' αὐτου as 'from the mast itself', e.g. Butcher and Lang "and from the mast let rope-ends be tied". (Not, with Heubeck 'on to it, i.e. the ἱστός' ('mast'): ἐκ ('from') will not bear that meaning. Heubeck has a picture of Odysseus tied to the mast: a picture, incidentally, not consistent with taking ἱστοπέδη as 'hole for fixing the mast' since Odysseus is to be in the hole, ἐν ἱστοπεδῃ, and there will hardly be room for him and the mast as well.) But (1) αὐτου taken as referring to the ἱστο-element in ἱστοπεδη is odd (the poet could easily have written ἱστοδοκῃ ('mast-holder')): and (2) if the idea is that Odyssey is to be tied to the mast, it is unnatural to talk of fastening cables from it.

From the description in 170 ff. the mast seems to remain in place: all the crew do is to furl the sails (170), put them in the ship and start rowing (171-72). That, of course, is not decisive; but it is in any case not plausible to take ἱστοπεδη as any kind of hole, and ἐν as 'inside it': for one thing, it is not likely that the hole for fitting a mast would be big enough to fit Odysseus. So we must take ἱστοπεδη to be something more substantial than a hole: something which, though no doubt containing a hole or hollow to receive the mast-foot (as with μεσόδμης ('mast-box'), 2.424), can be stood on. So we translate "Let them bind you... upright on the mast-block".

χεῖράς τε πόδας τε ('hands and feet') still leaves an incoherency; but that may be removed if we contrast it with αὐτου ('the man himself'): they are to bind Odysseus' hands and feet, and from Odysseus himself fasten ropes to hold him in place. That seems to me a more natural reading than any other, and makes syntactical sense of the phrase. We translate "Let them bind you in the swift ship, upright on the mast-block, hands and feet - and from you yourself let cables be fastened". That is still somewhat odd, because it is not clear where the cables are to be fastened to; but perhaps it saves the passage from total obscurity or incoherence.

12. 55-126

It is not necessary to give the text here in full: I shall quote only those passages which seem most relevant to the possibility of logical incoherence. There are of course many other problems with it (for which see Heubeck), mostly concerned with the poet's treatment of legendary topography. Our question is whether, or how, the text would make sense to the hearer/reader.

Circe says (55-51)

Αὐτὰρ ἐπὴν δὴ τάς γε παρὲξ ἐλάσωσιν ἑταῖροι,
ἔνθα τοι οὐκέτ' ἔπειτα διηνεκέως ἀγορεύσω
ὁπποτέρη δή τοι ὁδὸς ἔσσεται, ἀλλὰ καὶ αὐτὸς
θυμῷ βουλεύειν· ἐρέω δέ τοι ἀμφοτέρωθεν.
ἔνθεν μὲν γὰρ πέτραι ἐπηρεφέες, προτὶ δ' αὐτὰς

Then at that point, when your comrades have rowed past and outside these, I will no longer tell you unequivocally which of two ways will be yours - rather do yourself take counsel in your heart: but I will tell you of both. For, from thence, there are high-arching cliffs and to them...

ἔνθα in 56 seems to mean 'at that point', i.e. after Odysseus has passed the Sirens; and διηνεκέως something like 'directly' or 'unequivocally' (as in 4.836). Circe says that there are two routes, and he will have to decide between them himself: she will tell him of both.

The, main difficulty is that the distinction between the two routes is not clear in the text. Even more obviously, there is no point in the text in which Odysseus reflects (θυμῷ βουλεύειν ('plan in your heart')) about which route to take or is even given any chance to reflect: as soon as they leave the Sirens, they are immediately faced with the difficulties of Scylla and Charybdis (*et seq.*, 201 ff.).

'Αλλ' ὅτε δὴ τὴν νῆσον ἐλείπομεν, αὐτίκ' ἔπειτα
καπνὸν καὶ μέγα κῦμα ἴδον καὶ δοῦπον ἄκουσα·

(But when indeed we left the island, straightaway I saw smoke and a great wave, and heard a tumultuous noise.)

It is normally assumed that the two routes are (1) through the Planctai (59-72), and (2) through Scylla and Charybdis (73 ff.). We might then take ἐνθεν in 59 as meaning "For [following the assertion that there are two routes] on the one side, on the one hand (μεν)..." and then the description of the Planctai. But then this phrase is not properly answered (as it is answered in 235: ἐνθεν...Σκύλλη, ἐτερωθι δέ ... Χάρυβδις ('on this side...Skylla, and on the other side..Charybdis'): we have simply "the two rocks", οἱ δε δύω σκόπελοι (73), not even any phrase to mean "there are two rocks"; as if the rocks had already been mentioned. Moreover, it is clear that this is the route Odysseus is going to take: Circe says that he will see (ὄψει, 101) the lower rock, advises him to go past Scylla rather than Charybdis (108-10), and tells him to beseech Scylla's mother Krataiis (124-25). All this, plus the fact (noted above) that the text leaves no room (on this account) for Odysseus to choose one route rather than another, would certainly amount to considerable incoherence.

There is however an alternative. On this account ἐνθεν μεν γαρ might be taken as meaning something like "For from this point on there are [inescapable] high rocky, cliffs, and a great sea-surge (κυμα μέγα, 60). The μεν ('on the one hand') may be answered by the δε ('on the other hand') in οἱ δε δύω σκόπελοι as introducing a choice of routes: "there are these rocks, but there are two of them". Then there is another μεν and δε: ὁ μέν οὐρανον εὐρυν ἰκάνει ('the one reaches up to the broad sky') (73), contrasted with τεν δ'ἐτερον ...χθαμαλώτερον ('the other ... lower') (101). Then Odysseus' only choice is between Scylla and Charybdis; and this choice is made by Odysseus when he gives steering-instructions in 217 ff. (towards Scylla, though he does not tell the crew (223)). The choice is influenced by Circe's advice to prefer Scylla to Charybdis (108 ff.); but that might perhaps be thought to be consistent with διηνεκέως in 56 - she will not tell him which route to take unequivocally, but points out the advantages of Scylla as the lesser of two evils.

One obvious advantage of this interpretation is that it makes sense of what Odysseus experiences immediately after leaving the Sirens: καπνον ... μέγα κυμα ... δουπον ('smoke...a great wave...a tumultuous noise') 202. None of this is associated, in Circe's instructions, with Scylla or Charybdis, particularly the καπνον. On the other hand, as Heubeck (right here for once, p.130) sees, it does fit with her earlier depiction of the Planctai, especially with 60 (κυμα μέγα ῥοχθει ('a great wave surges')) and, for the κάπνος, the πυρός ὀλοοιο θύελλαι ('storms of deadly fire') of 68. The account has perhaps a further advantage in that it allows us to take τη μέν ('on the one side') in 62 and τη δ' ('on the other side') in 66 as referring to the two rocks, the πέτραι ('rocks') of 59, and κείνη ('that one') in 69 as referring to the latter: rather than as all referring to the same route (thus Butcher and Lang, p.194, 'By this way', 'Thereby', and 'That way': so too Heubeck). The first rock is sheer, a λις πέτρη ('a sheer cliff') (64). This rock is described again in 73 ff., in similar terms (πέτρη λίς, 79). But the main advantage of this interpretation is that it makes more sense of the choice between two routes.

To recapitulate this alternative account in translation: Circe says "At that point, I will no longer tell you unequivocally which of two routes to take - you must take counsel within yourself about that - but I will tell you about both. For your course from here (ἐνθεν) will involve high-arching rocks ... which the gods call Planctai. Past one of them, not even birds go.... Past the other, no ship has ever gone except the Argo... (56-72). Now of these two rocks, one of them rises up to heaven...it is a sheer rock...Scylla lives in it... (73-100). The other rock you will see to be lower ... there is a fig-tree under which Charybdis sucks in the water ... sail close to Scylla's rock, since that will be better.... (101-110)".

I take this account to represent the intended logic, as it were, of the poet in this passage, and thus save it from some incoherence: that is, I do not think the poet intended to offer the Planctai route as an alternative to the Scylla-Charybdis route. But the passage is still extremely awkward, and the choice of routes still not really clear. What has happened, I think, is that the poet wanted to get in the Planctai passage somehow and somewhere; and this insertion has confused the general logic. The text would read much more easily if 61-72 were excluded: we should move straight from the πέτραι of 59 to the σκόπελοι ('rocks') of 73, with a (comparatively) clear choice of alternative routes: though even then not as clear as the introductory 56-58 suggests.

Further obscurity arises from the fact that the Planctai passage is, so to speak, half-hearted: either the poet does not have an adequate knowledge of the details, or he does not make them clear. Hence certain passages and phrases seem random, or disconnected, or gratuitous. We are given no idea of how the sheer cliffs are supposed to 'take away' (ἀφαιρεῖται 64) the birds, or about the 'storms of deadly fire' (πυρός ὀλοοιο, 68) which destroy ships. Of course we can suggest how such sea-legends might have originated (by the volcanic action of Stromboli, for instance); but that is, as it were, to do the poet's work for him - it does not help to show that he had a coherent grasp of any legend (however unrealistic). Real sense returns only 69-72: he knows that the Argo came safe through the danger with Hera's help, but that is really all he is clear about.

We cannot, however, stigmatise parts of the Planctai passage as (in our sense) incoherent: they are too disconnected and mysterious to be either coherent or incoherent. The main incoherence of the whole account, 55-126, is as described earlier in this note; and it cannot be totally remedied on any interpretation.

12. 201-02, 219-20

Ἀλλ' ὅτε δὴ τὴν νῆσον ἐλείπομεν, αὐτίκ' ἔπειτα
καπνὸν καὶ μέγα κῦμα ἴδον καὶ δοῦπον ἄκουσα·

τούτου μὲν καπνοῦ καὶ κύματος ἐκτὸς ἔεργε
νῆα, σὺ δὲ σκοπέλου ἐπιμαίεο,

But when we left the island, straightaway I saw smoke and a great wave and heard a tumultuous noise...keep the ship away from that smoke and the wave, and do you make for the rock...

Whatever we may think of the problems in the previous note, there is certainly some carelessness here. In 201-02 Odysseus sees smoke and a great surge: nothing at all is said about any of the rocks in Circe's instructions (the Planctai in 59 ff. and/or the two rocks, the δύω σκοπελοι, in 73 ff.). Nor has Odysseus even mentioned them in talking to his crew. Yet in 219-20 the helmsman is told to 'make for the rocks' (σκοπέλω ἐπιμαίεο, 220). It makes no difference here whether we read σκοπέλω ('two rocks') or σκοπέλου ('rock'). It is just assumed, so to speak, that the rock or rocks have appeared: in 233 Odysseus is peering at one of them (Scylla's), and in 234-35 they enter the strait with Scylla on one side and Charybdis on the other. Failure to mention the rocks at all, before Odysseus tells the helmsman to steer for them, comes at least near incoherency in the narration. (It is not really possible to save it by translating σκοπέλου ἐπιμαίεο in 220 either as "steer for that rock", as if pointing it out for the first time, or as "steer for a rock [*sc.* which will appear shortly]".)

12. 251-55

ὡς δ' ὅτ' ἐπὶ προβόλῳ ἁλιεὺς περιμήκεϊ ῥάβδῳ
ἰχθύσι τοῖς ὀλίγοισι δόλον κατὰ εἴδατα βάλλων
ἐς πόντον προΐησι βοὸς κέρας ἀγραύλοιο,
ἀσπαίροντα δ' ἔπειτα λαβὼν ἔρριψε θύραζε,
ὣς οἵ γ' ἀσπαίροντες ἀείροντο προτὶ πέτρας·

As when on a promontory a fisherman with his long rod puts down bait to trick the little fishes, and sends into the sea the horn of an ox of the field, and then captures them as they gasp and throws them out of their home: even so they, gasping, were raised up to the rocks.

As with other passages (e.g. the 'mules' range' of 8.124), we have here to distinguish unintelligibility from logical incoherence. Thus a phrase or passage unintelligible to us might be perfectly intelligible to the poet's hearers who were familiar with certain practices: they might know at once, for instance, what the βοος κερας ('horn of an ox') in 253 was. But it is another question whether the text describes the practice in a logically coherent way. I do not, therefore, wish to become directly involved with questions about the technical details of Homeric fishing, but simply to see whether the text generates <u>some</u> coherent picture of what is going on.

Heubeck and other commentators take ῥάβδῳ ('staff', 'rod') with κατα...βάλλων ('putting down'). He says that "the fisherman is angling ... with his long rod ... and throws in morsels of food ... as bait". That is already confused: it looks as if Heubeck is thinking of the practice (common in modern angling) of first throwing in εἴδατα ('morsels', 'dainties', 'bait') to attract the fish generally, before using the rod at all. 252 may indeed mean that; and the plural argues for it, since if the bait were <u>on</u> the rod we might expect not more than one piece of bait. But if κατα...βάλλων goes with ῥάβδῳ, we must understand 'throwing (casting) in the bait on (with) his rod'.

That is at least a coherent possibility; but then we are in trouble with 254. The trouble is that, whatever the βοος κερας may be doing, the syntax suggests that this is a separate operation: the fisherman first casts his rod with the bait on it, and then προίησι ('sends forward') the κέρας. It is, at least, very awkward to translate with the sense of "The fisherman, casting his long rod with the bait, thereby (therein) projects into the sea the horn of a rustic ox". I emphasise that this is a point about how the text reads, not about the function of the βοος κέρας. (We would most naturally take it as some kind of float, for which an ox-horn would be very suitable. It would be too large to function as a hook; and Heubeck's idea that he 'uses a tube of horn set above the hook to protect the line from being bitten' seems absurd.)

So it is better to take κατα...βάλλων with εἴδατα. The fisherman casts his ox-horn into the sea, putting down bait for the little fish. On this interpretation the εἴδατα must of course be bait on the rod, not 'ground bait' thrown out before using the rod. That will make the passage coherent, whatever the βοὸς κέρας may be doing.

12. 315

γαῖαν ὁμοῦ καὶ πόντον· ὀρώρει δ' οὐρανόθεν νύξ.

...earth and sea alike: and night rushed down from the sky.

An incoherence in the narrative: it is already night (only three lines earlier, τρίχα νυκτὸς ἔην ('a third part of the night'), 312). It is no good saying, with Heubeck that ὀρώρει...νύξ (the night rushed down') "is less effective here, since it is still night. The meaning is probably that clouds cover the stars, so that there is total darkness". The plain fact is that the poet uses the formulaic lines, already used in 9.68-69, and has (as it were) forgotten that it is already night. This is a very obvious example of the kind of way in which formulaic composition may produce incoherence, as in 10.194 ff. (see note): any careful composer, reviser, or editor - certainly with the aid of a written text of any kind - would have noticed such cases.

13. 149-69

νῦν αὖ Φαιήκων ἐθέλω περικαλλέα νῆα
ἐκ πομπῆς ἀνιοῦσαν ἐν ἠεροειδέϊ πόντῳ
ῥαῖσαι, ἵν' ἤδη σχῶνται, ἀπολλήξωσι δὲ πομπῆς
ἀνθρώπων, μέγα δέ σφιν ὄρος πόλει ἀμφικαλύψαι."
  Τὸν δ' ἀπαμειβόμενος προσέφη νεφεληγερέτα Ζεύς·
" ὦ πέπον, ὡς μὲν ἐμῷ θυμῷ δοκεῖ εἶναι ἄριστα,
ὁππότε κεν δὴ πάντες ἐλαυνομένην προΐδωνται
λαοὶ ἀπὸ πτόλιος, θεῖναι λίθον ἐγγύθι γαίης
νηῒ θοῇ ἴκελον, ἵνα θαυμάζωσιν ἅπαντες
ἄνθρωποι, μέγα δέ σφιν ὄρος πόλει ἀμφικαλύψαι."
  Αὐτὰρ ἐπεὶ τό γ' ἄκουσε Ποσειδάων ἐνοσίχθων,
βῆ ῥ' ἴμεν ἐς Σχερίην, ὅθι Φαίηκες γεγάασιν.
ἔνθ' ἔμεν'· ἡ δὲ μάλα σχεδὸν ἤλυθε ποντοπόρος νηῦς
ῥίμφα διωκομένη· τῆς δὲ σχεδὸν ἦλθ' ἐνοσίχθων,
ὅς μιν λᾶαν θῆκε καὶ ἐρρίζωσεν ἔνερθε
χειρὶ καταπρηνεῖ ἐλάσας· ὁ δὲ νόσφι βεβήκει.
  Οἱ δὲ πρὸς ἀλλήλους ἔπεα πτερόεντ' ἀγόρευον
Φαίηκες δολιχήρετμοι, ναυσίκλυτοι ἄνδρες.
ὧδε δέ τις εἴπεσκεν ἰδὼν ἐς πλησίον ἄλλον·
" ὦ μοι, τίς δὴ νῆα θοὴν ἐπέδησ' ἐνὶ πόντῳ
οἴκαδ' ἐλαυνομένην; καὶ δὴ προὐφαίνετο πᾶσα."

"But now my desire is to shatter the beautiful ship of the Phaiecians as it comes back from its escort on the misty sea, so that they may now be checked and cease from giving escort to men: and also to cover up their city with a great mountain." Then in answer to him spoke cloud-gathering Zeus: "My dear friend, this is how it seems best to me in my heart: when indeed all the people are looking at the ship from the city as it is rowed on, turn it with a blow into stone near the land - a stone like a swift ship, so that all men may be amazed: and also cover the city with a great mountain". Then when earthshaking Poseidon heard that, he went off to Scheria, where the Phaiecians are. There he stayed; and the seafaring ship came very close, as it went swiftly on its way. The earthshaker came near to it, and struck it into stone and rooted it underneath, striking it with a downward blow of his hand; and then he went far away. And the Phaiecians of the long oars spoke winged words to each other, those sea-famed men: and thus would one look at his neighbour and say: "Alas, who then has bound this swift ship in the sea as it is being rowed home? Just now indeed it was entirely visible".

There seems to be some widespread incoherency here, but it is not clear. What Poseidon wants to do is simply to smash up the ship (ῥαῖσαι ('shatter', 'smite'), 151), and μέγα...ἀμφικαλύψαι ('a great ... to cover') (152), whatever that may mean. Zeus tells him to θεῖναι λίθον...ἴκελον ('establish a stone...like') (156-57), and that presumably is what he does (λᾶαν θῆκε ('he established a stone'), 163), though he does not μέγα....ἀμφικαλύψαι.

Zeus' words naturally read as meaning "Make (set up, establish) a stone like (in the shape of) a swift ship". But that will obviously not do, because Poseidon <u>turns</u> the ship <u>into</u> stone (163), which is a different thing. Hence editors have taken it to mean "Make a stone out of her" or "turn her to stone". But then ἴκελον ('like') is odd: if Poseidon is to turn the ship into stone, as in fact he does, then of course the result will look like a swift ship. There is something odd, too, about the way in which Poseidon does this, χειρὶ ... ἐλάσας ('with his hand...pressing down' or 'striking') (164), which must mean something like 'with a downward stroke of the hand', as if he were somehow submerging the ship or at least pressing it downwards - not a natural movement for turning something into stone. So there is some incoherence here.

"To put a great mountain as a cover round the city" (152, 158, 177 and earlier in 8.569) is of course obscure, but not in the context incoherent. In 178 Alcinoos says τὰ δὲ δὴ νῦν πάντα τελεῖται, which means "and all this is now in process of being accomplished". Only part of the prophecy has <u>been</u> accomplished, i.e. the turning of the ship to stone; and Alcinoos recommends sacrificing to Poseidon so that he may not accomplish the rest (181-83). So we do not expect Poseidon to do this, as in fact he does not, and Aristophanes' reading of μή in 158 instead of δή (to account for Poseidon's failure) is unnecessary. Of course we may wonder why this part of the prophecy, and the discussion of its possible fulfilment, is mentioned at all (since it never happens); but that is not an incoherency.

Nevertheless the incoherency of the poet's description of the actual process of turning the ship to stone remains; and it is increased rather than diminished by 168-69, where the Phaiecian onlookers say "Who has fettered (bound, chained up, ἐπέδησ') the swift ship? καὶ δὴ προεφαίνετο πᾶσα". This last phrase naturally means 'And just now it was entirely visible". But presumably if it has been turned to stone it (or the stone version of it) is still entirely visible. They talk as if the ship had wholly disappeared. It is tempting to take the phrase in a different sense, along the lines of "And indeed it has become entirely apparent", sc. as having been fettered or chained. But that hardly squares with the tense of προυφαίνετο. We do better to accept that this compounds the incoherence. Perhaps we are to imagine Poseidon pressing down with his hand on the ship, submerging it, temporarily leaving a vacuum which the Phaiecians marvel at, and then letting it reemerge as a stone. But that, besides being a rather elaborate scenario, does not square with Alcinoos' repetition of the prophecy: he says simply that the ship will be smitten (ῥαισέμεναι, 177) - there is nothing in his words, any more than in those of the Phaiecian onlookers, which implies that any stone now replaces the ship. In fact, apart from Zeus words νηῒ...ἴκελον, which must surely imply some visible ship-shaped stone (and of course fit with the later legend in Corcyra about the origin of the rock), there is no really clear idea of producing a ship-shaped stone at all: when in 163-64 Poseidon "makes it into a stone, rooting it underneath by pressing it downwards with his hand" he may just be sinking it without trace. Perhaps Poseidon did this, not following Zeus' instructions exactly. But it is hardly worthwhile trying to save the incoherence by such elaboration.

13. 187-93

ὁ δ' ἔγρετο δῖος Ὀδυσσεὺς
εὕδων ἐν γαίῃ πατρωΐῃ, οὐδέ μιν ἔγνω,
ἤδη δὴν ἀπεών· περὶ γὰρ θεὸς ἠέρα χεῦε
Παλλὰς Ἀθηναίη, κούρη Διός, ὄφρα μιν αὐτὸν
ἄγνωστον τεύξειεν ἕκαστά τε μυθήσαιτο,
μή μιν πρὶν ἄλοχος γνοίη ἀστοί τε φίλοι τε,
πρὶν πᾶσαν μνηστῆρας ὑπερβασίην ἀποτῖσαι.

And the godlike Odysseus woke up from his sleep in his native land, and did not recognise it - he had long been absent. For the goddess Pallas Athene, daughter of Zeus, poured mist around, so as to make it all unrecognisable in itself, and so that she could tell him everything: lest his wife and the townsmen and his friends might know who he was before he had taken full vengeance on the outrages of the suitors.

Most editors see incoherence or unintelligibility here, but there is neither.

There is first the problem of ἤδη...ἀπεών ('already...being absent') (189). Hoekstra rightly says that "it will not do to take the expression as an addition to εὕδων" (as if, to follow what Merry says, 'to make the situation more touching'); but wrong to say that its force cannot be causal 'since it is not apparent why his long absence should have prevented Odysseus from recognizing his own land'. So long an absence may easily have been thought, at least, to be a good reason. The natural sense, immediately after ἤδη δὴν ('for a long time already'), is indeed causal - "he did not recognise it, since he had been so long absent". That sense is not vitiated by the ensuing γάρ, we have to remember that γάρ ('for') is often elliptic. We should perhaps understand here something like "and there was another reason, that...".

More difficult is the problem about the mist which Athene pours (189). The key question is, round what/whom does she pour it? The options are:

(a) She pours it round about the environment, round about the topographical features of Ithaca. This is the first option one naturally takes up, because of the γαρ in 189: Odysseus did not recognise his native land, because Athene poured mist round it. But then of course it makes no sense to say that she poured mist round the land to make Odysseus (μιν αὐτον, 'the man himself', 190) unrecognisable (ἀγνωστον, 191). So then we shall read αὐτη (for which there is some authority) for αὐτῳ ('she'), and translate 'so that she might make it unrecognisable to him'. We now have the worry of how Athene's making the land or environment unrecognisable will prevent Odysseus' wife and friends from recognising him (192-93). But that is comparatively easy, and Hoekstra is wrong to say that 192 'makes no sense': it is precisely because he does not recognise the country that he addresses Athene (227 ff.) and hence gives her the opportunity to 'explain everything' (ἕκαστα μυθήσαιτο, 191), which of course includes the need to avoid being recognised (402-03). So that seems to be a coherent option; and it fits well with 194 ff.

τοὔνεκ' ἄρ' ἀλλοειδέα φαινέσκετο πάντα ανακτι,
ἀτραπιτοί τε διηνεκέες λιμένες τε πάνορμοι
πέτραι τ' ἠλίβατοι καὶ δένδρεα τηλεθάοντα.

Therefore everything appeared strange-seeming to the lord, the straight paths and the all-sheltering harbours, and the steep rocks and the flourishing trees.

Athene has poured mist over the land, and therefore the land looks different in respect of its various features. It also fits 352: Athene σκέδασ' αέρα, εἴσατο δε χθών: "she scattered the mist, and the land appeared". There is a problem about 194 and 352: if we translate in 352 'appeared' or 'became visible', it will not fit 194 where (whatever may plausibly be made of the MSS) there must be something about the land appearing, and about it appearing differently (ἀλλοειδέα). So we cannot say simply for 194 "The land appeared differently to him" if we say for 352 "The land now [for the first time] appeared/became visible to him", *sc.* having been shrouded in mist, hitherto. (Perhaps by εἴσατο in 352 we should understand 'appeared clearly' or 'appeared as it really was': but I think the poet has no clear or coherent picture at all: see below. In any case this particular problem does not affect the choice of options we are now discussing.)

(b) She pours the mist round about Odysseus. That of course fits much better with the normal purposes of mist-pouring, which Hoekstra rightly says "the gods use ... to conceal either themselves or mortals"; as for instance in 7.14 ff. But by the same token it does not fit Odysseus' inability to perceive the environment clearly (he perceives it quite clearly in 7.14 ff.). Of course it is possible to imagine that the mist round Odysseus would make his identification of the environment harder, obscure it, or make it ἀγνωστον ('unknown') - that it would be hard for him to see through his own mist, as it were. But there is no evidence for this in other cases of mist-wrapped gods or mortals in Homer. So, although this option does easy justice to 192-93 - he is wrapped in mist to make him unrecognisable, so that his wife and others will not recognise him - it runs up heavily against the αὐτον in 189: "He couldn't recognise his own land, because Athene shrouded him in a mist", as we have just argued, is not plausible. For the same reason it does not fit well with 194 ff. or 352.

Of these (a), though not popular with commentators, seems to me clearly preferable, and the only interpretation that preserves coherency and intelligibility. It might seem possible, as an alternative, to take ἠέρα χεύε ('she poured mist') with any particular object (neither the features of Ithaca nor Odysseus): she just pours mist around the place in general, as it were, and this mist both obscures the terrain and hides Odysseus. But this eirenic suggestion does not really help. We still have to choose whether to take the μιν ('it' or 'him') in 190 as referring (a) to the terrain or (b) to Odysseus. Either we say that Athene's purpose (γάρ ('for')) is to make the terrain unrecognisable to him, so that he will ask her about it, be told everything, and thus escape recognition by his wife or others: or we say that Athene's purpose is (directly) to ensure that Odysseus is unrecognisable, but that this has the side-effect of making the terrain unrecognisable to him. So we are forced between (a) and (b) once more, and I prefer (a).

13. 203-7

πῇ δὴ χρήματα πολλὰ φέρω τάδε; πῇ δὲ καὶ αὐτὸς
πλάζομαι; αἴθ' ὄφελον μεῖναι παρὰ Φαιήκεσσιν
αὐτοῦ· ἐγὼ δέ κεν ἄλλον ὑπερμενέων βασιλήων
ἐξικόμην, ὅς κέν μ' ἐφίλει καὶ ἔπεμπε νέεσθαι.
νῦν δ' οὔτ' ἄρ πῃ θέσθαι ἐπίσταμαι.

Where am I to carry all these many possessions? And where am I myself to wander? Would that I had stayed there among the Phaiecians: in that case I might have come to some other proud king, who would have entertained me and given me an escort to go. But now I do not know where to bestow them.

This is a much harder passage than most commentators seem to have realised. I think it may be incoherent, but I am not sure: in any case it merits discussion.

1. Odysseus has only just got up from sleep (εὕδων ('sleeping'), 188): he is not in the process of carrying anything anywhere. So φέρω ('am I to carry') in 203 must be deliberative, "Where am I to take all these many things?" But πλάζομαι ('am I to go' or 'wander') (204) is almost certainly not deliberative, because this verb always contains the idea of being

turned aside, beaten back, forced off a desired course (and hence, in the passive, the idea of wandering or roaming, rather than making straight for some goal). It must mean something like "Where have I been forced to this time?" or "Where is it I am now having to wander?"

2. That makes some, if not much, difference to how we interpret what follows. Odysseus has not asked the question, "Where ought I to make for?" or "Where am I to go to now?", and we shall not expect any kind of answer to that question in what follows. That fits with the general structure of the passage, which is threefold: (a) he asks the questions: (b) he wishes something else had happened, or envisages another scenario: (c), starting with νυνδ', 'as things are' (207), he describes his existing position. And in fact (c) deals only with the problem about his possessions, both in 207-08, and again in the last two lines of his speech, where he says he will count his possessions over in case of theft (215-16). So any alternative scenario in (b) must be chiefly designed to show how his possessions, rather than himself, would be better off than they are now.

3. So it looks as if we can happily go along with the majority of editors, who take 204 to refer to the possessions: thus Merry "would that they had abided where they were with the P., while I would have gone my way" (his italics). But there are difficulties. If we take that to mean (as I am sure that Merry and others do take it, though they do not say so) that the treasure was to remain Odysseus' property in Phaiecia, the obvious snag is that Odysseus would not have thought this safe. How could he have got back to Phaiecia? Did he even know where Phaiecia was? And anyway he now thinks the Phaiecians have tricked him by failing to land him in Ithaca - they are not νοήμονες ('intelligent') or δίκαιοι ('righteous') (209), and he hopes that Zeus will take vengeance on them (213-14). There is also a problem about exactly what is envisaged by ἐγω δέ κεν......('in that case'). Because of the κέν repeated in 206, this must have the force of the apodosis of a conditional: it must mean that if the treasure had stayed in Phaiecia, then Odysseus would have gone to some other powerful king. (It cannot translate as "Would that the treasure had stayed, and would that I had gone to some other king!", i.e. would that he had never landed in Phaiecia at all; that makes coherent sense, but does not fit the Greek.) But what is the sense of this? Are we to imagine the treasure remaining in Phaiecia until some other king received Odysseus, picked up the treasure from Phaiecia for him and then gave his escort home? No such elaborate and unlikely picture is suggested by ὅς...νέεσθαι ('who..to go') in 206.

4. We are just as badly stuck if we try the alternative of making 204 refer to Odysseus. On that account, there will be nothing in 204-06 which directly relates to the treasure problem, which (as we saw in 1 and 2 above) is Odysseus' main concern. Odysseus' movements, whatever on this interpretation they are supposed to be, are not or not obviously relevant. Moreover (and in my view more conclusively), it is not sense to say quite so baldly in the Greek "I wish I had stayed where I was there by the Phaiecians - in that case, I would have gone to some other king". It appears as a direct contradiction: there is no word in the apodosis meaning 'later' or 'afterwards'.

5. So now we go back to the basic idea in 3 above, that 204 refers to the treasure and the subject changes at 205. We may be encouraged to that idea by the prominent position of ἐγω ('I') in 205, which may be thought to mark the change. But to make sense of the passage we must take 204 to mean, not "I wish my treasure had stayed in the custody of the Phaiecians", but "I wish all these many things (πολλα τάδε, 203) had stayed in the possession of the Phaiecians (παρα Φαιήκεσσιν, 204)" - that is, he wishes he had never been given them in the first place. That might be taken as tantamount to the wish that he had never arrived at the Phaiecians' country in the first place, so that in that case (κεν) he would have arrived somewhere else, at some other king's home, and perhaps received presents, as well as entertainment and escort, from him. Or perhaps if he had gone to the land of the Phaiecians but not received presents, he would then have moved on to some other king.

I think that the Greek will bear the sense of 'staying in the Phaiecians' possession' (as against their custody); and that 205-06 do at least allow for the possibility of the interpretation that Odysseus is wishing that he had never had 'the Phaiecian experience', as one might call it, at all. But the chief point of that as regards the treasure, at least, is that he might have got treasure from going to some other king: and that, though allowed for (perhaps in ἐγω δέ....), is not specifically stated. "I wish they'd kept their blasted treasure" might have been followed by "and then I'd have gone to some other king who would have given me some", but hardly by "and then I'd have gone to some other king and got entertainment and escort from him". So this interpretation does not really get over the point that it is surely better for Odysseus to have his existing treasure, even at risk, than none at all: for the interpretation does not plausibly suggest that he would have got treasure from elsewhere.

So, though this suggestion is the best that one can do with the passage, it is perhaps not quite good enough, and we have to accept some incoherence.

13. 312-23

" ἀργαλέον σε, θεά, γνῶναι βροτῷ ἀντιάσαντι,
καὶ μάλ' ἐπισταμένῳ· σὲ γὰρ αὐτὴν παντὶ ἐΐσκεις.
τοῦτο δ' ἐγὼν εὖ οἶδ', ὅτι μοι πάρος ἠπίη ἦσθα,
ἧος ἐνὶ Τροίῃ πολεμίζομεν υἷες Ἀχαιῶν.

αὐτὰρ ἐπεὶ Πριάμοιο πόλιν διεπέρσαμεν αἰπήν,
βῆμεν δ' ἐν νήεσσι, θεὸς δ' ἐκέδασσεν Ἀχαιούς,
οὐ σέ γ' ἔπειτα ἴδον, κούρη Διός, οὐδ' ἐνόησα
νηὸς ἐμῆς ἐπιβᾶσαν, ὅπως τί μοι ἄλγος ἀλάλκοις.
ἀλλ' αἰεὶ φρεσὶν ᾗσιν ἔχων δεδαϊγμένον ἦτορ
ἠλώμην, ἧός με θεοὶ κακότητος ἔλυσαν·
πρίν γ' ὅτε Φαιήκων ἀνδρῶν ἐν πίονι δήμῳ
θάρσυνάς τε ἔπεσσι καὶ ἐς πόλιν ἤγαγες αὐτή.

"It is hard, goddess, for a mortal to recognise you when he meets you, even for a very perceptive mortal: for you can liken yourself to anything. That I knew well, when you were favourable towards me before, when we sons of Achaeans fought in Troy. But when we had sacked the steep city of Priam, and went in our ships, and the god scattered the Achaeans, then I never saw you, daughter of Zeus, nor perceived you on board my ship so that you could ward off any suffering from me. But always with a ravaged heart and with these thoughts I wandered, until the gods released me from evil, until in the rich land of the Phaiecian men you encouraged me with your words and yourself led me to the city."

A much-disputed passage, *mal vu* by virtually all editors from the Alexandrians onwards. Various cuts have been proposed, but (in my judgement) in the wrong places and for the 'wrong reasons. The OCT prints 312-23 in full, as above: I think it is ultimately incoherent as it stands, besides other difficulties with it.

In 313 παντί ('to everything') is not really a problem (*pace* Hoekstra, who considers no. other difficulty). It is not only that Odysseus has just had two examples in this very scene of Athene's disguises (the well-born shepherd, 222, and now the woman, 288), and may as it were 'remember' others from the Iliad (Hoekstra, *ibid.*), and hence may induce that Athene can use any and every disguise. Rather, this might be a piece of *a priori* knowledge either about gods in general or Athene in particular: that they can take any shape they please. There are plenty of examples in Homer. A particularly good case for Athene herself is the scene in 3.371 ff. where she changes into a bird from being Mentor. The striking thing is that Nestor immediately and without hesitation identifies this as an appearance of Athene, apparently on no evidence. Maybe Athene was shown as particularly adept in this respect.

320-323 have incurred a number of criticisms. (1) ᾗσιν cannot really mean 'my' and suggests some ignorant addition (Hoekstra is good on this). (2) Odysseus should not ascribe his rescue to the gods generally, in the presence of Athene; but that does not seem to me a serious criticism. (3) Odysseus did not recognise Athene in the land of the Phaiecians, so 322-23 cannot stand. (4) "we may add that πρίν δ'ὅτε ('until the time when') follows very awkwardly upon εἵως ('until')" (Merry). To this I myself would add (5) that in 321 θεοὶ κακότητος ἔλυσαν ('the gods released me from evil') are suspect, because the gods have not in fact released Odysseus from evil, either in reality or (more importantly, since Odysseus is speaking) in Odysseus' own understanding of his situation. He thinks he has been deceived by the Phaiecians (209 ff.), and that he is not in Ithaca (324 ff.): he has problems about what to do with his treasure (20 ff.): in general his situation is not a happy one.

Of these (3), (4) and (5) seem serious so far as coherency is concerned. Perhaps the most serious is the construction of πρίν in 322. We should have to take it as a kind of expansion of ἧος in 321:"I wandered, until the gods delivered me from evil - that is, until the time when …". Such syntax is a lot to swallow. The difficulty is reinforced by (5): Odysseus thinks that he is still wandering, so that it is not sense for him to say "I wandered until…". So something will have to go, if coherency is to be preserved. Traditionally (from Airistarchos onwards) the preference has been for deleting 322-23, because of (3) above. That will get rid of (3) and (4), but not (5); and not (1) and (2) either, for what they are worth.

There is however an alternative, which is to delete 319-21. That gets rid of all the difficulties except for (3), and also provides us with an admirably fluid syntax: "I never saw you, daughter of Zeus, or noticed you at least until the time when…". It may even be possible to look more tolerantly on (3). Certainly the text of Book 7 does not say Odysseus did recognise Athene in the shape of a young girl (παρθενικῇ νεάνιδι, 7.20), but neither does it say that he did not recognise her. (If this sounds like gross equivocation, let the reader try to decide when, towards the end of Book 24 for instance, Athene is and is not recognised or recognisable. It is not so easy.) She pretty soon stops talking like a young girl (49-77), and after her last line we are told simply that ἀπέβη γλαυκῶπις Ἀθήνη…λίπε δε Σχερίην ἐρατεινήν ('grey-eyed Athene departed, and left desirable Scherie') (78-79), suggesting perhaps a recognisably divine departure. Further, Odysseus is all the time wearing a mist, even in Alcinoos' palace (πολλὴν ἠέρ' ἔχων ('having much mist'), 140): he could hardly have been unaware that this was so, and might have ascribed it to Athenc. Finally, Athene's admission just before Odysseus' speech, that she was the one who made him dear to all the Phaiecians, and persuaded them to give him gifts (302-05), might in itself have enabled Odysseus to induce the truth of 322-23. That, I think, might save the passage as a whole from incoherence: otherwise we should have to delete at least 320-23.

13. 333-36

ἀσπασίως γάρ κ' ἄλλος ἀνὴρ ἀλαλήμενος ἐλθὼν
ἵετ' ἐνὶ μεγάροις ἰδέειν παῖδάς τ' ἄλοχόν τε·
σοὶ δ' οὔ πω φίλον ἐστὶ δαήμεναι οὐδὲ πυθέσθαι,
πρίν γ' ἔτι σῆς ἀλόχου πειρήσεαι,

For very strongly would any other man, who had wandered and returned, desire to see his children and wife in his house; but you do not wish to learn or find out this, until you make trial of your wife.

These lines have (since Aristarchus) been attacked 'on the ground that Odysseus has shown no sign of not wishing to rush off to Penelope and that 335-38 are at variance with his own words in 383-85' (Hoekstra), and defended against this attack. But the attack is too weak. The objection to the lines is simpler and stronger: Odysseus does not yet believe that he is in Ithaca, as 324 ff. make quite plain. But the lines make sense only on the assumption that he does believe this. They are grossly incoherent.

14. 495-98

' κλῦτε, φίλοι· θεῖός μοι ἐνύπνιον ἦλθεν ὄνειρος.
λίην γὰρ νηῶν ἑκὰς ἤλθομεν· ἀλλά τις εἴη
εἰπεῖν Ἀτρεΐδῃ Ἀγαμέμνονι, ποιμένι λαῶν,
εἰ πλέονας παρὰ ναῦφιν ἐποτρύνειε νέεσθαι.'

"Listen, friends; for a divine dream came to me when I was asleep. We have come too far from the ships; so let there be someone who will tell Atreus' son Agamemnon, shepherd of the people, to see if he will send more troops to come from the ships."

The passage in which Odysseus describes how he managed to acquire a cloak is often tersely narrated (e.g. 486-88), but at this particular point the poet becomes at least *prima facie* unintelligible. The difficulty is not so much that the words do not construe, but that it is hard to find any logical connection between the statements.

We have (1) 'a divine dream came to me', (2) 'we are too [or very] far from the ships', and (3) 'someone should go to Agamemnon to get more men'. The only logical help we have is the γαρ ('for') in (2). We may take this as (a) connecting (1) and (2), 'a divine dream came to me because we are too far from the ships'. That seems curt to the point of unintelligibility, though I suppose we could imagine the dream giving some kind of warning ("You are too far from the ships, Odysseus"). Or (b) the γαρ might (just) look forward to (3): "since we are too far from the ships, go to Agamemnon and get more men". But that strains even the elastic uses of γαρ, and still leaves it unclear <u>why</u> being too far from the ships requires the presence of more men - indeed why it is dangerous at all, or (worse still) why this danger is only now appreciated, since they knew perfectly well where they were going to (as 472 makes clear) and were quite happily asleep there.

We may of course imagine that Odysseus' words brought on the sudden reminder that they were very close to the enemy (the Trojans might make a sally, or whatever). But, short of sending the whole Greek army, it is still not clear why the presence of more men would help in this situation. Anyway the Greeks are supposed to be setting up an ambush (λόχον, 469): presumably they needed to be where they were. More men might make a more effective ambush, but what has that to do with being far from the ships?

I am not even sure that the poet had anything clearly in mind here: but whether he did or not, what he actually says is not coherent.

15. 69-71

νεμεσσῶμαι δὲ καὶ ἄλλῳ
ἀνδρὶ ξεινοδόκῳ, ὅς κ' ἔξοχα μὲν φιλέησιν,
ἔξοχα δ' ἐχθαίρῃσιν· ἀμείνω δ' αἴσιμα πάντα.
ἶσόν τοι κακόν ἐσθ', ὅς τ' οὐκ ἐθέλοντα νέεσθαι
ξεῖνον ἐποτρύνει καὶ ὃς ἐσσύμενον κατερύκει.
χρὴ ξεῖνον παρεόντα φιλεῖν, ἐθέλοντα δὲ πέμπειν

And I would be indignant with any other man, any other host, who showed either too much love or too much enmity: moderation is always best. It is equally bad if one urges on a guest to go against his will, and if one restrains a guest eager to go. One should entertain the guest who is present, and send him who wants to go on his way.

Hoekstra says of ἔξοχα δ' ἐχθαίρῃσιν ('excessively hates') "taken by itself this phrase can only mean that a host whose hate towards his guest does not exceed the average is not to blame. Since such a sense is out of the question, the expression is to be understood as (and in doing so behaves in the same way as a man) who shows hate to an excessive degree'. As this is not the natural interpretation of the relative clause, we probably have to do with a proverbial expression ('in love as well as in hate one should be moderate'), which came to mean something different by being brought into relation with a ξεινοδόκος ('host')". I must confess that I do not understand this at all; but perhaps I can be excused here, since Hoekstra's suggestion is not only 'not the natural interpretation', but clearly impossible (if only because the μεν and δ' must represent some kind of contrast).

We could follow Hoeckstra's implication that the phrase - perhaps the whole of ὅς κ' to ἐχθαίρῃσιν - has strayed in from some Hesiodic apothegm: that would clearly be an incoherence, if we assume that ἐχθαίρῃσιν means simply 'hate' and that hosts are not supposed to hate their guests at all. But it is not perhaps impossible that the rules of Homeric hospitality are laid down in such a way that personal emotions - love and hate - are not supposed to have much relevance. These rules are in fact quite formal and stringent (first the guest is given food, then he tells his name, and so on). Anyone with experience of such formal rules, for instance in contemporary Arab or even Greek societies, will appreciate this. In this light one may indeed feel towards the guest as towards a φίλος ('friend') or an ἐχθρός ('foe'), whilst still performing the duties of a host. What Menelaus is saying is that if one feels either too much, then things will go badly: if the guest is too much of a φίλος the host may keep him when he wants to go, and if he is too much of an ἐχθρος, the host may get rid of him when he wants to stay (as in 72-73). So we might perhaps translate 'who likes his guest too much, or dislikes him too much'. That would save the incoherence. At the same time, the whole passage (see below on 78 ff.) seems to have been, carelessly composed, and perhaps we should just accept the incoherence as it stands.

15. 78-82

ἀμφότερον κῦδός τε καὶ ἀγλαΐη καὶ ὄνειαρ
,δειπνήσαντας ἴμεν πολλὴν ἐπ' ἀπείρονα γαῖαν.
εἰ δ' ἐθέλεις τραφθῆναι ἀν' Ἑλλάδα καὶ μέσον Ἄργος,
ὄφρα τοι αὐτὸς ἕπωμαι, ὑποζεύξω δέ τοι ἵππους,
ἄστεα δ' ἀνθρώπων ἡγήσομαι·

It is in both ways a good thing to dine and then to go off over a long distance across the boundless land - it gives prestige and delight and advantage. And if you wish to go around in Greece and middle Argos, then for so long will I follow with you myself, and I will yoke horses for you, and lead the way to the cities of men.

Much of this passage is at least careless. (1) We expect two things after ἀμφότερον ('both') but get three (κυδος ('prestige'), ἀγλαιη ('delight'), ὄνειαρ ('advantage, 'benefit')). (2) πολλὴν ('much') makes no sense when joined with ἀπείρονα. ('boundless'). (3) The syntax of 80-82 is impossible. (4) Menelaus knows perfectly well that Telemachus wants to go home, and not τραφθηναι... Ἄργος ('to go...Argos').

Some of these, certainly (1) and (4), may be overlooked: even (2), though strictly nonsensical, may be forgiven (ἀπείρονα may be seen as a 'dead' epithet, so to speak: 'over a good deal of the infinitely-extending terrain' might just make sense). But (3) remains.

Merry says that "ὄφρα means 'so long', 'all that time' (as in Il. 15.547), while ἕπωμαι ('I will follow') is nearly equivalent to ὄψομαι". But that will hardly do: the Iliad parallel is not exact, and ὄφρα with the subjunctive ἕπωμαι must be a conjunction: 'whilst I myself will accompany you. We should then have to take the δέ in 81 as apodotic, and translate: "But if you want to travel throughout Hellas and Argos" (or whatever μέσον Ἄργος ('middle Argos') may mean) "whilst I myself accompany you, then I will yoke horses for you, and lead the way to the cities of men". That is not very convincing, and the idea of yoking horses is an additional oddity (Telemachus and Peisistratus already have horses).

A possible if somewhat desperate remedy would be to put a comma (rather than a full stop) after γαιαν ('land') in 79, and take ἴμεν as parallel to τραφθηναι ('to go', 'to travel'). We could then translate: "...to go over a good deal of boundless land - or, if you want, to travel throughout Hellas and Argos, while I myself accompany you: and I will yoke horses for you", etc. That saves the syntax: but I am not really convinced. It seems to me that the poet has carelessly thrown together a number of ideas, each perhaps intelligible in itself, but not grammatically coherent.

15. 111-122

" Τηλέμαχ', ἦ τοι νόστον, ὅπως φρεσὶ σῇσι μενοινᾷς,
ὥς τοι Ζεὺς τελέσειεν, ἐρίγδουπος πόσις Ἥρης.
δώρων δ', ὅσσ' ἐν ἐμῷ οἴκῳ κειμήλια κεῖται,
δώσω ὃ κάλλιστον καὶ τιμηέστατόν ἐστι.
δώσω τοι κρητῆρα τετυγμένον· ἀργύρεος δὲ
ἐστὶν ἅπας, χρυσῷ δ' ἐπὶ χείλεα κεκράανται,
ἔργον δ' Ἡφαίστοιο· πόρεν δέ ἑ Φαίδιμος ἥρως,
Σιδονίων βασιλεύς, ὅθ' ἑὸς δόμος ἀμφεκάλυψε
κεῖσ' ἐμὲ νοστήσαντα· τεῒν δ' ἐθέλω τόδ' ὀπάσσαι."
Ὣς εἰπὼν ἐν χειρὶ τίθει δέπας ἀμφικύπελλον
ἥρως Ἀτρεΐδης· ὁ δ' ἄρα κρητῆρα φαεινὸν
θῆκ' αὐτοῦ προπάροιθε φέρων κρατερὸς Μεγαπένθι,

"Telemachus, as to your return indeed, may Zeus the thundering husband of Here so accomplish it as you desire in your mind. Of the gifts that lie as possessions in my house I will give you that which is most beautiful and valuable. I will give you a wrought mixing-bowl: it is all of silver, and its rim is fashioned of gold: it is the work of Hephaistus. The hero Phaidimos gave it to me, the king of the Sidonians, when his house received me as I went there during my return. It is that which I wish to bestow on you". With these words the hero, the son of Atreus, placed the two-handled cup in his hands; and the strong Megapenthes brought the shining mixing-bowl and set it before him.

Pace Hoekstra there is here clear evidence of careless composition, if not a positive incoherence. Menelaus describes in great detail (115-19) the mixing-bowl he is going to give Telemachus; and directly after this we have "With these words the hero, Atreus' son, put into his hands the two-handled cup" (120-21). 113-19 is an exact repetition of 4.613-19, and the composer (or a composer) has re-inserted that passage here, where it does not fit with Menelaus' intention to give him the cup which he has taken from his treasure-chamber in 102. The composer has not forgotten about the mixing-bowl, which Megapenthes picks up in 103 and gives him in 121-22; and then Helen adds her own gift in 123 ff. So in this passage as a whole, 101-132, there is a kind of round-up of the gifts that Telemachus receives in general (Menelaus and Helen and Megapenthes go to the treasure-chamber, take the cup and the mixing-bowl and the robe and give them all to Telemachus: then Peisistratus puts them all into the chariot). The oddity is just that Menelaus' intention to give the mixing-bowl, and his detailed description of it, is repeated from 4.613 ff.: as if the poet had forgotten about it.

This passage shows us something, if nothing very clear, about the composition of at least this part of the poem. To someone who <u>heard</u> 113-121 (and *a fortiori* someone who <u>read</u> it carefully) Menelaus giving him the cup (120) would come as at least a slight surprise: and anyone who read carefully from Book 4 to the present book (15) would see that the repetition was inappropriate. The implication is that whoever composed this part of 15 did not have the passage in Book 4 clearly before his mind (otherwise he would not have made the repetition); or rather - since he did actually <u>use</u> the Book 4 passage as an exact repetition - did not see that it was here inappropriate. It is as if he just took the passage bodily and stuck it in: as if (to put it rather absurdly) he said to himself "Right, Menelaus is giving gifts to Telemachus: now, what have we got on that? Oh yes, the mixing-bowl - we have some lines about that, I'll put those in here". This shows at least how far away we are from a written text which the poet had clearly before him all the time as he proceeded. here, and perhaps often elsewhere, the idea of 'stitching' parts together seems on target.

15. 193-205

αἶψα δ' ἔπειθ' ἵκοντο Πύλου αἰπὺ πτολίεθρον·
καὶ τότε Τηλέμαχος προσεφώνεε Νέστορος υἱόν·
" Νεστορίδη, πῶς κέν μοι ὑποσχόμενος τελέσειας
μῦθον ἐμόν; ξεῖνοι δὲ διαμπερὲς εὐχόμεθ' εἶναι
ἐκ πατέρων φιλότητος, ἀτὰρ καὶ ὁμήλικές εἰμεν·
ἥδε δ' ὁδὸς καὶ μᾶλλον ὁμοφροσύνῃσιν ἐνήσει.
μή με παρὲξ ἄγε νῆα, διοτρεφές, ἀλλὰ λίπ' αὐτοῦ,
μή μ' ὁ γέρων ἀέκοντα κατάσχῃ ᾧ ἐνὶ οἴκῳ
ἱέμενος φιλέειν· ἐμὲ δὲ χρεὼ θᾶσσον ἱκέσθαι."
Ὣς φάτο, Νεστορίδης δ' ἄρ' ἑῷ συμφράσσατο θυμῷ,
ὅππως οἱ κατὰ μοῖραν ὑποσχόμενος τελέσειεν.
ὧδε δέ οἱ φρονέοντι δοάσσατο κέρδιον εἶναι·
στρέψ' ἵππους ἐπὶ νῆα θοὴν καὶ θῖνα θαλάσσης,

Straightaway they came to the steep city of Pylos. Then Telemachus spoke to the son of Nestor: "Son of Nestor, could you perhaps undertake to accomplish what I shall ask? We claim to be entirely friends to each other, because of our fathers' friendship, and also we are of like age: and this journey will make us even more like-minded. Do not drive me past the ship out of my way, Zeus-nurtured hero, but leave me here, in case the old man wants to entertain me and keeps me unwillingly in his house - but I have to get to my destination quickly". So he spoke, and the son of Nestor considered in his own heart how he might rightly undertake and accomplish that. And as he thought it seemed best to him to do this: he turned the horses towards the swift ship and the shore of the sea...

This passage may contain veridical memories of Pylian topography: in particular the knowledge, that the road from Sparta and Pherai went past the harbour before approaching the palace. That is why Telemachus asks Peisistratus not to drive him past his ship, παρεξ (199), and why Peisistratus has to turn the horses off the main road to the harbour (νηα ('ship'), 205). If this is right, the poet envisages Telemachus as speaking when they are close to the harbour, so that he asks Peisistratus to leave him there (αὐτου, 199). I think this survives the view of Hoekstra and other critics that (a) the palace is very close to the harbour (the text is ambiguous on this point); and that (b), if it were some distance away (at the Ano Englianos site), Telemachus would have plenty of time to escape before Nestor could detain him: for it might take some time for Telemachus to collect his companions and prepare his ship.

Anyway, if this view is correct, there is at least a *prima facie* inconsistency in 193, where they 'reached the high city of Pylos', before the point at which Telemachus says "Leave me here" (αὐτου, 199). That is indeed a problem on any account, since after Peisistratus leaves him he has to drive back to the city of Pylos (ἀψ Πυλίων ἐς ἀστυ, 216). But perhaps we need not take the idea of 'arriving at the high city' quite so strictly. In Book 3. 4-5 Telemachus' party, coming by sea, 'arrived at Pylos, the well-peopled city of Neleus' (Πύλον, Νηληος ἐυκτίμενον πτολίεθρον / ἰξον), where plainly the ship does not actually come to the city itself, but (as the ensuing scene in Book 3 makes clear) only to the seashore where the Pylians are feasting. Telemachus and Peisistratus may similarly be said, albeit loosely, to 'reach the city' when they are only in sight of it or in the immediate environs.

That would indeed be a bit easier if the poet had in mind not the Ano Englianos site (about four miles away from the sea), but the later city on Coryphasion which is very close to the sea. My own view is that the poet had himself no clear picture of Pylian topography, but that the text nevertheless incorporates veridical memories. But in any event I do not think there is a serious incoherence here.

15. 225 ff.

ἀτὰρ γενεήν γε Μελάμποδος ἔκγονος ἦεν,
ὃς πρὶν μέν ποτ' ἔναιε Πύλῳ ἔνι, μητέρι μήλων,
ἀφνειὸς Πυλίοισι μέγ' ἔξοχα δώματα ναίων·
δὴ τότε γ' ἄλλων δῆμον ἀφίκετο, πατρίδα φεύγων
Νηλέα τε μεγάθυμον, ἀγανότατον ζωόντων,
ὅς οἱ χρήματα πολλὰ τελεσφόρον εἰς ἐνιαυτὸν

εἶχε βίῃ. ὁ δὲ τῆος ἐνὶ μεγάροις Φυλάκοιο
δεσμῷ ἐν ἀργαλέῳ δέδετο, κρατέρ' ἄλγεα πάσχων
εἵνεκα Νηλῆος κούρης ἄτης τε βαρείης,
τήν οἱ ἐπὶ φρεσὶ θῆκε θεὰ δασπλῆτις Ἐρινύς.
ἀλλ' ὁ μὲν ἔκφυγε κῆρα καὶ ἤλασε βοῦς ἐριμύκους
ἐς Πύλον ἐκ Φυλάκης καὶ ἐτίσατο ἔργον ἀεικὲς
ἀντίθεον Νηλῆα, κασιγνήτῳ δὲ γυναῖκα
ἠγάγετο πρὸς δώμαθ'· ὁ δ' ἄλλων ἵκετο δῆμον,
Ἄργος ἐς ἱππόβοτον· τόθι γάρ νύ οἱ αἴσιμον ἦεν
ναιέμεναι πολλοῖσιν ἀνάσσοντ' Ἀργείοισιν.

But by birth he was the offspring of Melampus, who before that once dwelt in Pylos, mother of flocks: he was rich and lived in a very fine house amongst the Pylians. Then indeed he went to another country, going away from his fatherland and escaping from great-hearted Neleus, the proudest of living men, who held back much wealth from him by force for the space of a whole year. At that time he was constrained by harsh bonds in the house of Phylacus, suffering great pains for the sake of Neleus' daughter and his great folly, which the destructive goddess, the Erinus, had put into his mind. But he escaped his fate, and drove the lowing cattle from Phylake to Pylos, and he avenged the foul deed on godlike Neleus, and brought the woman as a wife for his brother to the house. Then he reached another country, and went to horse-pasturing Argos; for there it was now fated for him to live, ruling over many Argives.

Many scholars (e.g. Hoekstra) assume that the readers (or hearers) of this passage were sufficiently familiar with the story of Melampus, and also (a different thing) with the details of Melampus' descendants, to make this passage readily intelligible. I think that uncertain: but even if it were so, some parts of the passage at least border on unintelligibility, if not incoherence.

Thus it is not clear whether the ἄτης (233) belongs to Melampus or to Neleus: nor how Melampus' getting the cattle to Pylos counted as taking vengeance (ἐτίσατο, (236)) on Neleus - it enabled his brother to marry Neleus' daughter, but that in itself is hardly vengeance for Melampus. And it is odd that Theoklymenos should come from Argos, where he has many kinsmen and relatives in positions of power (πολλοι δὲ κασίγνησοι...μέγα δὲ κρατέουσιν Ἀχαιῶν ('many kinsmen....exercise great power over Achaeans'), 273-74), since his father Polypheides had gone to live in distant Hyperesie (254) and exercised his prophetic powers there (255).

Admittedly there are no overt logical contradictions here, and perhaps 'incoherence' is too strong a word. But the passage is, at least, more confused - as it were, hurried or rushed - than other passages which add background details to various characters or events. It reads more like a rapid or summary set of notes, put rather carelessly together by a composer who wanted to bring in his knowledge of the Melampus story, which (on any account) sticks out like a sore thumb. A borderline case, perhaps.

15. 368-88

αὐτὰρ ἐμὲ χλαῖνάν τε χιτῶνά τε εἵματ' ἐκείνη
καλὰ μάλ' ἀμφιέσασα, ποσὶν δ' ὑποδήματα δοῦσα
ἀγρόνδε προΐαλλε· φίλει δέ με κηρόθι μᾶλλον.

νῦν δ' ἤδη τούτων ἐπιδεύομαι· ἀλλά μοι αὐτῷ
ἔργον ἀέξουσιν μάκαρες θεοὶ ᾧ ἐπιμίμνω·
τῶν ἔφαγόν τ' ἔπιόν τε καὶ αἰδοίοισιν ἔδωκα.
ἐκ δ' ἄρα δεσποίνης οὐ μείλιχον ἔστιν ἀκοῦσαι
οὔτ' ἔπος οὔτε τι ἔργον, ἐπεὶ κακὸν ἔμπεσεν οἴκῳ,
ἄνδρες ὑπερφίαλοι· μέγα δὲ δμῶες χατέουσιν
ἀντία δεσποίνης φάσθαι καὶ ἕκαστα πυθέσθαι
καὶ φαγέμεν πιέμεν τε, ἔπειτα δὲ καί τι φέρεσθαι
ἀγρόνδ', οἷά τε θυμὸν ἀεὶ δμώεσσιν ἰαίνει."
Τὸν δ' ἀπαμειβόμενος προσέφη πολύμητις Ὀδυσσεύς·
" ὢ πόποι, ὡς ἄρα τυτθὸς ἐών, Εὔμαιε συβῶτα,
πολλὸν ἀπεπλάγχθης σῆς πατρίδος ἠδὲ τοκήων.
ἀλλ' ἄγε μοι τόδε εἰπὲ καὶ ἀτρεκέως κατάλεξον,
ἠὲ διεπράθετο πτόλις ἀνδρῶν εὐρυάγυια,
ᾗ ἔνι ναιετάασκε πατὴρ καὶ πότνια μήτηρ,
ἢ σέ γε μουνωθέντα παρ' οἴεσιν ἢ παρὰ βουσὶν
ἄνδρες δυσμενέες νηυσὶν λάβον ἠδ' ἐπέρασσαν
τοῦδ' ἀνδρὸς πρὸς δώμαθ', ὁ δ' ἄξιον ὦνον ἔδωκε."

"Then she dressed me in a cloak and tunic, very fine clothes, and gave me sandals for my feet, and sent me out to the country, loving me very deeply. Now I lack all these; yet the blessed gods prosper the work which I supervise. From this work I have food and drink, and give to revered guests. But I can hear nothing delightful from my mistress, neither word nor deed, since evil has fallen on the house – that is, these arrogant men. But slaves always long greatly to speak face to face with their mistress, and learn of everything, and to eat and drink, and then to take something away to the country, the kind of thing that always delights the spirit of slaves". Answering him then spoke ingenious Odysseus: "O alas, I see that just as a young boy, swineherd Eumaeos, you wandered far from your country and your parents. But come, tell me this and speak to me truly, whether the broad-pathed city of men in which your father and revered mother lived was sacked: or whether, as you were alone by the sheep or the oxen, foemen took you on their ships and brought you over to this man's house, and gave the price of you to them".

There are many difficulties in this passage, which I will first address in order. The most serious is 371-73, where it is not clear to what τούτων ('these things') (371) refers, and still less clear how we are to take των ('which') in 373, or why the verbs in that line are in the past tense. Almost as bad is 381: how does Odysseus know that Eumaios has come from another (distant) country? Then, what is the construction of νηυσιν in 387? And to whom does τουδ'ανδρος ('of this man') in 388 refer? (I should add that 374-75 presents no difficulty, *pace* some editors (e.g. Merry). ἀκοῦσαι need not mean simply 'hear', which would fit ἔπος ('word') but not ἔργον ('deed'): it means 'hear of', which fits either. Eumaios is saying that it is no pleasure to hear of what has been said or done in the palace.)

The last two difficulties are minor. νηυσιν ('ships') may construe as 'took you in their ships' or'...with their ships', though the construction is a bit loose in either case. And τουδ' ἀνδρος probably refers to Laertes, though it might refer to Odysseus. Certainly there is nothing like an incoherency here. They may suggest that the passage as a whole was carelessly put together, but no more.

But now consider 371-73. What exactly are the things which Eumaios now lacks? Not the cloak and the tunic and the sandals: he has these in his position as swineherd. Perhaps it may be taken to refer to the general favour and goodwill of Odysseus' mother. 373 is harder. Merry glosses των as 'of these (good) things, *sc.* ἃ μοι ἀέξουσι θεοί' ('which the gods prosper for me'): unconvincingly, since ἀέξουσι unequivocally governs ἔργον. More plausibly των refers to θεοι ('gods'), and perhaps we should translate 'from them', or 'from whose bounty'. But it is really unintelligible as it stands. The past tense (aorist, not perfect) is a little odd, since Eumaios still continues to eat and drink and give to strangers: and the absence of any noun with των odder still: but these are not incoherent in themselves. Only των deserves that description.

380 ff. remain incoherent, because Odysseus is quite clear that Eumaios must have come from a far country, yet nothing in Eumaios' speech suggests this. Nothing even suggests, so far, that he was sold as a slave, even though Odysseus knows that he is a slave (from δηωες ('slaves'), 376, δμώεσιν, 379, and elsewhere earlier). There is no reason why he should not have been a native-born Ithacan, whose parents had died: indeed the fact that Odysseus' mother brought him up, ἐτρεφόμην ('I was brought up') (365), suggests that he had something better than slave-status. It looks as if the poet just assumed that Odysseus knew of Eumaios' origin already, the details being filled out by Eumaios' speech that follows immediately in the text.

15. 434-445

Τὸν δ' αὖτε προσέειπε γυνὴ καὶ ἀμείβετο μύθῳ·
'εἴη κεν καὶ τοῦτ', εἴ μοι ἐθέλοιτέ γε, ναῦται,
ὅρκῳ πιστωθῆναι ἀπήμονά μ' οἴκαδ' ἀπάξειν.'
Ὣς ἔφαθ', οἱ δ' ἄρα πάντες ἐπώμνυον ὡς ἐκέλευεν.
αὐτὰρ ἐπεί ῥ' ὄμοσάν τε τελεύτησάν τε τὸν ὅρκον,
τοῖς δ' αὖτις μετέειπε γυνὴ καὶ ἀμείβετο μύθῳ·
'σιγῇ νῦν, μή τίς με προσαυδάτω ἐπέεσσιν
ὑμετέρων ἑτάρων, ξυμβλήμενος ἢ ἐν ἀγυιῇ
ἤ που ἐπὶ κρήνῃ· μή τις ποτὶ δῶμα γέροντι
ἐλθὼν ἐξείπῃ, ὁ δ' ὀϊσάμενος καταδήσῃ
δεσμῷ ἐν ἀργαλέῳ, ὑμῖν δ' ἐπιφράσσετ' ὄλεθρον.
ἀλλ' ἔχετ' ἐν φρεσὶ μῦθον, ἐπείγετε δ' ὦνον ὀδαίων.

Then the woman spoke to him in answer with a word: "Then let it be so, if you are willing, sailors, to pledge with an oath that you will take me back home without harming me". She spoke thus, and they all swore as she had bade them. Then when they had sworn and completed the oath, the woman spoke to them again, and answered in a word: "Be silent now, lest one of your comrades speaks words to me, meeting me either in the street or perhaps at the well: I fear that someone may go to the house and tell the old man, and learning of it he may bind me in a harsh bond, and plot destruction for you. But do you keep what I say in your minds, and press on with the journey-money."

Another passage which has been carelessly and sometimes incoherently constructed. (1) There is a (slight) difficulty about ἀμείβετο ('answered') in 439, since there is no immediately preceding direct speech to which the woman may answer. (Hoekstra raises this difficulty about the ἀμείβετο in 434: but that is absurd, since she is there directly answering the sailor's speech of 431-33. This must be just a clerical error in Hoekstra's edition.) However, in 437-38 the sailors swear an oath, and the woman may be loosely said to 'answer' that. (2) The real difficulty, which amounts to incoherence, is that the composer is muddled about whether the woman is addressing one sailor or many sailors. It will not do to say that her seducer has been joined by other sailors at some time before 434: the τον ('him') of 434 directly contradicts the plurals that begin with ἐθέλοιτέ ('you [all] are willing') and ναῦται ('sailors') in 435, and continue throughout. The position is further complicated by 440-41, where she appears now to be addressing a single person (σιγῆ νυν ('be silent now')), and where σιγῆ might be read as a 2nd singular imperative (Merry's 'σιγῆ sc. ἔχετε or μένετε' ('in silence...hold yourselves...remain') is unconvincing). Nor does it really help to say that she is here addressing only some of the sailors: that would explain ὑμετέρων ἑτάρων ('your companions'), and no doubt σιγῆ can be understood as a singular noun, but this does nothing to clear up the basic muddle.

15. 518-53

ἀλλά τοι ἄλλον φῶτα πιφαύσκομαι ὅν κεν ἵκοιο,
Εὐρύμαχον, Πολύβοιο δαΐφρονος ἀγλαὸν υἱόν,
τὸν νῦν ἶσα θεῷ Ἰθακήσιοι εἰσορόωσι·
καὶ γὰρ πολλὸν ἄριστος ἀνὴρ μέμονέν τε μάλιστα
μητέρ' ἐμὴν γαμέειν καὶ Ὀδυσσῆος γέρας ἕξειν,
ἀλλὰ τά γε Ζεὺς οἶδεν Ὀλύμπιος, αἰθέρι ναίων,
εἴ κέ σφι πρὸ γάμοιο τελευτήσει κακὸν ἦμαρ."

Ὣς ἄρα οἱ εἰπόντι ἐπέπτατο δεξιὸς ὄρνις,
κίρκος, Ἀπόλλωνος ταχὺς ἄγγελος· ἐν δὲ πόδεσσι
τίλλε πέλειαν ἔχων, κατὰ δὲ πτερὰ χεῦεν ἔραζε
μεσσηγὺς νηός τε καὶ αὐτοῦ Τηλεμάχοιο.
τὸν δὲ Θεοκλύμενος ἑτάρων ἀπονόσφι καλέσσας
ἔν τ' ἄρα οἱ φῦ χειρὶ ἔπος τ' ἔφατ' ἔκ τ' ὀνόμαζε·
" Τηλέμαχ', οὔ τοι ἄνευ θεοῦ ἔπτατο δεξιὸς ὄρνις·
ἔγνων γάρ μιν ἐσάντα ἰδὼν οἰωνὸν ἐόντα.
ὑμετέρου δ' οὐκ ἔστι γένεος βασιλεύτερον ἄλλο
ἐν δήμῳ Ἰθάκης, ἀλλ' ὑμεῖς καρτεροὶ αἰεί."

Τὸν δ' αὖ Τηλέμαχος πεπνυμένος ἀντίον ηὔδα·
" αἰ γὰρ τοῦτο, ξεῖνε, ἔπος τετελεσμένον εἴη·
τῷ κε τάχα γνοίης φιλότητά τε πολλά τε δῶρα
ἐξ ἐμεῦ, ὡς ἄν τίς σε συναντόμενος μακαρίζοι."

Ἦ καὶ Πείραιον προσεφώνεε, πιστὸν ἑταῖρον·
" Πείραιε Κλυτίδη, σὺ δέ μοι τά περ ἄλλα μάλιστα
πείθῃ ἐμῶν ἑτάρων, οἵ μοι Πύλον εἰς ἅμ' ἕποντο·
καὶ νῦν μοι τὸν ξεῖνον ἄγων ἐν δώμασι σοῖσιν
ἐνδυκέως φιλέειν καὶ τιέμεν, εἰς ὅ κεν ἔλθω."

Τὸν δ' αὖ Πείραιος δουρικλυτὸς ἀντίον ηὔδα·
" Τηλέμαχ', εἰ γάρ κεν σὺ πολὺν χρόνον ἐνθάδε μίμνοις,
τόνδε τ' ἐγὼ κομιῶ, ξενίων δέ οἱ οὐ ποθὴ ἔσται."

Ὣς εἰπὼν ἐπὶ νηὸς ἔβη, ἐκέλευσε δ' ἑταίρους
αὐτούς τ' ἀμβαίνειν ἀνά τε πρυμνήσια λῦσαι.
οἱ δ' αἶψ' εἴσβαινον καὶ ἐπὶ κληῖσι καθῖζον.

Τηλέμαχος δ' ὑπὸ ποσσὶν ἐδήσατο καλὰ πέδιλα,
εἵλετο δ' ἄλκιμον ἔγχος, ἀκαχμένον ὀξέι χαλκῷ,
νηὸς ἀπ' ἰκριόφιν· τοὶ δὲ πρυμνήσι' ἔλυσαν.
οἱ μὲν ἀνώσαντες πλέον ἐς πόλιν, ὡς ἐκέλευσε

"But I will tell you of another man whom you may come to, Eurymachos, the glorious son of warlike Polybos, whom now the men of Ithaca look on as a god. For indeed he is far the best man of them, and desires most strongly to wed my mother and have Odysseus' rights - yet Olympian Zeus who lives in the sky knows whether before his marriage he will meet a day of evil." As he spoke there flew past a bird on the right hand, a hawk, the swift messenger of Apollo. In its feet it clutched a dove, whose feathers poured down to the ground between the ship and Telemachus himself. Theoklymenos called him apart from his comrades: he grasped him by the hand and spoke a word and named him: "Telemachus, this bird has not flown on the right hand without the will of god: as I looked at it I knew it was an omen. There is no more royal race than yours in the land of Ithaca: you are always strong". Wise Telemachus spoke in answer to him: "Stranger, may that word of yours be accomplished. Then would you quickly know of my friendship, and have many gifts from me, so that anyone who met you would call you blessed". He spoke thus, and then spoke to Peiraios, his faithful comrade: "Peiraios son of Klytios, in all other things you are the most obedient of my comrades, those who have followed with me to Pylos; so now do you take this stranger in your house and entertain him with care and honour him, until I come". Spear-famed Peiraios answered back to him: "Telemachus, even if you stay there a long time, I will care for him, and there shall be no lack of entertainment". Saying this, he went on the ship and bade the comrades embark themselves and loose the mooring ropes. They at once embarked and sat on the benches. Telemachus bound his fair sandals beneath his feet, and took a strong spear, tipped with sharp bronze, from the decks of the ship; and they loosed the mooring-ropes. Then they pushed off and sailed to the city, as he had ordered.

I give the whole of this passage, because some of the difficulties only appear in context. The most glaring lie in Theoklymenos' remarks (531 ff.) and Telemachus' reply (536 ff.). Theoklymenos gives no <u>interpretation</u> of the omen at all, and that makes 534-35 incoherent - these lines have no connecting logic with the mere fact that he recognises the bird as an omen in 532. Equally 536 makes no sense: what is the ἔπος ('word', 'saying') that he hopes will be τετελεσμένον ('accomplished')? We might assume that some lines have been omitted between 532 and 533, something like "Just as this kingly hawk destroyed the dove, so will the kingly Odysseus..." etc., as with the analogous omen at Menelaus' palace (15.160 ff.). Even then to describe the hawk as a messenger of Apollo (rather than of Zeus, who characteristically sponsors kings) is odd: and the omission of such lines is even odder. As it stands, it is incoherent.

There are two minor oddities also, not perhaps incoherent in themselves, but suggesting extreme carelessness in the composition. (1) There appears to be (but perhaps not) some sort of muddle about the stem-cables (548, 552); however, the passage is not clear enough, and we do not know enough about standard Homeric practice for casting off ships, for there to be any very obvious incoherence. (2) We should expect ἀπώσαντες ('pushing off') rather than ἀνώσαντες ('pushing up') in 553, to mean 'pushing off, away from the shore; but this too is uncertain, and could be cured by a slight textual emendation.

However, in view of all this I am not inclined to accept various editors' suggestions for Telemachus' change of host for Theoklymenos as between 518 ff. and 540 ff., from Eurymachus (his enemy) to Peiraios (his friend). It is not so much that there could be no reason for the change, or reasons for recommending either host, but rather that there is no

COMMENTS ON THE ODYSSEY

indication of its being a change (let alone any indication of the reason for it). The passage just seems to have been put together incoherently.

16. 4-10

Τηλέμαχον δὲ περίσσαινον κύνες ὑλακόμωροι,
οὐδ' ὕλαον προσιόντα. νόησε δὲ δῖος Ὀδυσσεὺς
σαίνοντάς τε κύνας, περί τε κτύπος ἦλθε ποδοῖιν.
αἶψα δ' ἄρ' Εὔμαιον ἔπεα πτερόεντα προσηύδα·
" Εὔμαι', ἦ μάλα τίς τοι ἐλεύσεται ἐνθάδ' ἑταῖρος
ἢ καὶ γνώριμος ἄλλος, ἐπεὶ κύνες οὐχ ὑλάουσιν,
ἀλλὰ περισσαίνουσι· ποδῶν δ' ὑπὸ δοῦπον ἀκούω."

The mad-barking dogs fawned round Telemachus, and did not bark as he approached. Godlike Odysseus noticed it, and the fawning dogs, and a noise of footsteps came round his ears. At once he addressed winged words to Eumaios: "Eumaios, in truth it is some comrade who is coming here, or some other person you know, since the dogs do not bark but fawn around him; and I hear the noise of footsteps".

The incoherency in this passage, as with some others, only appears on a close reading, and it is perhaps unsurprising that it has escaped the notice of most commentators. περίσσαινον (4) must mean that the dogs <u>fawned</u> round Telemachus, so that both Telemachus and the dogs would be visible at the same time. Then 5-6 would naturally mean 'The godlike Odysseus noticed (actually <u>saw</u>) this, and (τε ('both', or 'and')) he saw the fawning dogs, and (τε) a noise of footsteps was audible". That is already a bit odd, since the audibility of the footsteps seems otiose if Odysseus has already seen Telemachus and the dogs together. Then Odysseus says (840) "Surely it must be some comrade or acquaintance who is on his way (will arrive, ἐλεύσεται) here, since the dogs aren't barking but fawning around him (περίσσαινον)' and I hear the noise of footsteps" (the meaning of ὑπο does not concern us here). That is also odd, because if (a) Odysseus has seen Telemachus then περισσαίνουσι makes sense but the noise of footsteps seems otiose, whereas if (b) Odysseus has not seen him (but is just guessing, as it were) then the footsteps are relevant but περισσαίνουσι is out of place (if the dogs are fawning around him then Telemachus must be visible).

8-10 might be saved if we assume that Odysseus has in fact seen Telemachus but wishes to conceal this from Eumaios. But we should have to take περισσαίνουσι in that case, just as 'are fawning about the place': i.e. not round Telemachus, but just visible by themselves whilst wagging their tails and doing whatever dogs do when a friend is approaching. That is odd enough, since then it must bear a different meaning to 4. We might also take 5-6 as meaning that Odysseus noticed the general situation (but did not see Telemachus): translating along the lines of "Odysseus noticed that the dogs were fawning, and also heard footsteps". But that leaves the first τε in 6 unexplained, and still does not meet the problem presented by 4 - that Telemachus and the dogs must have been simultaneously visible.

In fact the composer has no very clear picture in mind. He has, as it were, not settled either on a picture of Odysseus actually seeing Telemachus or on a picture of Odysseus just making a sensible guess about the person who is coming. At least a borderline case.

16. 93-111

οἷά φατε μνηστῆρας ἀτάσθαλα μηχανάασθαι
ἐν μεγάροις, ἀέκητι σέθεν τοιούτου ἐόντος.
εἰπέ μοι ἠὲ ἑκὼν ὑποδάμνασαι, ἦ σέ γε λαοὶ
ἐχθαίρουσ' ἀνὰ δῆμον, ἐπισπόμενοι θεοῦ ὀμφῇ,
ἦ τι κασιγνήτοις ἐπιμέμφεαι, οἷσί περ ἀνὴρ
μαρναμένοισι πέποιθε, καὶ εἰ μέγα νεῖκος ὄρηται.
αἲ γὰρ ἐγὼν οὕτω νέος εἴην τῷδ' ἐπὶ θυμῷ,
ἢ παῖς ἐξ Ὀδυσῆος ἀμύμονος ἠὲ καὶ αὐτὸς
ἔλθοι ἀλητεύων· ἔτι γὰρ καὶ ἐλπίδος αἶσα·
αὐτίκ' ἔπειτ' ἀπ' ἐμεῖο κάρη τάμοι ἀλλότριος φώς,
εἰ μὴ ἐγὼ κείνοισι κακὸν πάντεσσι γενοίμην
ἐλθὼν ἐς μέγαρον Λαερτιάδεω Ὀδυσῆος.
εἰ δ' αὖ με πληθυῖ δαμασαίατο μοῦνον ἐόντα,
βουλοίμην κ' ἐν ἐμοῖσι κατακτάμενος μεγάροισι
τεθνάμεν ἢ τάδε γ' αἰὲν ἀεικέα ἔργ' ὁράασθαι,
ξείνους τε στυφελιζομένους δμῳάς τε γυναῖκας
ῥυστάζοντας ἀεικελίως κατὰ δώματα καλά,
καὶ οἶνον διαφυσσόμενον, καὶ σῖτον ἔδοντας
μάψ αὔτως, ἀτέλεστον, ἀνηνύστῳ ἐπὶ ἔργῳ."

Such outrageous things you tell me that the suitors devise in the halls, against the will of yourself, being the sort of man you are. Tell me whether you are yielding voluntarily, or whether the people in the country hate you, in the light of some divine oracle; or do you blame your kinsmen, on whom a man relies to fight for him, even when a great quarrel arises? Would that I were young like you, if I had these feelings - either blameless Odysseus' son or Odysseus himself, if he came here in his wanderings: and there is still some hope of that. Then at once some other man could cut off my head if I did not prove a disaster to all those men, as I came to the hall of Odysseus son of Laertes. And even if they should overwhelm me, being but one man, with their numbers, I should prefer to be slain and lie dead in my halls rather than always see these revolting deeds: visitors ill-treated, the female slaves dragged through the fair house in an unseemly way, the wine drawn, and their eating the food without any restraint, without end, in an enterprise that has no resolution".

This passage is a mess, the same sort of mess as 15.518 ff. The only real difficulty commentators have seen is with 101; but if (with the Alexandrine critics) we reject that line, most of the difficulties and incoherences still remain.

We may get the general feel of it by first going through the difficulties in order. It is odd that in 94 Odysseus seems clear that Telemachus is unwilling to tolerate the situation (ἀέκητι ('against your will')), but in 95 asks whether he is willing (ἑκων). Then in 99 neither οὕτω νέος ('thus youthful') nor τωδ ἐπι θυμω ('on this spirit') is clear. Perhaps the former means 'young, as you are; and the latter something like 'in addition to (on top of) having these feelings' (*sc*. of anger or resentment at the situation: but whether Telemachus' or Odysseus' own feelings is not clear). Then 100 seems to mean "Would that I were either Odysseus' son or Odysseus himself", though Odysseus is not particularly young, certainly not οὕτω νέος (if that means as young as Telemachus). If we keep 101, then we have to take 100 as governing ἔλθοι ('come'): "Would that Telemachus or

49

Odysseus would come" - but as a wanderer or vagrant (ἀλητεύων)? And anyway Odysseus knows now that Telemachus is Odysseus' son: he is present with him and Eumaios in the cottage. Then (102 ff.) "if that were so I would go into Odysseus' house" (104) and (106) "I would rather die in my own (ἐμοῖσι) house": is Odysseus saying that, if he were young, he himself (in his present role as a vagrant) would fight the suitors, or that if he were Telemachus or Odysseus he would fight them? And finally (111), though ἀτέλεστον may mean 'without any point or 'to no good end', what exactly is the ἔργῳ ('work', 'enterprise') which will 'never be done/accomplished' (ἀνηνύστῳ)? The suitors' business is to marry Penelope, which might well be accomplished. The phrase might mean something like 'in a situation which may never be resolved', which would make some sense from Telemachus' viewpoint: but is an odd word to use here, and the line is at least very unclear.

So it is a mess; and there is certainly one incoherence in 99 ff. Suppose first that we keep 101: then we might take the ἢ in 100 as 'or that...' ("Would I were young, or that Odysseus' son or Odysseus himself might come as a wanderer", etc.) That will make sense of ἐμοῖσι ('my own') in 106: "I - i.e. as Odysseus' son or Odysseus - would rather die in my own house". But then 100-01 is odd: he refers to 'Odysseus' son' as if he did not know Telemachus was Odysseus son, and the idea of him coming as a vagrant is very strange. (Is he suggesting that Telemachus might dress up as a vagrant, and do what Odysseus himself is doing?) On the other hand, if we excise 101, we have a somewhat easier ride: but (1) it is still odd to talk to Telemachus about the πάϊς ('son'), and (2) the syntax is still unsatisfactory. Merry says that "With αὐτός ('himself') we must supply εἴην ('I might be') from above", but that is not good enough unless we also take ἢ in 100, as suggested above, as 'or that'. (Better sense would be made if we had ὡς ('as') instead of ἢ which would clarify νέος ('young'): "Would I were as young as Odysseus' son ......".)

16. 421-24

μάργε, τίη δὲ σὺ Τηλεμάχῳ θάνατόν τε μόρον τε
ῥάπτεις, οὐδ' ἱκέτας ἐμπάζεαι, οἷσιν ἄρα Ζεὺς
μάρτυρος; οὐδ' ὁσίη κακὰ ῥάπτειν ἀλλήλοισιν.
ἦ οὐκ οἶσθ' ὅτε δεῦρο πατὴρ τεὸς ἵκετο φεύγων,

Madman, why do you plan death and fate for Telemachus, and take no heed of suppliants, for whom Zeus is a witness? Nor is it holy to devise evil for each other. Do you not know that your father came here as a fugitive...?

This passage has been much discussed (see Hoekstra for references). The best we can do for it, following Hoekstra, is to take the main thrust of Penelope's argument to be that of 424-32, where she describes how Antinoos' father was protected as a suppliant by Odysseus: this puts Antinoos under an obligation, so that it is outrageous for him to behave so badly to Odysseus' family. That might allow us to take οὐδ' ἱκέτας ἐμπάζεαι (422) as "you care nothing for the moral principles governing suppliants" [*sc.* and their protectors]. We then have to translate οὐδ' ὁσίη ... ἀλλήλοισιν as something like "it is not right for the two parties [*sc.* suppliants and their protectors] "to devise harm for each other". But the trouble with this is that, besides being unbelievably elliptical, ἀλλήλοισιν ('for each other') can really only refer to the word ἱκέτας; it must be two suppliants, or at least two families of suppliants, who are not to harm each other.

The only alternative is to refer ἱκέτας ('suppliants') to both Antinoos (on the grounds mentioned above) and to Telemachus. But we cannot really see Telemachus as a suppliant to Antinoos, despite his requests to the suitors and the Ithacan assembly in Book 2. Supplication in Homer is a fairly formal institution, and generates moral duties (of the kind Penelope is talking about) only if the suppliant is received as such and offered protection - certainly not the case with Telemachus and Antinoos. So this alternative is worse than the former. The passage is incoherent.

17. 43

ἀλλ' ἄγε μοι κατάλεξον ὅπως ἤντησας ὀπωπῆς.

This must mean "Come, tell me how you came to see him". The phrase is used by Telemachus when talking to Nestor (3.97) and to Menelaus (4.327) about Odysseus, with good reason (Telemachus knows that they saw him), though it is admittedly a bit odd even there - if taken at face value, it would naturally be answered by "Well, of course we were at Troy together for ten years". But we can take it as meaning something like "Tell me of your face-to-face dealings with him". The trouble with the phrase as used by Penelope is that she has absolutely no reason for thinking that Telemachus has seen his father at all. Taken with the lines immediately preceding, we have to translate "...when you went in your ship to Pylos ... to get some news of your dear father: so come, tell me how you came to see him"; and that is, if not positively unintelligible, is at least bordering on the incoherent.

17. 160-61

οἷον ἐγὼν οἰωνὸν ἐϋσσέλμου ἐπὶ νηὸς
ἥμενος ἐφρασάμην καὶ Τηλεμάχῳ ἐγεγώνευν.

Such an omen did I perceive as I sat in the well-benched ship, and told it to Telemachus.

ἥμενος ('sitting') is careless ('incoherent' is too strong). It is clear from 15.499 ff. (where they all get out of the ship) and 529 (where Theoklymenos takes Telemachus aside) that Theoklymenos was not sitting, in the ship when the omen occurred.

I mention this passage chiefly to contrast it with, for instance, 17.492 ff. (see note *ad loc.*) where the poet's lack of clarity about the location of various *dramatis personae* does, I think, amount to incoherence. There are of course a lot of borderline cases here.

17. 205-07

ἄστεος ἐγγὺς ἔσαν καὶ ἐπὶ κρήνην ἀφίκοντο
τυκτὴν καλλίροον, ὅθεν ὑδρεύοντο πολῖται,
τὴν ποίησ᾽ Ἴθακος καὶ Νήριτος ἠδὲ Πολύκτωρ·

They were near the city, and arrived at the fountain: it was well-built and flowed fairly, and the citizens drew water from it. Ithakos and Neritos and Polyktor constructed it.

Perhaps a borderline case, though for a different reason: and perhaps worth mentioning as shedding some light on the origin of some other incoherences. the point is simply that it is hard to believe that three kings of Ithaca could all have made the well-spring. The poet seems to have felt obliged (a) to say that the well-spring is an old one, and therefore made by some ancient or traditional figure, and (b) to have filled out the line as best he could: 'Ithakos', an eponymous figure: 'Neritos', a name traditionally connected with Ithaca and its mountain: 'Polyktor', probably invented (-'wealthy') and used elsewhere only as a name for Peisandros' father (18.299, 22.243). He does this without much regard for plausibility.

17. 231-32

πολλά οἱ ἀμφὶ κάρη σφέλα ἀνδρῶν ἐκ παλαμάων
πλευραὶ ἀποτρίψουσι δόμον κάτα βαλλομένοιο.

And his ribs will break many stools about his head thrown by the hands of men, as he is smitten in the house.

It does not make much difference here whether we read πλευραι ("his ribs will break the stools") or some accusative ("the stools will break his ribs"). The incoherence is between either reading and ἀμφι κάρη, which must mean 'round his head', and represent quite a different idea or picture. Russo's suggestion that it is 'a phrase expressing the looser sense of "around you"' (he means, around him) is unconvincing.

17. 492-93 (512 ff., 541 ff.)

Τοῦ δ᾽ ὡς οὖν ἤκουσε περίφρων Πηνελόπεια
βλημένου ἐν μεγάρῳ, μετ᾽ ἄρα δμῳῇσιν ἔειπεν·

When prudent Penelope heard then that he was smitten in the hall, she spoke among maidservants.

These passages go beyond carelessness into incoherence. The last we have heard of Penelope is in 101 ff., where she tells Telemachus that she is going to her upper room (101), but says also that he has not told her his news: Telemachus then does this (108 ff.), Theoklymenos adds to it (151 ff.), Penelope answers (162-65), and the scene ends with ὡς οἱ μὲν τοιαῦτα ... ἀγόρευον ('such things they spoke to each other') (166). Then Antinoos hits Odysseus with the stool, and Penelope του ... ἤκουσε ('heard him') (492-93). Where is Penelope?

If (1) we translate ἤκουσε as 'heard him being hit' (as Russo says, 'she actually heard the sound and accompanying shouting'), we already have problems. She might indeed have heard enough to interpret what had happened: not just the noise of the stool hitting Odysseus, but the remarks made by various parties (particularly 483: οὐ μὲν κάλ᾽ ἔβαλες ... ἀλήτην ('wrongly did you smite the wanderer'), and Odysseus' own account in 473 ff., both of which actually say what has happened). But the use of ἤκουσε implies that she did not actually see what had happened; and then it is odd for her to address Antinoos as if he were present (σε in 494), 494 might be taken as a brief and bitter soliloquy, but as spoken in the company of her maid servants (μετ᾽ ἄρα δμῳῇσιν, 493) it is incoherent. Then if (2) we take ἤκουσε in the sense of 'got to know' (someone had told her) Penelope seems to be located even more remotely (out of earshot), and the direct address to Antinoos is even more odd.

There is in any case a contradiction between 506 (ἡμένη ἐν θαλάμῳ ('sitting in her chamber')) and Penelope's knowledge of just where Odysseus was hit (πρυμνὸν ... δεξιὸν ὦμον ('at the base of his right shoulder'), 504) and of what he looks like (πολυπλάγκτῳ ἔοικε ('he looks like a man who has wandered far'), 511); and it is not plausible to say that she is just repeating information given to her by someone else. Eumaios' remark in 513 ff. (in effect "I wish the Achaians would shut up, so that the beggar could tell you his story") suggests that Penelope is present amid the noise of the hall. Then further Penelope says that Eumaios should call the beggar to her, and the suitors can go and eat elsewhere (529-31), with the same implication: and, more conclusively, she must be present when Telemachus sneezes (541 ff.). Her being able to talk to Eumaios and hear Telemachus implies *prima facie* that she is in the same room, along with the suitors. But notwithstanding this she has perhaps to summon Eumaios (καλέσασα ('calling'), 507), some stress is laid on Eumaios having to go (some distance) to Odysseus, and we may even think that ὑπὲρ οὐδοῦ ('across the threshold') in 575 implies that he crosses some threshold into another room (where Penelope is).

Russo says that "the most plausible picture remains ... that she is here sitting in a ground-floor θάλαμος ('chamber') close enough to the μέγαρον ('hall') to hear and see what is happening". That is consistent with much of the text, but not with ἤκουσε in 492 or σε in 494. The former implies that she does not see what is happening, and the latter that she is near enough to the event for her to address Antinoos in the second person. To say with Russo that "we should not press the narrative too closely for verisimilitude and a strict consistency of architectural detail" does not help (it is not consistency of architectural detail that is at stake). The fact is that the poet is working with two radically inconsistent pictures.

18. 215-25

" Τηλέμαχ᾽, οὐκέτι τοι φρένες ἔμπεδοι οὐδὲ νόημα·
παῖς ἔτ᾽ ἐὼν καὶ μᾶλλον ἐνὶ φρεσὶ κέρδε᾽ ἐνώμας·
νῦν δ᾽ ὅτε δὴ μέγας ἐσσὶ καὶ ἥβης μέτρον ἱκάνεις,
καί κέν τις φαίη γόνον ἔμμεναι ὀλβίου ἀνδρός,
ἐς μέγεθος καὶ κάλλος ὁρώμενος, ἀλλότριος φώς.
οὐκέτι τοι φρένες εἰσὶν ἐναίσιμοι οὐδὲ νόημα,
οἷον δὴ τόδε ἔργον ἐνὶ μεγάροισιν ἐτύχθη,
ὃς τὸν ξεῖνον ἔασας ἀεικισθήμεναι οὕτως.

> πῶς νῦν, εἴ τι ξεῖνος ἐν ἡμετέροισι δόμοισιν
> ἥμενος ὧδε πάθοι ῥυστακτύος ἐξ ἀλεγεινῆς;
> σοί κ' αἶσχος λώβη τε μετ' ἀνθρώποισι πέλοιτο."

"Telemachus, your mind and intelligence are no longer firm. When you were yet a child you had more knowledge in your mind than this. But now indeed you are grown up and have reached the measure of manhood, and some other man would say that you were the son of a wealthy man, as he looked at your size and beauty. Your mind is no longer sensible, nor your thinking - such a deed has been done indeed in the hall: you who have allowed the guest to be ill-treated in this way. What now, if the guest sitting thus in our house were to suffer by being dragged around painfully? That would be a shame and disgrace to you amongst men."

I print (as usual) the OCT; but the full stop after 219 produces incoherence. "Telemachus, your wits and your thinking are no longer steady - you were more wise when you were a child. But now you're grown up, any stranger would say that you were the son of a man of substance": there is no logical connection. With a comma after 219 we can make sense at least up to the end of 220: "...But now you're grown up and (καί, 218) any stranger would say you were the son of a man of substance, your wits and thinking are no longer reasonable". But we cannot have a full stop after 220 either, because we have to keep the sentence going in order to make sense of 222, where the ὅς ('who') only construes if referred to τοι ('you') in 220: "...you have no longer reason in your wits and thoughts - for such a deed has been done in our house -, you who have allowed the stranger to be thus ill-treated".

That is still awkward, if not incoherent. But 223-25 are worse. The difficulty is to determine what exactly it is that Penelope is frightened that the stranger might suffer. Merry says that 'by πάθοι τι she means 'be killed'.... by way of euphemism', but that is unconvincing: there is no reason to think that being dragged painfully from the hall would result in death (it does not for the maid-servants who are dragged about in 16.109). Is it just the painful dragging itself that she fears? But what she actually says is 'suffer something (πάθοι τι) from a painful dragging. Can this mean simply 'suffer as a result of a painful dragging', in effect just 'suffer a painful dragging'? I doubt it, but it is perhaps the best we can do. (The ὧδε ('thus') in 224 would present a further problem if taken with πάθοι, though that might be taken as 'suffer in the same sort of way', i.e. just another case of being maltreated (ἀεικισθήμεναι). But it could be taken with ἥμενος ('sitting').)

18. 233-34

> οὐ μέν τοι ξείνου γε καὶ Ἴρου μῶλος ἐτύχθη
> μνηστήρων ἰότητι, βίῃ δ' ὅ γε φέρτερος ἦεν.

The combat between the stranger and Iros was not devised by the will of the suitors; but the stranger was the stronger.

All commentators translate ἐτύχθη ('was made') by reference to the <u>result</u> of the fight (Russo says, 'the fight did not turn out according to the will (or wish) of the suitors'); though they acknowledge that the suitors were in fact neutral, and ἐτύχθη normally means 'was made' rather than 'resulted in'.

The attraction of this interpretation is of course that it makes sense of μνηστήρων ἰότητι ('by the will of the suitors'): it did not turn out the way the suitors wanted, because Odysseus was the stronger. But my suspicion is that the passage means simply 'The fight between the stranger and Iros did not come about by the will of the suitors" (Telemachus at least gave it his blessing, 60-65): there is then some kind of elliptic thought, perhaps "It was Iros' aggravation in the first place" or 'The two just fell out with each other": and then he says that Odysseus proved the stronger. That admits the text to be incoherent because of the ellipsis, but I think it preferable to the orthodox interpretation.

18. 307-11, 317-19, 343-44

> αὐτίκα λαμπτῆρας τρεῖς ἵστασαν ἐν μεγάροισιν,
> ὄφρα φαείνοιεν· περὶ δὲ ξύλα κάγκανα θῆκαν,
> αὖα πάλαι, περίκηλα, νέον κεκεασμένα χαλκῷ,
> καὶ δαΐδας μετέμισγον· ἀμοιβηδὶς δ' ἀνέφαινον
> δμῳαὶ Ὀδυσσῆος ταλασίφρονος·
>
> αὐτὰρ ἐγὼ τούτοισι φάος πάντεσσι παρέξω.
> ἤν περ γάρ κ' ἐθέλωσιν ἐΰθρονον Ἠῶ μίμνειν,
> οὔ τί με νικήσουσι· πολυτλήμων δὲ μάλ' εἰμί.
>
> αὐτὰρ ὁ πὰρ λαμπτῆρσι φαείνων αἰθομένοισιν
> ἑστήκειν ἐς πάντας ὁρώμενος·

Straightaway they set up three lamps in the hall, so that they might give light; and around them they placed dry wood, long since withered, well-seasoned, recently cleft with the bronze; and they mixed torches with it. And in turns the maidservants of enduring Odysseus gave light... "And I will provide light for all these: even if they wish to go on till the lovely-throned Dawn, they will not overcome me: for I am very enduring"...then giving light by the burning braziers he stood looking at them all.

Most commentators take there to be only one kind of light-giving apparatus here, the λαμπτηρας ('lamps') (307). They then have problems about ξύλα ('wood'), which they take to be 'kindling, denoting small strips of wood coated with resin' (Russo), 'slips of pinewood' (Merry): these they think to be in the braziers, mixed in with the wood of 308-09.

But the trouble with this interpretation (apart from the odd sense of ξύλα) is that it goes against much else in the passage as a whole. The maid-servants ἀμοιβηδὶς ἀνέφαινον (310), which must mean 'took it in turns to produce the light'; but feeding three braziers would not require the energies of a number of maid-servants. Clearly 'producing the light' is an onerous task: Odysseus boasts that he can do it right up to dawn, because he is πολυτλήμων ('enduring') (318-19). And what Odysseus actually does is to 'produce the light' <u>by</u> (παρ) the burning braziers whilst <u>standing up</u> (ἑστήκειν) (343-44).

The implication is surely that, though the braziers produced both light and heat (φόος ἔμεν ἠδὲ θέρεσθαι ('to give light and to provide warmth') 19.64), there were also torches which had to be held upright by a standing person - certainly an onerous task. But this too runs into something like incoherence, in the original description of 308-10. it is odd that the wood is put round (περι) and not in the braziers; but the real difficulty is with δαίδας μετέμισγον "They mixed in torches" can hardly mean just "They used some torches as well". There is certainly some incoherence here.

19. 186-89, 199-201

καὶ γὰρ τὸν Κρήτηνδε κατήγαγεν ἲς ἀνέμοιο,
ἱέμενον Τροίηνδε παραπλάγξασα Μαλειῶν·
στῆσε δ' ἐν Ἀμνισῷ, ὅθι τε σπέος Εἰλειθυίης,
ἐν λιμέσιν χαλεποῖσι, μόγις δ' ὑπάλυξεν ἀέλλας.

ἔνθα δυώδεκα μὲν μένον ἤματα δῖοι Ἀχαιοί·
εἴλει γὰρ Βορέης ἄνεμος μέγας οὐδ' ἐπὶ γαίη
εἴα ἵστασθαι, χαλεπὸς δέ τις ὦρορε δαίμων·

For indeed the force of the wind bore him off to Crete, beating him off past Cape Maleia as he desired to reach Troy. He stopped at Amnisos, where is the cave of Eileithuie, in a difficult harbour, and only just escaped the storms...there the godlike Achaeans stayed for twelve days; for the great gale of the north wind did not allow them to stand up on land - some evil spirit had roused it.

This is in one way the most baffling incoherence I have come across. Not only does one meet εἴα ἵστασθαι ('allowed to stand') (200) with blank incomprehension, but also it is very hard to think of any way in which the incoherence could have arisen.

Odysseus' fleet is making for Troy, and is beaten off from Cape Malea (187). παραπλάγξασα Μαλειῶν ('beaten away from Cape Maleia'), as in the (rather different) case of Agamemnon's voyage (4.514 ff.), requires some sympathetic interpretation: it must mean that the fleet was beaten off by the north wind (Boreas, 200) from actually rounding Maleia and setting a natural course to the north-east for Troy: the wind forced it on a more southerly course in Crete. That is all in good order. Odysseus 'stops', i.e. anchors, the fleet ἐν Ἀμνισῷ. Whether this means 'at the town Amnisos' or 'in the river Amnisos' does not for our purposes much matter: in either case they are anchored in a harbour, ἐν λιμέσι (189), and Odysseus and is crew are entertained on land (clear from 185 and from 190 ff.). But now the poet says that the north wind 'penned them in' and 'did not allow them to stay (anchored) on land'; then the wind drops and they put to sea (202). What can this possibly mean?

I can think of no plausible answer to this. Nor can I think of any plausible emendation. Two lesser MSS read γαίης ('land'); one might try reading ἀπό ('from') for ἐπί ('on'), but even then ἵστασθαι can hardly have the required (natural) meaning ('set sail', 'start their voyage'). I suppose it might just mean 'stand off from the land', i.e. put to sea; but even that is not very convincing. One or two editors take ἵστασθαι literally, 'to stand upright': thus Monro "...did not allow them even to stand up on land - much less to put to sea". But (1) the 'even' is not in the text: it must mean "...penned them in and did not allow them...": (2) 'penned them in', on this interpretation, does not make much sense (whereas the idea of penning the fleet in makes good sense): (3) the picture of a strong wind making it impossible for people to stand upright is unparalleled in Homer (despite the frequent mention of very strong winds): and (4) given Greek winds, the picture is implausible in itself. Translators do no better (e.g. Butcher and Lang, who render ἐπὶ γαίῃ ἵστασθαι as 'to stay on that coast', which leaves the incoherence untouched).

The origin of the incoherence is also baffling. I suppose the poet might have had a picture in mind (or a formula to hand), whereby a fleet at sea is shut off (if εἴλει can bear this sense) from a land anchorage: the wind 'shut them off and did not allow them to anchor on land'. But that is, of course, still incoherent in the context.

19. 325-34

πῶς γὰρ ἐμεῦ σύ, ξεῖνε, δαήσεαι εἴ τι γυναικῶν
ἀλλάων περίειμι νόον καὶ ἐπίφρονα μῆτιν,
εἴ κεν ἀϋσταλέος κακὰ εἱμένος ἐν μεγάροισι
δαινύῃ; ἄνθρωποι δὲ μινυνθάδιοι τελέθουσιν.
ὃς μὲν ἀπηνὴς αὐτὸς ἔῃ καὶ ἀπηνέα εἰδῇ,
τῷ δὲ καταρῶνται πάντες βροτοὶ ἄλγε' ὀπίσσω
ζωῷ, ἀτὰρ τεθνεῶτί γ' ἐφεψιόωνται ἅπαντες·
ὃς δ' ἂν ἀμύμων αὐτὸς ἔῃ καὶ ἀμύμονα εἰδῇ,
τοῦ μέν τε κλέος εὐρὺ διὰ ξεῖνοι φορέουσι
πάντας ἐπ' ἀνθρώπους, πολλοί τέ μιν ἐσθλὸν ἔειπον."

For how will you learn of me, stranger, if I surpass other women in my intelligence and prudent counsel, if you take your food being all unkempt and with foul clothes in the hall? Men do not live very long. Whoever is himself harsh and thinks harsh thoughts, on him do all men call down curses to give him pain for the future, whilst he is alive: and when he is dead, they all scoff at him. But whosoever is himself blameless and thinks blameless thoughts, strangers carry his fame widely throughout all men, and many men call him good.

In many ways a strange passage (e.g. the sense of ἀμύμων ('blameless') in 332: see Russo). The *sententiae* of 329 ff. are unexceptional, though they do not quite fit the ἐπίφρονα μῆτιν ('prudent counsel') of 326 or Penelope's particular position, and the introduction of ὃς μεν... ('he who on the one hand') is syntactically harsh. But 325-28 are distinctly odd. "How will you learn, stranger, whether I am superior to other women in intelligence and wise counsel, if you dine in the hall unrefreshed and with foul clothes?" Odysseus is going to dine in the hall in any case, and will have the opportunity to judge of Penelope's virtues. So it must mean not so much "How will you be able to learn/judge whether ... ?" but rather "How will you come to appreciate that ... ?": That is, he will not be able to think Penelope to be virtuous if she lets him dine unrefreshed and with foul clothes, since no generous hostess would do such a thing. This is clumsily expressed: certainly on the borderline of incoherence.

19. 536-53

χῆνές μοι κατὰ οἶκον ἐείκοσι πυρὸν ἔδουσιν
ἐξ ὕδατος, καί τέ σφιν ἰαίνομαι εἰσορόωσα·
ἐλθὼν δ' ἐξ ὄρεος μέγας αἰετὸς ἀγκυλοχείλης
πᾶσι κατ' αὐχέν' ἔαξε καὶ ἔκτανεν· οἱ δ' ἐκέχυντο
ἀθρόοι ἐν μεγάροις, ὁ δ' ἐς αἰθέρα δῖαν ἀέρθη.
αὐτὰρ ἐγὼ κλαῖον καὶ ἐκώκυον ἔν περ ὀνείρῳ,
ἀμφὶ δ' ἔμ' ἠγερέθοντο ἐϋπλοκαμῖδες Ἀχαιαί,
οἴκτρ' ὀλοφυρομένην ὅ μοι αἰετὸς ἔκτανε χῆνας.

ἂψ δ' ἐλθὼν κατ' ἄρ' ἕζετ' ἐπὶ προὔχοντι μελάθρῳ,
φωνῇ δὲ βροτέῃ κατερήτυε φώνησέν τε·
' θάρσει, Ἰκαρίου κούρη τηλεκλειτοῖο·
οὐκ ὄναρ, ἀλλ' ὕπαρ ἐσθλόν, ὅ τοι τετελεσμένον ἔσται.
χῆνες μὲν μνηστῆρες, ἐγὼ δέ τοι αἰετὸς ὄρνις
ἦα πάρος, νῦν αὖτε τεὸς πόσις εἰλήλουθα,
ὃς πᾶσι μνηστῆρσιν ἀεικέα πότμον ἐφήσω.'
ὣς ἔφατ', αὐτὰρ ἐμὲ μελιηδὴς ὕπνος ἀνῆκε·
παπτήνασα δὲ χῆνας ἐνὶ μεγάροισι νόησα
πυρὸν ἐρεπτομένους παρὰ πύελον, ἧχι πάρος περ."

I saw twenty geese eating corn in the house from the water-trough, and my spirit was warmed as I saw them. Then coming down from the mountain a great crooked-beaked eagle broke all their necks and killed them; and they were strewn in a heap in the hall, and the eagle flew up into the divine air. Then I wept and wailed even in my dream, and around me were gathered the fair-haired women of Achaea, as I lamented piteously because the eagle had killed my geese. Returning, the eagle sat on a projecting beam, and speaking with human voice it detained me and said: "Be of good cheer, daughter of far-famed Icarius. This is not a dream, but a true vision, a good one, which shall be accomplished for you. The geese are the suitors: I was before an eagle, but now am your own husband who has come to you, who will fasten an evil fate on the suitors". So it spoke, and then sweet sleep left me; and looking around I saw geese in the hall eating corn at the trough, as before.

Yet another strange passage, particularly surprising when the creature says "I was previously an eagle, but I am now your husband who has come" (549). So far as any logical incoherence is at stake, there are two difficulties: (1) Just where are the geese? 536-37 are somewhat odd in themselves. Russo says: "ἐξ ὕδατος ('from the water'): construe either with πυρον ('corn'), as if the grain was in the trough (the πύελον of 553), or in a general sense with χηνες ('geese') describing their location, 'away from (out of) the water', as seen in ἐκ καπνου κατέθηκα ('I put away out of the smoke'), xix.7..." But the former is unconvincing: it is hard to believe that there is a water-trough which they throw grain into for the geese to eat (nobody does this with geese, that I know of), and harder still to believe that this happens indoors (κατα οἰκον, 536). And the latter is at least harsh: Russo's parallel is not a true one, since ἐκ καπνου depends on κατέθηκα in a way that ἐξ ὕδατος does not, on this view, depend on ἐδουσι ('they eat'). Perhaps ἐξ ὕδατος just means something like 'coming from the pond', or whatever water the geese came from (outside the house). However, this is perhaps elliptic or otherwise mysterious rather than positively incoherent.

But there is a more general problem with the picture. If the geese are inside the house in the sense of being actually under some roof (and this is suggested by ἐν μεγάροις ('in the hall') in 540 and ἐνι μεγάροισι in 552) we should naturally expect something about the eagle coming into the hall in order to kill them, and then coming back into the hall (ἀψ ἐλθων ('coming back'), 544) to speak to Penelope: eagles do not usually come into houses. If on the other hand the scene takes place outside the house, then perhaps we may take κατα οἰκον ('in the house') and even the two mentions of μεγάροις to refer to the palace buildings in general, including the outer (unroofed) courtyard. That is a more plausible location for geese and troughs; but then Penelope wakes up and sees the geese (νόησα ('I saw'), 552) at the trough, presumably from her bedroom, which is slightly odd; and anyway this interpretation goes against the natural meaning of οἰκος or at least of the repeated μεγάροις. (The eagle's perch ἐπι προυχοντι μελάθρῳ 'on a projecting beam') (544) is neutral as between these, since the beam may project either inside or outside the house.) The difficulties here cannot be entirely dissipated by the fact that Penelope (at least up to 552) is dreaming, and may hence be imagined to view the scene from any point of vantage.

(2) What does οὐκ ὄναρ ἀλλ' ὕπαρ mean (547)? Russo says "ὄναρ is a dream, ὕπαρ, as the scholiasts say, 'a dream that appears in the daytime'". That will not do, for two reasons. First, it does not square with 20.90, where Penelope's dream is a night-time dream (νύκτας ('nights')) and secondly, the contrast is clearly between a deceptive vision and a true vision, a vision to be τετελεσμένον ('accomplished') (Though that does not solve the difficulties in 20.85-90: see note on that passage.) The problem is that Penelope's vision is in fact an ὄναρ or an ὄνειρος ('a dream') (we have no reason for distinguishing the sense of these two words), and she knows, as we do, that there are false and true dreams, as she indeed explains in 560 ff. The eagle must of course mean that it is not a false dream; but that is not what the eagle actually says.

19. 572 ff. 21. 420 ff. and elsewhere

νῦν γὰρ καταθήσω ἄεθλον,
τοὺς πελέκεας, τοὺς κεῖνος ἐνὶ μεγάροισιν ἑοῖσιν
ἵστασχ' ἑξείης, δρυόχους ὥς, δώδεκα πάντας·

αὐτόθεν ἐκ δίφροιο καθήμενος, ἧκε δ' ὀϊστὸν
ἄντα τιτυσκόμενος, πελέκεων δ' οὐκ ἤμβροτε πάντων
πρώτης στειλειῆς, διὰ δ' ἀμπερὲς ἦλθε θύραζε

"For now I will set up a contest - the axes, which that man used to stand up in a row in his hall, like woodcutters' axes, twelve in all..." Then from his stool where he sat he aimed directly and sent an arrow, and it did not miss any of the axes from the first handle onwards, but went right through them and away.

Problems about the bow and the axes are of course notorious (see Fernandez-Galiano, for a very full account). But while there is much difficulty in establishing an empirically plausible picture of what occurs, there is (I think) only one point at which there crops up any question of logical incoherence in the text. Briefly, the axes (of, whatever kind they are) are set up (probably in the hall or οἰκος ('house') itself, but it makes no matter) (21.120 ff.): Odysseus with his great strength strings the bow easily (405 ff.), and then shoots through the axes (420 ff.).

The difficulty is with 421-22. This must mean, in general, 'He did not miss any of the axes" (since the "bronze-tipped arrow went right through them all and out at the other end"). But, *pace* implausible theories that have Odysseus' arrow actually breaking through some part of the axes, Odysseus did not actually hit or strike anything substantial: the arrow went through some kind of open space in the axes. (Nor could it have grazed or touched parts of them, as some commentators think, which would have altered the arrow's direction.) πρώτης στειλειῆς ('first handle') must depend in some way on οὐκ ἤμβροτε ('he did not miss'), it is something that the arrow did not miss. So the natural translation must be of the form "He did not miss the πρώτης στειλείης of all the axes". But now, to make sense, the στειλείη must be some kind of space or hole. That goes against what we know of the word, which almost certainly means 'handle'. Worse, to make the best sense of πρώτης, ('first') we should have to translate 'the first hole', as if each axe had more than one hole.

It may just be possible to save this if we translate 'He did not miss any of the axes, right from the first στειλείη onwards - the bronze-tipped arrow went right through them all". That is odd Greek, even for Homer. But we would then be able either (a) to take στειλείη as a technical term (otherwise unknown) meaning some kind of hole or space in the axes: or (b) to keep something of the known meaning of στειλείη handle', and take it to be used here as 'part for whole': 'right from the first axe-handle onwards' - i.e. in effect 'right from the first axe onwards'. That is the best I can do; but I think the poet either had no coherent picture in mind at all, or that he did not bother to produce it in the text.

20. 87-90

αὐτὰρ ἐμοὶ καὶ ὀνείρατ' ἐπέσσευεν κακὰ δαίμων.
τῇδε γὰρ αὖ μοι νυκτὶ παρέδραθεν εἴκελος αὐτῷ,
τοῖος ἐὼν οἷος ἦεν ἅμα στρατῷ· αὐτὰρ ἐμὸν κῆρ
χαῖρ', ἐπεὶ οὐκ ἐφάμην ὄναρ ἔμμεναι, ἀλλ' ὕπαρ ἤδη."

"But the god laid bad dreams on me; for on that night he slept beside me looking like himself, just such as he was in the army. And my heart rejoiced, because I did not think it a dream only, but really a true vision".

Some logical tolerance is required here. Penelope says that the god laid bad dreams upon her (87), yet her heart rejoiced at her dream (90): it was, then, only a bad dream inasmuch as it was deceptive: she thought it was a ὕπαρ and not an ὄναρ. But what do ὄναρ and ὕπαρ mean here? Where these words are used in 19.547 (see note), the contrast must be between a deceptive or misleading dream and a dream that will come true: the eagle tells her, whilst she is dreaming, that the dream will come true, it is a ὕπαρ and not an ὄναρ. If we apply this to the present passage, however, there is a problem. Suppose we think (1) that Penelope, whilst still asleep, thought (ἐφάμην) that Odysseus' being with her was not a dream but an actual reality - and ὕπαρ might be thought to suggest this - then that makes sense, and it is unsurprising that she rejoiced: but then ὕπαρ must have a different meaning from 19.547: it now refers not to a dream at all, and does not square with 87. Then if we think (2) that Penelope believed (either whilst asleep or awake) that it was indeed a dream, but a dream that would come true (rather than a deceptive dream), this will preserve the senses of ὕπαρ and ὄναρ; but then why should she see this as a case of the god sending her a bad dream? She rejoices at it because she takes it to be a dream that will come true: and what has happened to make her change her mind?

I suppose we could say that she believed, in her sleep, that it was a dream or vision that would come true, hence rejoiced at it (still in her sleep), but that when she awoke she reverted to her general pessimism about Odysseus ever returning, hence saw it as a bad and deceptive dream. But that is not in the text, and I suspect the poet had not thought the logic out properly.

20. 92-96

τῆς δ' ἄρα κλαιούσης ὄπα σύνθετο δῖος Ὀδυσσεύς·
μερμήριζε δ' ἔπειτα, δόκησε δέ οἱ κατὰ θυμὸν
ἤδη γιγνώσκουσα παρεστάμεναι κεφαλῆφι.
χλαῖναν μὲν συνελὼν καὶ κώεα, τοῖσιν ἐνεῦδεν,
ἐς μέγαρον κατέθηκεν ἐπὶ θρόνου,

Godlike Odysseus recognised her voice as she wept; and then he pondered, and it seemed to him in his spirit that she already recognised him and stood by his head. Taking the cloak and the blankets in which he slept, he went to the hall and put them on a stool.

A highly compressed and strange passage, if not positively incoherent. We can assume readily enough (though the text does not say this) that Odysseus is only half awake, and imagines Penelope to have recognised him and to be standing over him. But then why does he take up his bedding and move? If he is still asleep, we should expect some words from him to the (imaginary) Penelope: if he is now awake, some reason for the move. The poet leaves us quite in the air about Odysseus' intentions. To say with Merry 'that he was fain to hasten to some place where the voice could not be heard' does not help.

20. 97-101

θῆκε θύραζε φέρων, Διὶ δ' εὔξατο χεῖρας ἀνασχών·
" Ζεῦ πάτερ, εἴ μ' ἐθέλοντες ἐπὶ τραφερήν τε καὶ ὑγρὴν
ἤγετ' ἐμὴν ἐς γαῖαν, ἐπεί μ' ἐκακώσατε λίην,
φήμην τίς μοι φάσθω ἐγειρομένων ἀνθρώπων
ἔνδοθεν, ἐκτοσθεν δὲ Διὸς τέρας ἄλλο φανήτω."

He carried it out of doors, and prayed to Zeus, holding up his hands: "Father Zeus, if by your will have brought me to my own land across much land and sea - since you have made me suffer much -, then let some word be spoken as a sign from thise men who are awake within, and outside may some other portent of Zeus be shown".

The incoherence here does not so much lie in the plurals themselves (when Odysseus is supposed to be addressing a singular Zeus): we may readily understand 'if you (gods) have...'. It lies rather in the fact that he starts by addressing Zeus in the second person but ends by referring to him in the third person (Διος, 101), so that it is not clear whether he is really addressing Zeus or the gods in general.

20. 104 and 114 ff.

αὐτίκα δ' ἐβρόντησεν ἀπ' αἰγλήεντος Ὀλύμπου,
ὑψόθεν ἐκ νεφέων·

" Ζεῦ πάτερ, ὅς τε θεοῖσι καὶ ἀνθρώποισιν ἀνάσσεις
ἦ μεγάλ' ἐβρόντησας ἀπ' οὐρανοῦ ἀστερόεντος,
οὐδέ ποθι νέφος ἐστί·

Straightaway he thundered from shining Olympus, from high up in the clouds...
"Father Zeus, who rules over gods and men, indeed you have thundered from the starry sky - and there is no cloud at all."

Commentators have seized on this avidly enough, but it is at worst a case of carelessness. It might anyway be argued that the clouds in 104 were not visible, or that the woman grinding meal did not see them.

20. 241-46

μνηστῆρες δ' ἄρα Τηλεμάχῳ θάνατόν τε μόρον τε
ἤρτυον· αὐτὰρ ὁ τοῖσιν ἀριστερὸς ἤλυθεν ὄρνις,
αἰετὸς ὑψιπέτης, ἔχε δὲ τρήρωνα πέλειαν.
τοῖσιν δ' Ἀμφίνομος ἀγορήσατο καὶ μετέειπεν·
" ὦ φίλοι, οὐχ ἡμῖν συνθεύσεται ἥδε γε βουλή,
Τηλεμάχοιο φόνος· ἀλλὰ μνησώμεθα δαιτός."

The suitors were preparing death and fate for Telemachus. Then a bird came to them on the left hand, a high-flying eagle, and it held a timid dove. Amphinomos spoke and addressed them: "O friends, this plan will not go well for us - I mean, to murder Telemachus: let us rather think of feasting".

This is again compressed to the point of incoherence. The nature or force of the omen is quite unexplained. *Prima facie* it is either neutral, or else might be taken as encouraging (Telemachus being the defenceless dove). Perhaps the fact that it appears on the left (ἀριστερός, 242) rather than the right makes it a bad omen, discouraging to any intended enterprise.

20. 361-62

ἀλλά μιν αἶψα, νέοι, δόμου ἐκπέμψασθε θύραζε
εἰς ἀγορὴν ἔρχεσθαι, ἐπεὶ τάδε νυκτὶ ἐΐσκει."

But quickly, young men, we'll send him out of doors, to go off to the market-place, since it is like night here.

ἐς ἀγορὴν ('to the market-place' or 'place of assembly') is strange: why should he be escorted there in particular? Something more must be meant than that Theoklymenos should simply go out of the house into the light, and go with an escort (which he says he has no need of, 364). Perhaps the idea (ironically) is that he should be taken εἰς ἀγορὴν in the hope that someone there would help him recover his senses. But the passage is again too compressed for the sense to be clear. A borderline case.

21. 152-62

πολλοὺς γὰρ τόδε τόξον ἀριστῆας κεκαδήσει
θυμοῦ καὶ ψυχῆς, ἐπεὶ ἦ πολὺ φέρτερόν ἐστι
τεθνάμεν ἢ ζώοντας ἁμαρτεῖν, οὗ θ' ἕνεκ' αἰεὶ
ἐνθάδ' ὁμιλέομεν, ποτιδέγμενοι ἤματα πάντα.
νῦν μέν τις καὶ ἔλπετ' ἐνὶ φρεσὶν ἠδὲ μενοινᾷ
γῆμαι Πηνελόπειαν, Ὀδυσσῆος παράκοιτιν.
αὐτὰρ ἐπὴν τόξου πειρήσεται ἠδὲ ἴδηται,
ἄλλην δή τιν' ἔπειτα Ἀχαιϊάδων εὐπέπλων
μνάσθω ἐέδνοισιν διζήμενος· ἡ δέ κ' ἔπειτα
γήμαιθ' ὅς κε πλεῖστα πόροι καὶ μόρσιμος ἔλθοι."

For this bow will give trouble to many noble men in respect of their spirit and life; since it is much better to die than to live and sin - just as now we always gather here and wait for all our days. For now someone may even hope and desire in his heart to marry Penelope, Odysseus' wife; but when he tries the bow and sees it, then let him woo some other of the fair-robed Achaean women and seek her out with gifts; and Penelope can then marry whoever gives her the most and comes as her destined husband".

Fernandez-Galiano says that Leodes' words 'are coherent up to xxi.159', and that at 160 'there is evidently some contamination'. The opposite seems to me true. 159 ff. translate "But when he actually tries the bow and looks at it, then let him seek out with gifts and wed some other of the well-robed Achaian women - and then let Penelope marry whoever gives her the most, and comes as her destined husband". That is, when all the suitors fail the test of the bow, the test will become null and void: the situation will revert to normal, with Penelope marrying whoever she marries by a different criterion of selection. (The criterion is repeated from 16.391-92.) It is rather 153-56 that are odd: what does Leodes mean by κεκαδήσει ... ψυχῆς ('give trouble' ... 'life')?

Prima facie this looks as if it meant 'will give them trouble in respect of their spirit and life': that is, perhaps, will cause them shame and a great expense of moral effort. But that (in itself rather odd) does not square with τεθνάμεν ('die') in 154. He must rather mean 'will rob them of spirit and life', or at least (keeping closer to κεκαδήσει) 'will give them trouble about' (or 'will put at risk') their spirit and life'. Merry says., "he probably means that many a one will 'break his heart' over it, in fruitless efforts to string it; or even might fairly make away with himself in mortification at his failure"; but that is not convincing. The suitors may be mortified and 'break their hearts', but τεθνάμεν is stronger than that idea: and the suitors are not the sort of people actually to commit suicide over the test. Nor does the fact that the words represent an unconscious prophecy (Odysseus will in fact kill them) help to make the words in themselves coherent.

It is tempting to make the prophecy conscious, particularly since Leodes was a θυοσκόος (diviner') (145); but the context hardly justifies this. We are told (146-47) that

ἀτασθαλίαι δέ οἱ οἴῳ
ἐχθραὶ ἔσαν, πᾶσιν δὲ νεμέσσα μνηστήρεσσιν·

To him alone were their follies hateful, and he was indignant about all the suitors.

and whatever that means exactly (it seems to mean that he was foolishly hostile to the other suitors or had some personal grudge against them): it certainly does not imply that he is prophesying for their benefit. Indeed this brief character-sketch hardly squares with the noble (if over-dramatic) idea that it is better to die than to fail in their attempts at wooing. I suspect the poet just wished to bring in the idea of the suitors' death without bothering about whether that idea, as expressed by Leodes, made any sense.

22. 208-10, 233-40

" Μέντορ, ἄμυνον ἀρήν, μνῆσαι δ' ἑτάροιο φίλοιο,
ὅς σ' ἀγαθὰ ῥέζεσκον· ὁμηλικίη δέ μοί ἐσσι."
Ὣς φάτ', ὀιόμενος λαοσσόον ἔμμεν' Ἀθήνην.

ἀλλ' ἄγε δεῦρο, πέπον, παρ' ἔμ' ἵστασο καὶ ἴδε ἔργον,
ὄφρ' εἰδῇς οἷός τοι ἐν ἀνδράσι δυσμενέεσσι
Μέντωρ Ἀλκιμίδης εὐεργεσίας ἀποτίνειν."
Ἦ ῥα, καὶ οὔ πω πάγχυ δίδου ἑτεραλκέα νίκην,
ἀλλ' ἔτ' ἄρα σθένεός τε καὶ ἀλκῆς πειρήτιζεν
ἠμὲν Ὀδυσσῆος ἠδ' υἱοῦ κυδαλίμοιο.
αὐτὴ δ' αἰθαλόεντος ἀνὰ μεγάροιο μέλαθρον
ἕζετ' ἀναΐξασα, χελιδόνι εἰκέλη ἄντην.

"Mentor, defend me in this fight, and remember your dear comrade, who has done good to you: and you are the same age as me". So he spoke, thinking that it was Athene who saves the army...
"But come hither, my dear friend, stand by me and observe my deeds, so that you may know what sort of man Mentor the son of Alkimos is amongst foemen to repay kindness". He spoke and not yet did she altogether give him a victorywon by another's strength, but still tested out the strength and valour both of Odysseus and of his glorious son. She herself darted up and sat on a beam of the blazing hall, looking like a swallow.

The text appears to get increasingly casual about Athene's appearances towards the end of the Odyssey. Because of the lack of realism or verisimilitude, these passages at least border on the incoherent. Why does Odysseus talk to her as if she were really Mentor (mentioning Mentor's age and the benefits he has received from Odysseus in the past, 209) if he thinks that Mentor is really Athene? And why does Athene in 233-35 say that Mentor is going to stand by them and repay these benefits, when in fact Mentor-Athene is going to disappear into the roof like a swallow (239-40)? We have to assume a rather complex convention: (1) that Odysseus knows that Mentor is really Athene, (2) that Athene knows that Odysseus knows this (otherwise he would be baffled and disheartened by a Mentor who, as it were, switched himself on and off), and (3) nevertheless Odysseus was not supposed to admit to this knowledge (perhaps because this might seem to be taking Athene's help too much for granted?). That is possible, but puts a good deal of strain on the reader/hearer.

22. 312, 318-25

" γουνοῦμαί σ', Ὀδυσεῦ· σὺ δέ μ' αἴδεο καί μ' ἐλέησον·

αὐτὰρ ἐγὼ μετὰ τοῖσι θυοσκόος οὐδὲν ἐοργὼς
κείσομαι, ὡς οὐκ ἔστι χάρις μετόπισθ' εὐεργέων."
Τὸν δ' ἄρ' ὑπόδρα ἰδὼν προσέφη πολύμητις Ὀδυσσεύς·
" εἰ μὲν δὴ μετὰ τοῖσι θυοσκόος εὔχεαι εἶναι,
πολλάκι που μέλλεις ἀρήμεναι ἐν μεγάροισι
τηλοῦ ἐμοὶ νόστοιο τέλος γλυκεροῖο γενέσθαι,
σοὶ δ' ἄλοχόν τε φίλην σπέσθαι καὶ τέκνα τεκέσθαι·
τῷ οὐκ ἂν θάνατόν γε δυσηλεγέα προφύγοισθα."

"I beseech you, Odysseus: have respect for me and pity me. I am a diviner amongst these men and have done nothing - shall I lie dead, so that there is no gratitude later for good deeds?" Looking at him askance ingenious Odysseus addressed him: "If indeed you claim to be their diviner, you must often have prayed in the halls that the accomplishment of my sweet return should be far distant, and that you would gain my dear wife and beget children. Therefore you will not escape death which lays men low".

There is a clash between Leodes' speech (particularly its first line, 312) and his awareness of its futility (318-19): what is the point of his asking for mercy if he knows he is not going to get it? That is tolerable; but Odysseus' reply is incoherent. The basic idea must be that, if Leodes has been their θυοσκόος ('diviner'), he must have given the suitors favourable prophecies to the effect that Odysseus would not return (323). That. is already a bit odd, since ἀρήμεναι in 322 means 'pray', not 'prophesy': no doubt Leodes, like the other suitors, did pray for Odysseus' absence -but hardly in his capacity as θυοσκόος. In fact this capacity has been muddled up with Leodes' personal prayer or wish that Penelope should marry him (σοι ('you'), 324). he could hardly have prayed for this outcome in any public capacity in front of the suitors, who of course each wanted Penelope for himself.

22. 465-73

Ὣς ἄρ' ἔφη, καὶ πεῖσμα νεὸς κυανοπρῴροιο
κίονος ἐξάψας μεγάλης περίβαλλε θόλοιο,
ὑψόσ' ἐπεντανύσας, μή τις ποσὶν οὖδας ἵκοιτο.
ὡς δ' ὅτ' ἂν ἢ κίχλαι τανυσίπτεροι ἠὲ πέλειαι
ἕρκει ἐνιπλήξωσι, τό θ' ἕστηκῃ ἐνὶ θάμνῳ,
αὖλιν ἐσιέμεναι, στυγερὸς δ' ὑπεδέξατο κοῖτος,
ὣς αἵ γ' ἑξείης κεφαλὰς ἔχον, ἀμφὶ δὲ πάσαις
δειρῇσι βρόχοι ἦσαν, ὅπως οἴκτιστα θάνοιεν.
ἤσπαιρον δὲ πόδεσσι μίνυνθά περ, οὔ τι μάλα δήν.

So he spoke, and he fastened a rope from a dark-prowed ship to a pillar of the great building, and tied it round, stretching it high up, so that none of them should touch the ground with her feet. And as when long-winged thrushes or doves are crammed into a trap which is set up in a thicket, as they go to roost, and a foul place of rest receives them, so they all iin turn held up their heads, and there were nooses around the necks of all of them, so that they might die most piteously. They kicked with their feet for a little, but not for long.

Nearly all commentators make a fuss about this passage (see Fernandez-Galiano), but there is nothing wrong with it despite some ellipsis in the description. Telemachus strings the rope up very high so that the girls' feet cannot touch the ground (467) when they are hanged from it. Each girl has a rope/noose round her neck (471-72), and they kick with their feet for a little (473). This last detail suggests that they are suffocated, rather than having their necks broken (as with modem hangings, where a trap-door opens beneath the victim, or the support of a chair, horse, etc. is suddenly removed). We assume that the girls were simply lifted off the ground so as to have their heads in nooses suspended from the main rope, and then let go.

23. 177-84

ἀλλ' ἄγε οἱ στόρεσον πυκινὸν λέχος, Εὐρύκλεια,
ἐκτὸς ἐϋσταθέος θαλάμου, τόν ῥ' αὐτὸς ἐποίει·
ἔνθα οἱ ἐκθεῖσαι πυκινὸν λέχος ἐμβάλετ' εὐνήν,
κώεα καὶ χλαίνας καὶ ῥήγεα σιγαλόεντα."

> Ὣς ἄρ' ἔφη πόσιος πειρωμένη· αὐτὰρ Ὀδυσσεὺς
> ὀχθήσας ἄλοχον προσεφώνεε κεδνὰ ἰδυῖαν·
> "ὦ γύναι, ἦ μάλα τοῦτο ἔπος θυμαλγὲς ἔειπες.
> τίς δέ μοι ἄλλοσε θῆκε λέχος;

"But come now Eurykleia, make up the solid bed outside the well-measured chamber, which he himself made. There carry out bedding, and put it on the solid bed - rugs and cloaks and shining blankets." Thus she spoke, testing her husband; and Odysseus was vexed, and spoke to his wife: "Wife, the word you have spoken is painful to my spirit: who has put my bed in another place?"

Commentators are (for once) right about the incoherence here: 179, if not 177-78, implies that the bed is to be moved, whereas 184 (and 204) imply that it has already been. (See Fernandez-Galiano for attempts to remedy this, none at all plausible.) It is additionally odd that Penelope wants to make up her husband's bed outside the bed-chamber at all. Just possibly we might take ἄλλοσε θηκε ('placed elsewhere') more broadly to mean something like 'made it different' (*sc.* in terms of its position), as opposed to ἐτ' ἐμπεδόν (203), or 'made it moveable'; but that is somewhat desperate: it is better to assume a careless incoherence.

23. 215-24

> αἰεὶ γάρ μοι θυμὸς ἐνὶ στήθεσσι φίλοισιν
> ἐρρίγει μή τίς με βροτῶν ἀπάφοιτο ἔπεσσιν
> ἐλθών· πολλοὶ γὰρ κακὰ κέρδεα βουλεύουσιν.
> οὐδέ κεν Ἀργείη Ἑλένη, Διὸς ἐκγεγαυῖα,
> ἀνδρὶ παρ' ἀλλοδαπῷ ἐμίγη φιλότητι καὶ εὐνῇ,
> εἰ ᾔδη ὅ μιν αὖτις ἀρήιοι υἷες Ἀχαιῶν
> ἀξέμεναι οἰκόνδε φίλην ἐς πατρίδ' ἔμελλον.
> τὴν δ' ἦ τοι ῥέξαι θεὸς ὤρορεν ἔργον ἀεικές·
> τὴν δ' ἄτην οὐ πρόσθεν ἑῷ ἐγκάτθετο θυμῷ
> λυγρήν, ἐξ ἧς πρῶτα καὶ ἡμέας ἵκετο πένθος.

For always my spirit in my breast was fearful lest some one of mortals might come and deceive me with words: for many men plan evi, cunning counsels. Nor would Argive Helen, born from Zeus, have made love with a foreign man, if she had known that the warlike sons of the Achaeans were going to bring her home to her native land. The god spurred her on to do a foul deed; nor did she imagine in advance the terrible folly in her heart, the folly from which first this suffering came upon us too.

There is no real problem here, despite the vast majority of commentators (see Fernandez-Galiano: he rightly retains them as coherent, but does not quite bring out the point). The point is simple: Penelope says in effect I did not want to be deceived" (*sc.* because that would have led to trouble): "nor would Helen have been seduced if she had known the trouble that led to".

24. 118-19

> μηνὶ δ' ἄρ' οὔλῳ πάντα περήσαμεν εὐρέα πόντον,
> σπουδῇ παρπεπιθόντες Ὀδυσσῆα πτολίπορθον."

"For a whole month in all we crossed the wide sea, only with difficulty persuading Odysseus the sacker of cities."

118 is certainly incoherent as it stands: it has no plausible sense or syntax. It looks as if the sense should be something like "It took a whole month to persuade him, before we could cross the wide sea", but that would require wholesale emendation.

24. 196-201

> τεύξουσι δ' ἐπιχθονίοισιν ἀοιδὴν
> ἀθάνατοι χαρίεσσαν ἐχέφρονι Πηνελοπείῃ,
> οὐχ ὡς Τυνδαρέου κούρη κακὰ μήσατο ἔργα,
> κουρίδιον κτείνασα πόσιν, στυγερὴ δέ τ' ἀοιδὴ
> ἔσσετ' ἐπ' ἀνθρώπους, χαλεπὴν δέ τε φῆμιν ὀπάσσει
> θηλυτέρῃσι γυναιξί, καὶ ἥ κ' εὐεργὸς ἔῃσιν."

The immortals will fashion a pleasing song for men about the prudent Penelope: not as the daughter of Tyndareus planned evil deeds, killing her wedded husband - and the song about her will go out to men as hateful; and she will give a bad reputation to women, even to one whose deeds are good.

The general sense is clear, though it is a bit odd to say that the immortals (ἀθάνατοι, 198) will make the song: perhaps we are to understand that the Muses will do the job. But Πηνελοπείῃ is hard to construe. Some commentators think that the song is supposed to delight Penelope herself: e.g. Merry '...to bring joy for chaste Penelope', taking the dative to depend on χαρίεσσαν ('pleasing'). But the parallel with Helen's χαλεπην φημιν ('bad repute') (200) suggests rather that the songs will be, as it were, laudatory or pejorative in general. We naturally expect something like 'a pleasing (laudatory) song <u>about</u> chaste Penelope'; but then the dative does not really fit. The immortals are not making the song for Penelope's benefit.

24. 244-49

> "ὦ γέρον, οὐκ ἀδαημονίη σ' ἔχει ἀμφιπολεύειν
> ὄρχατον, ἀλλ' εὖ τοι κομιδὴ ἔχει, οὐδέ τι πάμπαν,
> οὐ φυτόν, οὐ συκέη, οὐκ ἄμπελος, οὐ μὲν ἐλαίη,
> οὐκ ὄγχνη, οὐ πρασιή τοι ἄνευ κομιδῆς κατὰ κῆπον.
> ἄλλο δέ τοι ἐρέω, σὺ δὲ μὴ χόλον ἔνθεο θυμῷ·
> αὐτόν σ' οὐκ ἀγαθὴ κομιδὴ ἔχει,

"O old man, no lack of skill besets you in tending your orchard: but you have great care for it - nothing at all, no plant, no fig, no vine, no olive, no pear or leek in your garden is without care. But I will say another thing, and do not feel anger in your spirit: you yours elf have no good care.

The poet has got into a muddle with ἔχει ('has') here. σ' ἔχει in 244, and σ' ἔχει in 249, are both in order, but how are we to take εὖ τοι κομιδὴ ἔχει in 245? The sense must of course be that the orchard receives plenty of care: nothing in it is ἄνευ κομιδῆς (247). But the idea of 'care' (κομιδη in the nominative) 'occupying' (ἔχει) the orchard does not square with this. If we read κομιδὴν so as to mean simply "It has plenty of care" we should have sense and syntax: though even then the change of meaning in ἔχει is at least clumsy. A careless if not positively incoherent passage.

24. 502-08, 529-30, 548

Τοῖσι δ' ἐπ' ἀγχίμολον θυγάτηρ Διὸς ἦλθεν Ἀθήνη,
Μέντορι εἰδομένη ἠμὲν δέμας ἠδὲ καὶ αὐδήν.
τὴν μὲν ἰδὼν γήθησε πολύτλας δῖος Ὀδυσσεύς·
αἶψα δὲ Τηλέμαχον προσεφώνεεν ὃν φίλον υἱόν·
" Τηλέμαχ', ἤδη μὲν τόδε γ' εἴσεαι αὐτὸς ἐπελθών,
ἀνδρῶν μαρναμένων ἵνα τε κρίνονται ἄριστοι,
μή τι καταισχύνειν πατέρων γένος, οἳ τὸ πάρος περ
ἀλκῇ τ' ἠνορέῃ τε κεκάσμεθα πᾶσαν ἐπ' αἶαν."

εἰ μὴ Ἀθηναίη, κούρη Διὸς αἰγιόχοιο,
ἤϋσεν φωνῇ, κατὰ δ' ἔσχεθε λαὸν ἅπαντα·

Μέντορι εἰδομένη ἠμὲν δέμας ἠδὲ καὶ αὐδήν.

Athene daughter of Zeus came near to them, looking like Mentor in shape and with his voice. Seeing her the enduring godlike Odysseus rejoiced, and straightaway spoke to Telemachus his dear son: "Telemachus, soon you will go yourself and learn this, when men are fighting in combat where the best men are assessed - not to shame the ancestry of your fathers, who were always before this superior over the whole earth in strength and valour"
... had not Athene, daughter of aegis-bearing Zeus, shouted with her voice, and restrained the whole host, looking like Mentor in shape and with his voice.

On this see earlier note on 22.208 ff. In 502-03 Athene approaches in the appearance of Mentor. In 504 Odysseus 'rejoices' at the appearance (does he know it is really Athene?) Then what he says to Telemachus bears no apparent relation to the appearance, and is also syntactically incoherent: "soon you will know how not to put shame upon..." is the best we can do for it, but it is unconvincing. We naturally expect something like "soon we shall see if you shame your ancestry or not", and Telemachus answers (511-12) "You will see me not putting shame on my ancestry". In 516 Athene, presumably still q*ua* Mentor, tells Laertes to pray to Athene. Then in 529-30 Athene must surely appear in her own shape, otherwise they would not be terrified as they are in 533-36. Then Athene (as Mentor or not?) tells Odysseus to stop fighting in case it makes Zeus angry (541 ff.); and finally arranges a treaty in the appearance of Mentor (547). All this is casual to the point of incoherence.

A Note on 21-24

Nearly all commentators (see Fernandez-Galiano, p. 131 ff., with references) assume some degree of multiple authorship for these books. They tie up this assumption with very long and detailed discussions of various problems: in particular the test of the twelve axes, the hanging of the slave-girls, and the topography of Odysseus' palace. There are also discussions of the general structure and aesthetic appropriateness of large parts of the text, particularly Book 24.

I have not thought it right to enter into these discussions, for a number of reasons. First, I am not convinced that the text can be convicted of any very obvious or certain incoherence (other than the particular logical incoherencies mentioned in the foregoing notes): thus there is no doubt much that is obscure about the axes, or the hanging, or the palace topography, but nothing that is palpably absurd or incoherent in our sense. These seem to be cases, like some other topographical or geographical cases, where we should not expect the text to paint a full and detailed picture: at worst there may be some kind of muddle or uncertainty. Secondly, despite Fernandez-Galiano's "It is now widely accepted that the poem had two main authors" (*ibid.*) and remarks by other commentators, it seems to me premature to base any decision about multiple authorship on an analysis of these books alone: we need some adequate overall theory in the light of which they may then be viewed and assessed. And thirdly, any reasons <u>other</u> than logical incoherence that may be adduced are outside the scope of the present work.

These discussions seem to me to start from the wrong place, so to speak. They are conducted mostly in terms of a polarity between a 'unitarian' or 'anti-unitarian' viewpoint, with the onus nowadays placed firmly on the anti-unitarians. Both the polarity and the onus are questionable. So far as logical incoherence goes, those who (on the basis of some theory about these books) might naturally expect a higher count of incoherence in them will, in my judgement, find their expectation defeated.

PART 3

CONCLUSIONS

The foregoing analyses of incoherencies raise questions about their origin and persistence - about how they arose in the first place, and how they came to remain in place so as to form part of the texts as we have them; and also about their distribution in the two texts, which is far from random. These questions obviously connect with very general, difficult and well-rehearsed issues in Homeric studies as a whole. I am only too painfully aware that these issues have been for long researched by very capable scholars; but the fact that such scholars still differ very widely amongst themselves emboldens me to say something here. At least it is possible that approaching the texts from the particular angle of logical incoherency may be suggestive.

A. <u>Nature and Distribution</u>

I have stressed throughout that I am concerned with incoherencies in a fairly strict sense of the term: that is, with passages where what is said does not actually <u>make sense</u>, where there is some kind of contradiction or blatant inconsistency. That still makes it possible to classify them in different ways. Thus the description of Ithaca's location in Od. 9.21 ff. is incoherent because two inconsistent facts about it are given in a few lines (there are many islands all round it, but also it stands alone and apart). Telemachus' speech is Od. 1.384 ff. is incoherent in a different way (he says in effect "There are other kings in Ithaca, let one of them have the privilege of being king"). Different again is Od. 15.518 ff., where the whole passage seems to be in a mess (see my note *ad loc.*) and to contain various kinds of muddle. Then again, there are quite a few cases of what might be called topographical or pictorial incoherences or obscurity: where the text gives no single clear picture of where some particular person is, or just what is happening to whom at a particular time, and where we can speak of incoherence if the text is not only obscure but internally contradictory.

I have been tempted to try to classify these, since it might reasonably be thought that different kinds of incoherency shed different kinds of light on Homeric composition. But that would have involved a much more detailed, and much more controversial, analysis than I have felt able to undertake here; and it would also, I think, repay study only with the help of other weapons in the armoury of Homeric scholarship (particularly a closer analysis of language-use and style), which I am not qualified to wield. For our purposes here it will be most useful to classify them by the single criterion of <u>extensiveness</u>. By that I mean (to put it roughly, and in advance) that we can ask some such question as "How deeply-rooted is this or that incoherence in the text? With what ease or difficulty could it have got into the text? How much alteration of the text would it need to be cleared up and made coherent?" I hope that both the nature of this criterion, and the reason why I take it to be important, will become clearer in what follows.

This criterion really operates on a sort of sliding scale, rather than yielding entirely discrete categories. Nevertheless, even wielding too sharp an axe, we can usefully distinguish the following:

1. There are some cases where the incoherence is minimally extensive (of course it may still be <u>blatant),</u> in the sense that it is confined perhaps to a single line or phrase. It could in principle be adjusted, for instance, by simple textual emendation of a word or two, or by the insertion or deletion of a single line, or by reversing the order of lines. In some of these cases - though I think not all, or even most - we may think that Homer simply nodded: more precisely, that they are consistent with the idea of a single composer who was just rather careless (and that might be thought to apply particularly to oral composition, where the reciter could get away with incoherencies which would be much more visible with a written text). That is, to some degree, a matter of subjective judgement: though I have to

add here that such judgement must be exercised in comparison with those parts of the text - the vast bulk of it, in fact - where there are no incoherencies of this kind. If Homer did not nod at all in these parts, at least the question arises of why he nodded elsewhere.

2. Then there are cases where the incoherency is rather more extensive - where it is, so to speak, more structural. In these cases we can hardly imagine, even in principle, how any simple textual emendation could clear them up, or that they could have passed muster as the finished product of any composer with his wits about him. Such passages often give the impression of being self-contained, in a general sense 'integrated', perhaps even 'finished' - they are not just a mess: only, they contain internal contradictions. Here we might naturally think in terms of some additions to an original text, or perhaps an amalgam of different lines or parts, quite closely woven together. (Thus Od. 9.21 ff. may be thought to read all of a piece: it is independent, self-contained, not grammatically or syntactically confused: it is just that bits of it are contradictory.)

3. Finally, there are cases where the incoherency is more extensive, perhaps extending over 20 or more lines, and where any unbiased observer receives the strong impression that the whole thing is in an unfinished state - a state in which unsurprisingly, there are not only contradictions but mysterious gaps, oddities, obscurities and uncertainties. These passages, if not those in 1 and 2 above, strongly suggest the idea of something being unfinished, perhaps of 'work in progress' rather than of a complete and polished product.

I think these categories can stand, even though different scholars may differ in respect of what particular items fall within each. Any theory that attempts to explain the incoherencies, however, must also take account of their distribution in the text. Here again it would be inappropriate for me to try to go into too much detail, but one major fact stands out: there are far more of them in the Odyssey than in the Iliad. That very obvious fact turns out to be a useful guide for any satisfactory theory.

I print below a simple chart showing the distribution of the incoherencies. Borderline cases are marked with a query (?): single incoherencies with an I; and passages which seem to me in a general mess with an M.

As I have said earlier, all these judgements are of course controversial; but I should like to draw particular attention to the distinction between I and M passages, where the identification is even more a matter of subjective judgement. I have tried to confine M to extended passages which seem to be confused or incoherent as a whole, as opposed to I-passages where a single incoherence sticks out like a sore thumb (so to speak). But that distinction is hard to make in practice, since it often depends on the 'feel' of the whole passage rather than on any demonstrable failure of logic. I do in fact believe that many passages which I have marked as I-passages are likely to be M passages: I mean, examples of 'work in progress' where the inconsistency or inconsistencies did not arise from 'one-off' cases of carelessness or interpolation or addition, but rather from the passage still being in an unfinished state. But that cannot be always proved beyond doubt from the actual text, and so I have confined the M-marking to those examples where I believe it is plainly visible.

Even so, of course many readers will disagree with these and other identifications. I hope only to have established the general propositions
(1) that there are at least some cases of M, and
(2) that there are far more cases both of M and of I in the Odyssey than the Iliad.

ILIAD

2.291 ?	2.356 ?	5.134 ?
5.181 I	5.885 I	7.116 ?
7.312 I	7.322 M	7.351 I
7.446 ?	8.166 ?	8.530 I
9.182 M	10.408 I	10.496 ?
10.498 I	11.100 I	11.127 ?
13.71 ?	13.363 I	13.775 ?
14.484 I	14.668 I	16.367 ?
16.614 I	17.91 ?	17.327 I
18.221 I	18.470 ?	18.498 ?
18.509 I	20.200 I	23.103 I
23.323 ?	23.638 ?	23.874 I
24.53 ?	24.139 I	

TOTAL: 2 M, 21 I, 17 ?

ODYSSEY

1.358 ?	1.386 M	2.240 I
2.312 ?	4.795 M	5.140 I
5.154 ?	6.119 I	6.263 I
6.278 ?	7.31 I	7.205 ?
8.109 I	8.192 I	8.278 ?
8.370 ?	9.482 I	9.501 I
10.1 ?	10.190 M	10.282 M
10.403 I	11.142 I	11.156 I
11.330 I	11.313 I	11.363 I
11.572 I	12.50 ?	12.55 M
12.201 ?	12.315 I	13.156 M
13.203 I	13.312 I	13.333 I
14.495 I	15.69 I	15.78 I
15.111 ?	15.225 ?	15.368 I
15.434 I	15.518 M	16.4 ?
16.94 M	16.421 I	17.43 ?
17.160 ?	17.205 ?	17.231 I

CONCLUSIONS

17.492 I	18.215 I	18.233 I
18.307 I	19.187 I	19.325 ?
19.536 M	19.572 I	20.87 I
20.92 ?	20.97 I	20.241 I
20.361 ?	21.152 I	22.208 ?
22.312 I	23.177 I	24.118 I
24.196 I	24.244 ?	24.502 ?

TOTAL: 8 M, 42 I, 24 ?

B. <u>Origin and Persistence</u>

Any, adequate theory must account not only for how these incoherencies originated, but also for their persistence in the text. At some point, the text was allowed to <u>go forward</u>. so to speak - to be published and established as more or less authoritative under the name of 'Homer' - even though parts of it were incoherent. Before that stage, nobody took it upon himself to produce a totally coherent text: though later on some at least of the incoherencies were of course noted and criticised in the long history of Homeric scholarship. That fact is not in itself mysterious or without parallel: there is a sort of parallel (not of course exact) with the way in which early Christian authorities established the canonical scriptures which now form the Christian bible, but did not iron out the incoherencies and inconsistencies (both between particular books and within individual books) at that time - though of course later commentators have been much concerned with these. But we have to give some account of how and when that happened.

So far as the origin of the incoherencies goes, one thing seems entirely clear. No <u>single</u> author or composer, whether oral or literate, could have produced them - not, at least, if such a composer is conceived of as taking final or overall responsibility for the relevant passages. I mean this: if I, a single composer, am trying to say something about (for instance) the location of Ithaca, I could not be solely responsible for Od. 9.21 ff. - the contradictions are too blatant, it cannot be put down to carelessness; and so with many other passages. We may perhaps imagine a single person who had <u>available</u> the lines and phrases of Od. 9.21 ff., some of which indeed he might have composed himself: we are seeing such a person now not or not only as a 'composer' but as some sort of 'assembler' or 'redactor': but still, be could not with his wits about him have taken <u>responsibility</u> for the final passage. And *a fortiori* with the passages in our third category, those which I have described as 'a mess'. Indeed, in one clear sense nobody, no single person and no group of people, took on or at least fulfilled such responsibility (otherwise the incoherencies would not have been allowed to stand): and no <u>single</u> person could have composed them, for the reason given above.

How, then, are we to account for them? In some cases we may regard the passage as a composite creation, and account for the incoherency by the idea of <u>addition</u> or expansion. Thus consider our example from Od. 9.21 ff. (together with 10.196). We have (see my note *ad loc.*) the very clear incoherence between ἀμφι ('around') and ἀνευθε ('apart') (that is, between Ithaca being surrounded by νησοι ('islands') and being πανυπερτάτη ('last of all') and located in a different area): plus the oddity of the Doulichion-Samos-Zacynthos line, which does not square with πολλαι ('many') (three islands are hardly πολλαι): plus the uncertainty about what χθαμαλη ('low') means in 9.25, which turns into an unintelligibility in 10.196, where Odysseus is actually <u>on</u> the island. How could all this have arisen?

Well, of course, we can only guess. But it might be that poet A composed something about Ithaca: perhaps just that there was a mountain in it called Neriton, perhaps also that there were other islands close to it. Poet B received this, but wished to add more information (perhaps from some genuine source, such as the knowledge of seafarers in the area, perhaps just from some common stock of traditional topography, perhaps merely invented). He has the formulary line about Doulichion-Samos-Zacynthos, so he puts that in. Then he (or a poet C) puts in the contradictory bit about Ithaca being separated from the other islands. In doing this he uses what seems to be also the formulary phrase αὐτη δε χθαμαλη κειται, which here makes sense ("it lies low" *sc.* presumably as viewed from far off). Then in 10.196 the poet has, as it were, forgotten that Odysseus is actually <u>on</u> the island, and speaks as if he is viewing another island from far off, using the formulary of αὐτη...κέιται contrasts with 10.148-49, where Odysseus (*in propria persona*) says simply

ἔστην δὲ σκοπιὴν ἐς παιπαλόεσσαν ἀνελθών,
καί μοι ἐείσατο καπνὸς ἀπὸ χθονὸς εὐρυοδείης

I went up and stood on a look-out point amongst the crags, and smoke appeared to me coming up from the broad earth.

with no mention of any island, low-lying or otherwise, at all. The <u>same</u> poet could hardly have forgotten this within fifty lines; we have to assume another poet who may have received a (coherent) repeat of 148-49 but decided to alter and add to it. The striking thing about all this (whether or not this particular picture is anywhere near the truth) is the extent to which the composers were, so to speak, <u>carried away</u> by the availability and magnetism of particular phrases (perhaps especially formulaic ones), at the price of coherence: something not too surprising in composition of a composite kind. Certain phrases were at hand, and they simply put them in: as if they lived a life of their own. The underlying motive must have been, characteristically at least, to add and expand.

Consider in this light the incoherency in Od. 1.384 ff. It is barely possible that a single oral composer should have muddled up the different ideas of (a) being a βασιλεύς ('king') one amongst many, and (b) being the βασιλεύς, a special position which Odysseus alone held, and which some ordinary existing βασιλεύς might take on now that Odysseus is dead (396). But it seems more likely that the original oral passage was coherent. Perhaps it was only about being the βασιλεύς, taking over Odysseus' position (ὅ τοι ... πατρώον ἐστιν ('which is your ancestral right'), 387). Then if we omit 394-96 the passage is wholly coherent: Telemachus says in effect "Yes, I wouldn't mind taking that on if Zeus granted it - being a king brings wealth and honour: but I'll just stick to running my own household". So we may assume a second composer with a different concept of βασιλεύς who put in the incoherent βασιληες in 394: as if he wanted to say "There are other nobles in Ithaca, let one of them be king, since Odysseus is dead".

Most of the items in our first and second categories may perhaps be thus explained; but the really difficult problem arises with incoherencies in the third category, those which occur over an extended passage which is nevertheless not extended enough to allow for simple forgetfulness. Od. 15.518 ff. is a fair example (see my note *ad loc*.). In this we have an incoherency about the omen itself, Theoklymenos' failure to interpret it, and Telemachus' reply (as if he had in fact interpreted it): and also the strangeness, if not the positive incoherence, of Telemachus' change of host for Theoklymenos. How could this passage have been produced, or (a different point) allowed to stand as it was? When reading the passage with the incoherencies in mind, we feel not so much that the composer(s) has/have slipped up, so to speak, or that there have been additions to an originally coherent text, but rather that the whole passage is half-baked: as if no single person had really given the whole of this serious attention either during its composition or afterwards. And that is a very striking fact, when compared with other parts of the text which (whether or not they contain single incoherencies) hang together quite well.

I think we are forced to say here simply that the passages are half-baked, and were not given enough serious attention; and if that is so, the question again arises of what conditions of composition that implies. Here, *par excellence*, we cannot plausibly say that any single composer, whether oral or literate, would have made such a mess of things: there must have been more than one hand (or voice) at work. But we have to go rather further than this.

We have surely to imagine conditions under which a number of composers simply weighed in, as it were, with various lines or short passages, to make a deeply incoherent amalgam which was nevertheless allowed to stand. It is as if such a passage represented 'work in progress': no doubt if more work had been done the incoherencies would have been ironed out. And if that picture is on the right lines, it may shed some light on the other incoherencies. We shall say that there were some parts of the poem which had not been worked over to the extent that other parts had been.

I think we can go even further than this, if we try to envisage more clearly the conditions of this 'work in progress'. On the one hand it could not, as I have already said, be in this state if the text were just the result of dictation from a single bard who had composed it orally: no such bard would have produced such a mess. On the other hand, it could not be in such a state if there were some single literate editor, redactor or composer who wrote it out and took overall responsibility for it. In either case, the incoherencies would have been too glaring. So we can only assume a state of affairs in which contradictory parts of the passage were allowed, at least temporarily, to stand side by side. It is hard to think of any parallel which might clarify this; but imagine a Renaissance painting on a very large scale, constructed by a number of workers in a particular 'school'. At a certain stage of the painting different workers might put in various features which were in fact not consistent with each other, features which might have been ironed out later by the master of the school, or whoever took final responsibility for the painting.

This is, or could be, just a synchronic rather than a diachronic picture: I mean, that different composers or editors could have been responsible for putting in different (and mutually inconsistent) lines or phrases more or less at the same time. We do not have to believe in temporally different 'strata', even on a small scale. Indeed, for such passages as these, a synchronic interpretation seems much more plausible. For it is hard to believe that if some composer or redactor already had in front of him some sort of text, or even a memorised composition, his additions would have been so glaringly at odds with what he had. The idea of diachronic additions or alterations fits better with other passages, where there may have been an existing text or memorised composition, and another bard added to it inconsistently - but in a way pardonably: there might be one or two incoherencies, but the whole passage would not be a mess.

The picture of the incoherencies that I have so far presented is clearly at odds with other pictures. Such pictures are usually painted *a priori*, and sometimes connected with opinions on more general matters (single or multiple authorship, for instance). Thus Kirk (1965, p.183), who believes in a single (oral) composer, claims a very high degree of general consistency in the text and says that "certain minor Homeric lapses were probably corrected in the course of transmission through antiquity": hence what he calls the 'rare precision of the Iliad and Odyssey'. But in terms of semantic incoherency, at any rate, that seems false: there are too many incoherencies, and they are often too well-integrated in the text. Conversely, it might be thought that the poems may have been perfectly coherent, but were made incoherent later, just by carelessness or misunderstanding naturally arising from their long-term transmission. But this idea also has to be rejected, for three reasons. The first is obvious: the greater coherence of the Iliad over the Odyssey suggests strongly that a longer transmission produced less, rather than more, errors. Secondly, this picture is most plausible where there appear to be gaps or compressions which produce the incoherence, and where we might think that a transmitter had just omitted something: and also in cases where some alternative reading, or some other minor adjustment, would restore coherence. But most of the incoherencies are simply not like that: they are more integral and often more extensive, so that it is hard to see how any process of transmission could have produced them - whereas it is easy to see how some process of addition, and still more some attempt at a new creation which had not yet been adequately organised ('work in progress'), could have this effect. And thirdly, both poems are for the most part free from incoherency, and no general theory about the effects of long-term transmission can account for this. So for the time being I shall stick to the picture I have suggested, and see where it leads us.

I think it may not be too much to say that some of the points made above would have allowed us to predict at least the major and most obvious feature in the distribution of incoherencies - namely, that there are far more of them in the Odyssey than in the Iliad. For once we have the idea of 'work in progress', which is necessary to account for some of the incoherencies, and given (what no-one denies) that the Odyssey is a later work constructed with reference to an already existing Iliad, it is easy to see that more of such 'work in progress' would have been going on, and that such work could have been interrupted - as it were, frozen with the incoherencies in it unresolved - at some particular time, a time at which the Iliad had already been made much more coherent.

We may speculate about just what froze it in this way, and when. That, as I said earlier, is a problem which we have to face anyway: at some point in time the text, incoherent or not, became established and authoritative. It was allowed to go forward in the name of Homer with all its sins (and virtues) upon it. How did this happen? One thing at least seems tolerably clear: that those responsible for the construction of the Odyssey would not, without due cause, simply have downed tools at a certain point and allowed the poem to go forward as it was - it contains too many incoherencies, too much 'work in progress', for that. They were, after all, trying to produce for public hearing or reading something which was supposed to rival the Iliad. The implication must be that their work was somehow interrupted. And it was interrupted at a point when much of it was more or less complete, so that it could be seen in general as an acceptable construction (which in fact did come to rival the Iliad), but when many parts were still incoherent and in need of further work.

Of course many things might in principle have interrupted it: but any plausible candidate must account for the fact that the guilds or committees of bards or whatever person or people were engaged in the construction must have been willing to let their work go forward in an unfinished state. (Thus the advent of full literacy *per se* would not have been enough: they would still have wished, as with the Iliad, to use literacy to produce a polished work.) They needed a *quid pro quo*. The only *quid* I can think of (in default of other evidence) is the so-called Peisistratean recension. Whatever that may have involved, it certainly involved giving individual bards and guilds of bards a market for their work: the work would be organised, established, made authoritative, and (as it were) distributed, for instance at the Panathenaea, very widely: it would be published. That would be a big temptation, even though they might have handed over the copyright, so to speak, to the authorities at Athens.

If that is right, it gives us some idea about the timing of the Odyssey's composition. Up to the Peisistratean recension, there must have been some bards still engaged on such composition, there was still some work in progress; and for most of the time, at least in the seventh century, they must have been doing so with the aid of some kind of literacy. That does not of course tell us very much. Most of the work may - indeed surely must - have been done a good deal before the recension, perhaps at least a century before it. A good deal of substantial oral composition, probably for the most part coherent in itself, may have been received and transcribed at a quite early stage: by the time the work got into the hands of the Peisistratids, the vast majority of it was already in place and coherent. But there were still some parts left unfinished.

It may of course be asked why these unfinished passages, and indeed the incoherencies in general, were not tidied up after the texts had been handed over (as it were) to the Athenian authorities: why the 'work in progress' was not continued. We do not know enough either about the recension or about the guilds of bards to give a detailed answer. But the general answer must surely be that the recension itself established some text as authoritative: thereafter 'Homer' more or less meant what the Athenian authorities had collected and (to some extent) organised. Such details as we have (if indeed we can rely on these) about the recension accord with this idea. (See West, p.37, who rightly interprets the relevant passage in Plutarch as implying that Hipparchus acquired a text and 'established it as the version to be followed at the Panathenaea', as well as making the recited text coherent in the basic sense that there were no gaps or overlaps - reciter B started where reciter A left off.) There is no mention of any further or more thorough organisation of the texts so collected; and since the incoherencies in fact remained, there could not have been any. Again, there is some sort of parallel with the authorities of the early Christian church establishing a canon of scriptures, deciding in general what was authoritative and canonical, but not purging the scriptures of all incoherency.

This general picture must surely apply to the Iliad as well as the Odyssey, even though the Odyssey provides the stronger evidence for it. The greater coherence of the Iliad will most obviously be due to the simple fact that more time had been spent on its composition and arrangement; but it also allows for the possibility that a single composer, or single composers, could have generated at least very large parts of the text more or less as we have it -that is, in a coherent form. But such judgements must relate to some overall view on Homeric composition: I shall discuss this below.

I said that we can make an educated guess about which parts of the text were left unfinished; but the matter is rather more complex than that. We can indeed see easily enough (from the charting of the distribution of the incoherencies) where the incoherencies cluster most thickly: and that certainly suggests a lack of finish, 'work in progress'. But it does not at all follow that most of the substance of such passages was not composed or transcribed much earlier. It may be, for instance, that this substance formed part of the original composition, but was somehow overlaid by a rival version or even just by one or two additions by individual bards. We do not have to believe that the whole passage was composed at a late date. It was 'left unfinished' in the sense that more work was needed (to iron out the incoherencies); but that does not imply that the passage as a whole was only worked at towards the end of our time-scale. If we are trying to date 'early' and 'late' passages in the Odyssey, for instance, there will of course be other considerations besides that of coherency and incoherency (considerations of language, consistency of plot, etc.: we shall not think Book 24 of the Odyssey 'late' only, or perhaps at all, because it contains incoherencies in my sense).

For that reason I would not venture to make any suggestions about which particular passages, in either poem, are 'early' or late'. To repeat: the fact that the bards were still working on a particular passage in itself tells us nothing. One passage may have been composed very late, but quite coherently: another very early, but (for one reason or another) become liable to incoherency, and hence still 'in progress'. The most we can say - and even this may be too much - is that the incoherent passages may deserve particular attention, and that it may be possible to see them as 'late' if there are other grounds for doing so. And that may be largely a matter of subjective stylistic judgement. For instance, it seems to me reasonably clear that certain passages do not just contain more than their fair share of incoherencies, but also stand out as being composed carelessly, in a hurry, jerkily, or in a style which strongly suggests that they were rapidly and confusedly run up, so to speak, in order to fill in gaps in a composition already existing in a more coherent and well-organised form. I have occasionally commented on this (see notes *ad loc.*). But here I begin to go outside my terms of reference: I must leave such matters to those better able to wield the other weapons of Homeric scholarship that are relevant.

One important issue here relates to the general question of literate as against oral composition. That question is still unsettled, and scholars are divided on it. On any reasonable account, much of the material which originally existed only in the mind of some bard or bards was subsequently put into written form: and that raises the possibility that this process itself may account for at least some of the incoherencies. Thus it is possible that much of it was carried out by a 'master poet' dictating the material to a number of scribes who may well have transcribed it incorrectly. Or the process may have been much more complicated, with scribes writing down the memorised material from a great many bards, and perhaps adding material of their own as composers rather than just as transcribers. Could this process (whatever it was) account for the kind of muddles and obscurities which we have looked at?

I think that the answer to this must be in the negative, for reasons in part already given. First, since the vast majority of the text is free from incoherency, we should have to believe that for the incoherent passages a different process was operative (or perhaps the same process but carried out much more incompetently), which seems *a priori* unlikely. Secondly, the kind of incoherence would have to be such that it could reasonably be ascribed to incompetent transcription: cases for instances where the dictating bard was misheard, or part of what he dictated was omitted. But very few of the relevant passages are of that kind: the incoherencies are, as I remarked earlier, more structural (as it were, deeper) than that, and it is hard or impossible to think of alterations or additions that would clear them up.

That is not to say that the complex process of oral and literate composition played no part in generating incoherency: it is to say only that incompetence in transcription alone cannot account for it. Much more plausibly, in my view, we may ascribe the incoherencies to the fact that some at least of the 'transcribers' were also themselves composers: that they added to, subtracted from, or in general 'stitched' the text as we have it rather than just transmitted it. That is the general picture which I am presenting here, in opposition to the idea of a 'monumental bard' whose memorised material was transcribed more or less as it stood. Certainly that may have been the case with some of the text; but it cannot have been the case with those parts of the text which contain the incoherencies, and may indeed not have been the case with the text as a whole.

It will be clear from what I have said so far that this picture, at least as it applies to the Odyssey, implies that quite substantial portions of the text were not composed - or at least not composed in any finished form - by any single, 'monumental' composer. I think it may be worthwhile considering (despite the immense amount of existing literature) whether that picture may not apply more widely:

CONCLUSIONS

that is, whether the idea of corporate and synchronic (as well as diachronic) composition might be appropriate to the Iliad and the Odyssey in general - or, at least, need not be confined to the incoherent passages. This is of course, no more than a hypothesis which may account for the facts about the incoherencies. Obviously it runs into the whole set of problems about (a) how far each poem should be seen as 'monumental', and/or the work of a single composer of genius, and (b) what part, if any, literacy played in its composition: together with (c), the question of what date we are to assign to various stages of composition or transcription or redaction. But in trying to see how our hypothesis fares in respect of these problems, it is important to keep firmly in mind that what we have recently learned about the *Kunstsprache* -briefly, the methods of formulaic composition which lightened the task of the oral or improvising composer - does not settle any of them. It shows indeed that oral composition was much more possible than we might have supposed; but that is a two-edged weapon. For it implies a common tradition and style of composition, available over a fairly lengthy period of time to any competent bard. The impersonality of the *Kunstsprache,* so far from suggesting a single oral composer, leaves open the possibility that any such bard or bards could have used it at any time whilst the tradition lasted and was practised. And it also leaves open the possibility of using just the same *Kunstsprache* with the additional help of literacy. In the same way, to use an admittedly imperfect parallel, the existence of an established tradition of certain architectural techniques (the arch, the rib-vault, the flying buttress, etc.) in itself tells us nothing about (a) whether such techniques were used by only a single 'monumental' architect, nor about (b) whether the techniques were or were not assisted by plans, drawings, architectural schedules or other forms of literacy, nor even (c) about just when these techniques were used in certain buildings.

To judge from most modern commentaries, nearly all the arguments about particular passages revolve between two poles. At one pole are the 'Analytic' scholars, now mostly out of fashion, who believe(d) in various historical layers or 'strata', as if the poems were built up diachronically by various hands/voices: at the other pole are the monumentalists or unitarians, who hold to the picture of a single composer who organised the whole text, even though he may have had some difficulty in incorporating some of the material. But it is at least possible, as I have argued, that these are not the only nor perhaps the most important categories within which we can view the text. If substantial or at least significant amounts of it were corporately and synchronically constructed, by groups of bards working with the *Kunstsprache*, then the most important dimension would rather be the extent to which such construction had succeeded in producing a finished and unexceptionable text: that is, the stage of development to which various passages may be assigned. Of course we have no hope of adjudicating this in many or most cases, but the existence of seriously incoherent passages, to which the idea of 'work in progress' must surely apply, may be seen as at least the tip of an iceberg whose depths we cannot now plumb.

C. Some wider issues

How far, then, is this hypothesis tenable in the light of what we actually know (not, perhaps, very much) in a wider or more general way about Homeric composition? It will be convenient to begin with the question of literacy: and it is a daunting fact that scholars diverge very widely on this question. Thus Kirk goes pretty well the whole way down the road of oral composition (p.10 ff.), whilst Heubeck and West (p.12 ff., 33 ff.) go the other way. Kirk summarises at least some of the arguments very fairly; and his points about the difficulties of written composition in the eighth century (p.13) are well taken. So Kirk thinks that the poems were composed orally, more or less as we have them, and were recited on specially-arranged occasions, over 'two or three or four days': he thinks this possible because "Homer must have had an extraordinary reputation in order to be able to impose his epic on audiences despite its unnatural size; but then an extraordinary reputation for such a man of genius is only to be expected" (p.13).

But there is a major difficulty here. It is not, perhaps, wholly incredible that an unusually gifted poet should have been able to create, and remember, the 16,000 lines which constitute our Iliad (and similarly for the Odyssey): nor that he should have found an audience willing to spend the considerable time needed in order to listen to them. What is incredible is that this, representing as it does something very new and striking - a radical departure from the one-off performances of bards in various contexts - should have left absolutely no trace in the tradition. If there was such a man, and if he actually did this (presumably on more than one occasion), we should surely have heard about it. The Greeks were quick enough to invent things about Homer; but if this had happened, they would not even have needed to invent. We are talking, after all, about (supposed) historical facts: performances that could hardly have been forgotten by Homer's contemporaries or by later generations, but would (if anything) have been celebrated and advertised. They would surely also have been continued after Homer's lifetime. Nothing in the Homeric tradition comes anywhere near this, at least before the Peisistratids. Indeed, even if we overlook the actual performances, it is very striking that the amount which the Greeks actually knew about Homer is more or less negligible: he is almost as dim a figure as Orpheus. And that does not square with the 'man of genius' idea at all.

Even if the 'man of genius' gave no actual performances, it is still hard to believe that he would have remained so dim a figure: a figure about whom practically everything, even his birthplace, was in dispute. Nothing in the tradition, or speculation, about Homer comes anywhere near diminishing this dimness. Yet, on any account, he would have been responsible for an entirely new, and extremely daring and remarkable, enterprise - the construction of an epic poem quite different in scale and complexity from anything that had gone before. Would not such a man have advertised himself? Would not those who had a vested interest in him, particularly the *soi-disant* Homeridai, have advertised him? Yet there is nothing either in the poems themselves, nor in the external tradition, which offers any serious information about his life or circumstances - or offers even an invented picture of them.

That difficulty seems to me insuperable. There is also the suggestion, though I do not regard it as conclusive, which has been made by many writers and. which Kirk acknowledges (p.13) - that the length, complexity and coherence of the poems themselves seem outside the range of any oral composer, even a genius. Thus Heubeck says "Their most important characteristic is the structure of form and content, the ordering of the material, which is planned precisely and in detail from the very beginning": though he goes much too far in saying that "nothing can change places and nothing can be added or left out" (*ibid.*).Yet we may still have to accept the fact that a wholly written composition, which would be needed to take care of such complexity and ordering, was barely practicable in the eighth century: and we know, in any case, that a good deal of oral poetry was available at that time.

This naturally suggests the possibility that some of the text was indeed composed or organised in a written form, but later than the eighth century. Some person or persons unknown inherited an amount of orally-composed poetry, added to it, and put it together with the aid of writing so as to produce something like the text as we have it. Unsurprisingly, particularly if this was a joint effort (perhaps by a guild of bards) they did not claim originality of authorship - they were in fact not the sole authors: they ascribed it to an earlier figure in a characteristically Greek way (*cf.* the ascriptions to Lycurgos in Sparta), to 'Homer', who may indeed have been an outstanding oral composer in the previous century. This will also account for the Greeks' ignorance of Homer's personal identity and history.

That such a guild or corporation would have had an incentive to produce the texts is not hard to see. Kirk's arguments (1965, p.182 ff.) against plural composition are not strictly relevant to our thesis here, since he is considering only oral composition. They are, briefly (1) that there was no audience, and (2) that the high degree of consistency in the epics argues for a single composer. "In short it is difficult to see what sort of aim, function or opportunity could have induced the progressive development of a monumental epic by a plurality of singers" (p.182). But, given a corporation of composers who could both compose orally in the *Kunstsprache* and also make use of literacy, the answer to these questions is clear enough: they wanted to ensure the permanence of the epics by having them in written form, and to ensure their authoritative status. That indeed is the main function of literacy; and it would be hardly surprising if the corporation did not seize upon literacy as soon as it was available. And for this latter reason it seems sensible to ascribe at least some part of the process to the earliest practicable stages of literacy.

Even without literacy, the idea of the 'development of a monumental epic' (or two such epics) seems far from strange. That idea is indeed already inherent in the text; there are references to other epic material concerning Thebes and the Argonauts, which must have covered quite a lot of ground, and to the possibility of a bard (Demodokos) being able to take up a long story (what happened at Troy) at some requested point (Od.8.492). The desire to have such long stories or epics available in some form - whether written or memorised, and whether memorised by a number of people or by a single bard - is surely understandable. Those who worked at realising this desire were trying to produce some sort of authorised or standardised or publicly accepted version; and they would have hoped to get some public recognition of this in some institutionalised form - as in fact they did in Athens under the Peisistratids.

Before that, recitations of the story would have almost certainly been 'one-off' performances, to audiences whose nature we can only guess at. For it is no more likely that any guild or collective organisation could have persuaded any audience to listen over 'two or three or four days' than that a single bard could have. More decisively, if that had happened we should certainly have heard of it. We should consider the 'monumental epic' as a kind of repertoire from which parts of different lengths and suitability were drawn, in a way wholly familiar to many traditions of acting and recitation ("Tonight we give you Wotan's farewell/the sleepwalking scene from Macbeth/the Wooden Horse"). In the absence of the theatre at Bayreuth or the Globe that picture is quite a natural one.

Of course the question of monumentality (or plural as against singular composition) has to be separated, so far as possible, from the question of literary as against oral composition. As will be clear from what I have already said, I disagree with both Kirk and Heubeck on the former, and indeed with most other modem Homericists. Kirk says (p.xv) that "Most scholars now accept that the Homeric epics are the result of a developing oral epic tradition on the one

CONCLUSIONS

hand, and the unifying and creative work of an exceptional monumental composer on the other". The former proposition is beyond doubt: but whether or not we are to accept the latter must depend on the two questions (1) how far the poems are in fact coherent and integrated (and, just as important, whether they are coherent and integrated in the way that only a single person could have achieved under any conditions whatsoever): and (2) which approaches the problem from the other end, whether it is possible that a group of people could have produced such coherence. It seems to me (1) that the poems are not all that coherent and integrated (so that we do not positively require a single genius), and (2) that a joint or corporate effort is not only possible but probable.

Those scholars who favour literate composition do so mostly on the grounds that the complex and monumental nature of the epics requires a monumental composer - it is just that they think that such a composer must have been literate. These grounds seem to me unacceptable. The aesthetic merits of the two poems, despite what has been said by many critics like Heubeck, do not lie primarily in their monumentality, or integration. The basic plots (see below) are, after all, pretty simple (though effective enough, indeed); nor is the characterisation especially subtle or complex or profound. It seems to me, at least, that any 'monumental' qualities which stick in the mind (and that only after a good many readings of the text) consist of a number of general themes or ideas, highlighted in particular scenes or episodes that derive their force partly from the straightforward, almost naïve, way in which whoever composed them actually wrote, but chiefly because they are set in a background and plot which conveys ideas of this general kind with enormous force. I have in mind those scenes where such general ideas as the horrors and also the inevitability of war, the necessity of defending one's country, the sudden and fearful vengeance of a returning hero whose home and wife have been besieged, or that hero's self-revelation when, without the need for more lies or tricks, he can declare himself in a friendly atmosphere, are as it were brought to a head in Achilles' meeting with Priam, Hector's parting from Andromache, Odysseus' slaying of the suitors, and his self-revelation in the palace of Alcinoos. Those scenes derive their force from the vast environment of each poem, which constantly harps on them in a more indirect way. In that sense, if it is a sense, the poems are monumental. But that is less a matter of complex structure than of strength and consistency of theme.

Similarly, Griffin (1980, p.13 ff.) rightly stresses the important differences between ways in which the Iliad and Odyssey differ from other early epics, and it is partly this, I think, which leads him (along with many other scholars) to the idea of a monumental genius (or two *genii*, one for each epic). He then has to play down any internal difficulties: "it is right to insist that they contain in reality very few significant discrepancies" (p. 13). But there are in fact quite a lot of 'discrepancies' of various kinds. He admits "that we know nothing of the author; we must add that we know as little of his audience" (p.15), and so has to claim that

> "Whatever his hearers were, the poet had established an ascendancy over them which made it possible for him to impose upon them a very long poem, instead of complying with their more natural demand for something which could be heard complete in one or two sittings, like the songs which Demodocus sings in the Odyssey. Once he was embarked on something of the Iliad's scale, the poet and not the audience was in control. We are to think of a singer, conscious of his own powers and the attention of his audience, conceiving a massive poem, concerned with the subject-matter and drawing on the resources of the oral tradition.... The whole conception, in scale and originality, was so bold and individual that we can be confident that it was that of one man. The days when romantic scholars believed in 'folk poetry', producing the Iliad by collective action, are over" (ibid.).

But that is itself a very 'romantic' view. It is not in dispute that the poems represent a considerable departure from short-term epics and songs; but the absence of any evidence, or even any coherent tradition, either about the poet or about his supposed performance argues strongly (as I have said) against the view. It is much more natural to accept the impression which the poems leave on the unsophisticated reader who is not *parti pris*. Such a reader (I have made the experiment with several) will naturally take it that the poems, despite some general coherence in plot and structure, have been put together, sometimes clumsily and often with much repetition. And it is also natural to think that the existence of literacy offered an appropriate opportunity and incentive to do this, so as to produce a permanent and durable body of work which was not at the mercy of particular bards or particular audiences: in Thucydides' words, a κτημα ἐς ἀεί, ('an eternal possession, not just a production to hear for a particular occasion') not just a ἀγώνισμα ἐς τὸ παραχρῆμα ἀκούειν. In the same way it would be wrong (though romantic) to suppose that the difference in kind between Romanesque and Gothic architecture must be due to some monumental genius, rather than on the development of an existing tradition by many hands.

Just how 'monumental' or 'integrated' is the plot of either poem? The authors of the Odyssey faced a problem that those of the Iliad did not have. The story of the Iliad contains quite a lot of ready-made 'plot', which does indeed centre round the wrath of Achilles (as the preface, 1.1 ff., makes clear) and extends quite naturally from that basic idea. Agamemnon upsets Apollo, is forced to return his priest's daughter, takes Achilles' prize Briseis as a substitute, and thus offends Achilles; Achilles withdraws, and as a natural consequence the Greeks are hard put to it, Hector and the Trojans prevail and get close to capturing the Greek camp; Patroclus wants to save them and enters the battle, and is killed; Achilles reacts predictably, gets new armour, enters the battle and kills Hector; Priam dares to recover Hector's body from Achilles, and Hector is given a proper funeral. Moreover, most of the scenes which are, strictly speaking, not essential for this plot naturally support it.

The basic plot of the Odyssey - I mean, the basic idea of it, before the authors got to work in adding to it and complicating it - is much simpler. As the preface (1.1 ff.) says, it is the story of a much-enduring and ingenious man who has a long and difficult journey home and loses all his companions. So the problem will be how to spin out this simple theme into the length of an epic equal to the Iliad. One may ask why that should be thought necessary; and the answer must be, not that the basic plot demands it (it does not), but that the poem was meant to rival the Iliad, at least in the sense of being equally long. One may also ask why that particular theme should be chosen (Odysseus' return). That is a more difficult question. Part of the answer may lie in the actual availability of the original oral material: it is conceivable that there was plenty about Odysseus' *nostos* and not so much about any other theme. But a more important reason may be that the authors wanted the poem not only to rival, but also in a sense to depend on or follow on from the Iliad, yet at the same time to be reasonably distinct from it - as it were, not just more of the same (as would have been the case if the poem had just continued the Trojan story, like Arctinus' *Aethiopis*). And that in effect limits the choice of subject to the subsequent fortunes of some hero or heroes already prominent in the Iliad.

Some of these met sticky, and too early, ends: Achilles, Ajax, Agamemnon. Others came home without sufficient heroic difficulty: Nestor, Philoktetes, Diomede, Idomeneus. More or less the only other candidate is Menelaus; and his *nostos* is in fact described in the Odyssey (Book 4) at some length, in a way that resembles a sort of microcosm of Odysseus' own (he wanders for eight years, visits Cyprus, Phoenicia, Egypt, etc., and has a typical seafarer's scenario with Proteus). But perhaps Menelaus was not chosen for two reasons: first, and more important, because he was not, like Odysseus, famed for both cunning and endurance, both heroic qualities (or at least qualities of the 'new hero': see Heubeck, p.21 ff.); second, because no other heroic qualities were required by his *nostos* - he did not often have to display .heroic prowess in battle, for instance.

So Odysseus may have been the natural candidate. But the plot had to be, and was, filled out. This is done in two ways, very different from each other. The first was of course the succession of magic tales. Some elements of these may derive from the Argonautic material: most of them are to be found in the folk-tales of many countries: there would in any case have been plenty of material to draw on. Apart from the Calypso episode, and Odysseus' dealings with the Phaiecians (who stand half-way between the world of magic and the normal heroic world), these tales are recounted in Books 8-12 - over a quarter of the whole poem. They are germane to the basic plot only in a broad sense, in that they serve to reinforce Odysseus' endurance and resourcefulness; but they certainly fill the poem out, albeit in a picaresque rather than structural way.

The second way of expanding (rather than just filling out) the plot was to jack up the part played by Telemachus (who was known to the Iliad), and here the skill of the authors comes more into question. The last part of Book 1 and Book 2 serve well to show the state of affairs in Ithaca, a background clearly relevant to Odysseus' eventual return. Books 3 and 4, however, are not really about Telemachus at all: rather, they give the reader (hearer) a chance to see and learn of other Iliadic heroes and their *nostoi* from the mouths of Nestor and Menelaus, and to see Menelaus and Helen, Nestor and his well-organised household, in their own right. At this point indeed the authors seem to have got into a muddle about Telemachus, or perhaps even to have lost interest in him. Thus, though having declined Menelaus' offer to stay for 11 or 12 days, he in fact stays for a month. Athene only goes to Sparta to get him moving after she has greeted Odysseus on his return to Ithaca: bad timing. In Book 15 there is the wholly mysterious accession of Theoclymenos to Telemachus' party, followed by a highly unsatisfactory account of the geography of Telemachus' own return to Ithaca (both the route and the landing-point are not made clear either in themselves or in relation to the suitors' ambush). Thereafter Telemachus, after being united with his father, does not play a significantly greater part in the plan for vengeance than Eumaeus does.

With the Iliad the whole problem of plot is entirely different, because there is nothing like so clear a distinction between what is essential to the plot or

CONCLUSIONS

'organic' and what is unessential or 'inorganic'. Indeed it is much less easy than in the case of the Odyssey to say just what 'the plot' actually is. As we saw, the basic plot of the Odyssey is simple: Odysseus has a long and difficult *nostos,* returns home to find that home besieged, and takes his revenge. Other features may be said to support, reinforce or (occasionally) complicate this, but are not integral to it. But what is 'the plot' of the Iliad? If we go along with many critics (Leaf, for instance), we shall say that the plot is (as the preface says) the wrath of Achilles; and then we shall find ourselves excluding such elements as the embassy to Achilles, the capture of the wall, the making of Achilles' arms, Patroclos' funeral, and Priam's recovery of Hector's body (all of which Leaf condemns to his 'Third Stratum': Leaf, p.xx). But then we might say "Hang on a minute, surely some or all of these elements are pretty directly connected with Achilles' wrath, so why not include those?" - and clearly there is a case for this.

We may stop there and still exclude elements like the scenes in Troy, the Catalogue, and the various *aristeiai* (Diomede, Idomeneus, Menelaus). But we may also not stop and say "But these are still connected with Achilles' wrath, if taken in context: it affects the Trojans, and brings other heroes and their *aristeiai* into prominence by Achilles' absence"; or we shall say "Well, the plot is not just about Achilles' wrath, this is a national epic about (a part of) the Trojan War in general, so that the Catalogue is integral because after all it tells us who was there, and we need the *theomachiai* to give some sort of supernatural weight to all this", and so on. And clearly there is a case for this too.

Suppose we accept something like the above view of the Odyssey and Iliad as (more or less integrated) stories or plots. What does this tell us about the manner of their composition? I regret to say, absolutely nothing. If there were many serious incoherencies of plot, it would be a different matter: then we should be able to say, "Look, no single composer with any sense could have written both X and Y, because they are grossly contradictory" or "There is a terrible gap in the plot between A and B - any monumental composer would surely have filled it in". But arguably there are very few such cases. What we have, in both poems, are plots from which a good many features could have been left out (with whatever aesthetic loss); and we cannot argue from that to any conclusions about whether they came from a single composer, or even about the order of their composition.

One fallacy we have to beware of is that of taking 'the essential plot' as primary, and assigning it either to a single author and/or to an earlier stage of composition than the less 'essential' features. Then we shall argue about what 'the essential plot' actually is, and proceed accordingly. Thus both Heubeck and Kirk argue that the whole text of each poem is more or less an integral whole: Heubeck going so far as to say that nothing can be omitted from the Odyssey, and Kirk saying of the Iliad that "one comes to feel the overriding cohesion of the whole structure" (p.46). And of course, if that is taken as given - if one feels that the structure would collapse, so to speak, if certain elements were omitted - then some person or persons must have put the whole thing together very carefully. But no serious person (I hope not Heubeck or Kirk) can think that the omission of quite a lot of elements would make the plot incoherent or self-contradictory or obscure. Such omission might weaken the plot, or diminish it, or change 'the plot' into what we might want to call another plot: but that is a different thing.

The simple fact is that most elements of the Iliad and Odyssey could have been composed by any person or persons, at any time when the *Kunstsprache* was still available, and - to some extent at least - in any order. Since we no longer have much reason to believe in chronological 'strata', we shall not say that the 'kernel' of the plot of either poem was composed first, with subsequent additions by later bards. And, since the style, language, and other features of the *Kunstsprache* are (for the most part) comparatively uniform, it will be anybody's guess who composed what and when. Of course there are limits to this, but fairly loose ones. Without some such limits we could hardly talk of any coherent plot at all. But within those limits, nothing is certain: nor can I see that there could be any internal evidence obtainable by inspection of the plot to achieve certainty.

Nor can we detect additions to any 'basic plot' by trying to assess the motives of bards who may have added to it, since such motives may have been very various. A bard may have composed, or drawn and inserted from existing material, a particular passage for any of these reasons: (1) because he thought it would round the plot off nicely (the end of the Odyssey); (2) to gratify local patriotism or curiosity (the Catalogue); (3) to make the most of known and admired heroes (the *aristeiai*; (4) to display some ideal state of affairs (the Phaiecians); (5) to make some general comment on life, war, or whatever (Priam's visit to Achilles); (6) to gratify the hearers' taste for esoteric adventure or for displays of supernatural power (Odysseus' 'Sinbad' adventures, the *theomachiai*; (7) to display his knowledge of events not connected with the plot at all (the nostoi related by Nestor and Menelaus to Telemachus); or (8) just for fun (the deceiving of Zeus by Hera).

That both the Iliad and the Odyssey are reasonably coherent, fairly unified, and exceptionally powerful artistic creations is not in dispute (though the extent of that coherence and unity, and even of the aesthetic merits of large parts of the poems, may reasonably be doubted). Certainly this may tempt one to the idea of a monumental composer, but the words which Kirk applies (p.13) to the belief that this must have involved written composition can also be applied to the idea of a monumental composer itself. We may have the feeling that only such a composer could have done the job; but "That kind of feeling, which some Homerists experience all the time and all must experience some of the time, is one belonging to habitual literates, which is a reason for regarding it with some suspicion". It is perhaps as if we felt that some city (Venice, for instance) must have been centrally planned by some architectural genius, since it now seems so aesthetically coherent and beautiful: we are apt to think this in an age of central town planning, and neglect the possibility that it was the result of a group effort by people working in a similar tradition and with similar materials.

Let me now try to present a coherent picture which stands up in the light of these and other considerations. We are to suppose a substantial body of orally composed poetry about the Trojan War, or part of that war. At this stage there may have been a single outstanding poet, 'Homer', but it is unlikely (for reasons already given) that any single person put together or performed the whole, or anything like the whole, of what we now have as the Iliad. The production of the Iliad (not all or most of its original composition) was the joint effort of some guild or community of bards able to deploy the *Kunstsprache*. They produced it perhaps with the aid of some kind of primitive literacy, and ironed out most of the incoherencies that would naturally exist in purely oral composition. Insofar as they added anything of their own, they usually (not always) did so with sufficient care to avoid incoherency, or ironed out incoherencies as their work progressed. Most if not all of this body of oral poetry may have already existed in the repertoire of various bards, who (like Demodokos) could take up the story on request at various points and allow it to be transcribed. The guild or community of bards produced the Iliad, or something very like it, in order to achieve permanence and authoritative status for the epic: and, characteristically, assigned it to a single figure, 'Homer'.

Later (perhaps within a generation) this venture encouraged a similar group of bards to produce a rival epic, the Odyssey. Existing oral poetry for this epic may have been thinner and more disjointed; and there may have been fewer or less orally competent bards who had it in their repertoire. They used what material there was, but had to add a good deal of their own, and to use a good deal of 'stitching' and 'bridging' so as to produce a reasonably coherent poem of equal length to the Iliad. Being adequately versed in the *Kunstsprache*, they may have composed their own material orally, but with the help of a very primitive literacy. The complex process of interrelating existing oral material, combining it with their own, and 'stitching' and 'bridging' understandably involved them in some degree of logical incoherency at various points, perhaps those points in particular where they were not transcribing coherent existing oral material. They also had less time to work on it than on the Iliad. It is most plausible to assume two stages in this process: a first stage in which, as with the Iliad, they transcribed oral material with sufficient care to avoid incoherency, and a second stage in which, as they added to it themselves and interrelated it, some incoherencies were unresolved. This version together with the Iliad was then taken over by the Athenian authorities without being subject to critical analysis, and regarded as having some kind of authoritative status, also under the name of 'Homer'.

At what time was all this done? Arguments (e.g. Kirk, p.4) based on literary or archaeological fragments which seem to derive from the texts, and which can be dated to the middle of the eighth century, do not in fact give us *a terminus ante quem*: for it is not only possible but probable that much of the contents of what was eventually to appear as the complete text were widely known, in oral form, at quite an early date, and were hence available both for 'quotation' by other poets and for artistic representation, e.g. on vases. A better *terminus* argument derives from the well-established belief that 'Homer' came at the beginning of Greek literary history, and before Archilochus, Hesiod and Tyrtaeus, who must have composed their works in writing some time before c.625 BC.

It is perhaps worth adding that this point applies more widely, indeed to (almost) any attempt to date the epics from particular features in them or connected with them. For the passages in which those features occur - knowledge (or ignorance) of cultural or geographical features, mentions of various types of military equipment or practices, etc. - may have been composed or added at more or less any time (within reason). There may be Mycenean memories and Mycenean formulae: and at the other end of the time-scale, there may be additions or interpolations by some bard in the late seventh century anxious to show off his knowledge - or even whole passages inserted later still to gratify local feeling (for instance, the Peisistratid connection with Pylos). We can of course try to date those passages themselves, but that is a very far cry from trying to date the epic as a whole.

The 'stitching' required would have been a considerable task, not because those responsible for it need have added all that much of their own by way of original material, but simply because of the difficulties of correlating and coordinating the existing oral material. It must have taken some time. After this time - and perhaps also during it - nothing prevented individual poets - given, now, the availability of written composition - from producing other work of their own; and we should naturally expect, what in fact we get, a number of such works - including the cyclic poems and the Homeric hymns. Some of these represent a parallel aesthetic endeavour, so to speak, in an age which now made allowance for individual effort and in which the individual authors could be named; though naturally they imitated much of the existing oral material. But they did not, in general, pretend to Homeric status - to be Homer, so to speak. That task, the production of the Iliad and the Odyssey,

CONCLUSIONS

in a sense the creation of 'Homer', or at least the organisation of the oral material relevant to the Iliad and the Odyssey round the name of Homer, was a quite different one.

A further point is that, given (what cannot reasonably be denied) much of the original material of the texts was orally composed, somebody, somewhere, at some time, must have written it down, with sufficient care to generate very long epics with the coherence of plots which they show: and given this length, this general coherence, and the primitive state of literacy (including the shortage of papyrus and/or other materials), it must have been a long and difficult business. It seems *prima facie* unlikely that any one person, with a working life of not more than a few decades, could have done it. This again points to a group or team effort conducted by people who were collectively (a) familiar with the oral material, (b) able to add to it or stitch it together both (i) in the same style and (ii) with something like the same poetic competence, and (c) possessed of enough literacy to produce a complete written version.

There are two ways or senses in which this picture does not wholly preclude the idea of a 'monumental composer'. First, there will have been bards who, even if their actual recitations were (like Demodokos') confined to short periods of time, wished and were able on their own account to generate longer poems. Some bards might in some sense have had in their minds the whole history of the Trojan War (or a large part of it), or of some hero's *nostos*, from which (again like Demodokos) they could draw as required by a particular audience. Such a long poem might have been memorised, or perhaps improvised as needed. One such bard might thus already have a repertoire which formed at least the kernel of the Iliad and the Odyssey: perhaps a good deal more than that. Second, in the process of group composition (with or without the use of literacy), there may well have been one leading ('monumental') figure primarily responsible for the arrangement of the oral material: much as, with monuments like Chartres cathedral, there will have been an architect with overall responsibility for the general plan, though particular parts of that plan will have been carried out by colleagues or subordinates. That is, I think, as far as we can go to satisfy the monumentalists, though I would not myself wish to go so far.

That is not to deny an excellent aesthetic taste, as one might rather preciously call it, to the arrangers who did this: there is not much which is palpably inferior in quality in some parts of the epic as opposed to others. But the reduplications, extensions, repetitions and irrelevancies do exist: and not only in cases, like the end of the Odyssey, where we feel confident in saying that someone is trying to round off the plot. Of course it is true that a 'monumental' composer, whether oral or literate, might well have had a quite different conception of relevance, repetition or reduplication than the conception we entertain nowadays. He might have wanted to produce something which, whilst also being a coherent plot with a clear general theme and story, also included a sort of pastiche (as it were) or picaresque series of episodes, much less tightly constructed than modern taste would consider appropriate. Our difficulty in adjudicating this arises partly from the entire lack of parallels (certainly not in later epics like the Aeneid, if only because they were largely imitative of Homer): we have very little idea of how a 'monumental composer' in the eighth or seventh century would actually think about these matters. But it still seems to me that the idea of a 'single genius', as Homer has sometimes been described, does not fit the actual texts. And certainly - the only point on which I feel confident - it does not square with the incoherencies.

REFERENCES

TEXTS

Iliad (1902) Oxford Classical Text (ed. D. B. Monro & T. W. Allen), Oxford University Press, 1902 onwards.

Odyssey (1908) Oxford Classical Text (ed. T. W. Allen), Oxford University Press, 1908 onwards.

COMMENTARIES AND OTHER WORKS

Ameis-Hentze-Cauer (1940) *Homer Odysee* Leipzig.

Apthorp, M.J. (1980) *The Manuscript Evidence for Interpolation in Homer* Heidelberg.

Bolling, G.M. (1925) *The External Evidence for Interpolation in Homer* OUP: Oxford.

Chantraine, P. (1958-63) *Grammaire Homerique* Paris.

Butcher, S. H. and Lang, A. (1935) *The Odyssey* (translation), Macmillan: London.

Eisenberger, H. (1973) *Studien zu Odysee* Wiesbaden.

Fenik, B. (1974) *Studies in the Odyssey* Wiesbaden.

Finlay, M.I. (1979) *The World of Odysseus* Harmondsworth.

Griffin, J. (1980) *Homer*, OUP: Oxford.

---------- (1995) Iliad Book IX, OUP: Oxford.

Heubeck, A. et al. (1988 onwards), *A Commentary on Homer's Odyssey* OUP: Oxford.

Kirk, G.S. (1962) *The Songs of Homer* CUP: Cambridge.

---------- (1965), *Homer and the Epic*, CUP: Cambridge.

Kirk, G. S. *et al.* (1985 onwards), *The Iliad: A Commentary*, CUP: Cambridge

Leaf, W. and Bayfield, M. A. (1959), *The Iliad of Homer*, Macmillan: London.

Merry, W. W. (1935), *The Odyssey* (edition), OUP: Oxford.

Monro, D. B. (1884). *Iliad* OUP: Oxford.

Page, D.L. (1955) *The Homeric Odyssey* OUP: Oxford.

--------- (1959) *History and the Homeric Iliad*, Berkeley & Los Angeles

Rieu, E. V. (1959), *The Iliad* (translation), Penguin: London.

---------- (1950), *The Odyssey* (translation), Penguin: London.

Shipp, G.P. (1972) *Studies in the Language of Homer* CUP: Cambridge.

van der Valk, M. (1949) *Textual Criticism of the Odyssey* Leiden

---------- (1963-64) *Researches on the Text and Scholia of the Iliad* Leiden

Willcock, M.M. (1978) *The Iliad of Homer* London.

Willcock, M. M. (1984), *Iliad* Macmillan: London.

Woodhouse, W.J. (1969) *The composition of Homer's Odyssey* OUP: Oxford.

www.ingramcontent.com/pod-product-compliance
Ingram Content Group UK Ltd.
Pitfield, Milton Keynes, MK11 3LW, UK
UKHW061213180426
11947UKWH00029B/2016